We Will Never Forget

A National Book of Remembrance

Containing The Names of Those Who Lost Their Lives in The September 11, 2001 Terrorist Attack on The United States of America

Text by Charles W. Wibel
Edited by Charles W. Wibel

J. Tumeroll Press
P.O. Box 546
Farmington, NH 03835

Graphics and Layout by Bryan Upson

Acknowledgements and Credits

All photographs copyright by Associated Press International and supplied under purchase rights agreement.

Victims' names and related information developed from a variety of sources and
compared against Associated Press International list as supplied under purchase rights agreement.

Published by J. Tumeroll Press
P. O. Box 546
Farmington, NH 03835

ISBN 0–9715238–0–0

Printed in Canada

First Edition

God Bless America

An American flag is posted in the rubble of the World Trade Center Thursday, Sept. 13, 2001, in New York. The search for survivors and the recovery of the victims continues since Tuesday's terrorist attack. (AP/WideWorld Photos)

"GOD BLESS AMERICA"
Words and Music by Irving Berlin

God Bless America, land that I love.
Stand beside her and guide her
Thru the night with a light from above.
From the mountains, to the prairies,
To the oceans white with foam.
God Bless America, my home sweet home.
God Bless America, my home sweet home.

INTRODUCTION

Not since Pearl Harbor was attacked by the Japanese on December 7, 1941 has the United States of America been subjected to such a level of violence and destruction as occurred on Tuesday, September 11, 2001.

While we all are certain to remember where we were on this infamous day when the Twin Towers of the World Trade Center in New York City were hit, there is no way that we can individually know or remember all of the people who died that day at the hands of terrorists. It is with this in mind that we have prepared and dedicated this Book of Remembrance. On the following pages, to the best of our ability, are the names of those who were killed in the four separate instances of terror: two in New York City; one in Washington, D.C.; and one in Shanksville, PA. The lists were developed from numerous sources. The Associated Press list was used exclusively for the civilian World Trade Center names and as a verifying source for the other lists.

According to AP classification criteria, the World Trade Center victims are divided into these groups:

CONFIRMED DEAD. Includes those who have been confirmed dead by a coroner's office or the Defense Department. It also includes those for whom death certificates have been issued, even if no body has been recovered.

REPORTED DEAD. Includes those whose deaths have been reported by family, employers, mortuaries, places of worship or by the airlines that listed them as aboard one of the four flights. Includes people for whom memorial services have been held, even if their bodies have not been recovered or positively identified. (Those identified by federal authorities as the hijackers are not included in the database.)

REPORTED MISSING. People identified by family, official agencies or employers as missing.

As time passes and memory of the events slowly fades into the shadows of your mind, we hope that you will frequently return to this *Book of Remembrance* so that "We Will Never Forget" those who died on September 11, 2001.

Charles W. Wibel

FOREWORD

We may never know exactly when, where or with whom the first idea for this horrible series of attacks originated. However, we do know when the vehicles of mass destruction (in this case, commercial airplanes) left their "launch sites" and when they arrived at their targets.

It is at these four "launch sites" that we begin our timelines. Following each of the three attacks and the one heroically aborted attack is a list of those who either died on the planes used in the attacks or on the ground. In the case of the attacks on the Twin Towers of the World Trade Center in New York City and the Pentagon in Washington, D.C., we have divided the civilians killed and the various uniformed services. All lists are in last name alphabetical order, but each individual name is presented in first name, last name order as we want to remember each person as an individual, not a statistic.

We have made a sincere effort to include everyone who died as a result of these attacks. However, it has been particularly difficult to compile the list of everyone involved in the attacks in New York City. The exact names and the total number of victims involved may never be known because of the total devastation and the fact that some victims may not have had family who would be capable of reporting them missing.

If we have missed anyone who should have been listed or if we have listed inaccurate information, please write to us with the correct information. One year from the publication date of this edition of the "National Book of Remembrance" we will issue a supplement to any and all persons who have completed and mailed in a written request. Please address your request to: J. Tumeroll Press, P.O. Box 546, Farmington, NH 03835.

AMERICAN AIRLINES FLIGHT 11
BOSTON TO LOS ANGELES

Fire and smoke billow from the north tower of New York's World Trade Center, Tuesday Sept. 11, 2001. Mounting an audacious attack against the United States, terrorists crashed two hijacked airliners into the World Trade Center and brought down the twin 110-story towers. (AP/WideWorld Photos)

September 11, 2001 dawned bright and clear across the eastern portion of the United States. At Logan Airport in Boston, thousands of passengers were arriving for flights to all parts of the world. Little did they know that, in just a short period of time, some of them would become the first victims in what would become the worst terrorist attack ever carried out on American soil.

Shortly before 8:00 a.m. American Airlines Flight 11, a Boeing 767-200 scheduled from Boston to Los Angeles and loaded with approximately 60,000 pounds of highly explosive aviation fuel, pushed away from its gate and began to taxi along the runway and up into the skies. There were 81 passengers and a crew of 11 on board. Five of those passengers had terrorism and murder on their minds.

At approximately 8:20 a.m., ground controllers noticed that the plane had failed to climb to its assigned cruising altitude as it crossed over western Massachusetts. As the plane reached Amsterdam, New York, it suddenly turned and headed south towards New York City. It was 8:29 a.m.

Now flying on a collision course, Flight 11 crashed into the North Tower of the World Trade Center. It was 8:48 a.m. All people on board the plane and an unknown number in the tower were killed as the plane's load of fuel exploded. The first World Trade tower was on fire and mortally wounded. The day of horror that we shall never forget had begun.

American Airlines Flight 11
Crew and Passenger List

CREW:

John Ogonowski, captain
Thomas McGuinness, first officer
Barbara Arestegui, flight attendant
Jeffrey Collman, flight attendant
Sara Low, flight attendant
Karen A. Martin, flight attendant
Kathleen Nicosia, flight attendant
Betty Ann Ong, flight attendant
Jean Roger, flight attendant
Dianne Bulls Snyder, flight attendant
Madeline Sweeney, flight attendant

PASSENGERS:

Anna Williams Allison
David Lawrence Angell
Lynn Edwards Angell
Seima Aoyama
Myra Joy Aronson
Christine Barbuto
Carolyn Beug
Kelly Ann Booms
Carol Marie Bouchard
Nellie Anne Heffernan Casey
Jeffrey W. Coombs
Tara Kathleen Creamer
Thelma Cuccinello
Patrick Currivan
Brian P. Dale
David DiMeglio
Donald Americo D. Tullio
Albert Dominguez, *Australia*
Alexander M. Filipov
Carol Flyzik
Paul Friedman
Karleton D.B. Fyfe
Peter Alan Gay
Linda M. George
Edmund Glazer
Lisa Reinhart Fenn Gordenstein
Andrew Peter Charles Curry Green
Paige Farley-Hackel
Peter Hashem
Robert Hayes
Edward (Ted) R. Hennessey
Cora Hidalgo Holland
John Nicholas Humber
John Charles Jenkins
Charles E. Jones
Robin Kaplan
Barbara Keating
David Kovalcin
Judy Larocque
Jude Larson
Natalie Larson
N. Janis Lasden
Daniel John Lee
Daniel C. Lewin
Susan A. MacKay
Christopher D. Mello
Jeffrey Peter Mladenik
Antoni Montoya
Carlos Alaerto Montoya
Laura Lee Morabito
Mildred Naiman
Laurie Ann Neira
Renee Lucille Newell
Jacqueline J. Norton
Robert Grant Norton
Jane Orth
Thomas Nicholas Pecorelli
Berinthia Berenson Perkins
Sonia Morales Puopolo
David E. Retik
Philip M. Rosenzweig
Richard Barry Ross
Jessica Leigh Sachs
Rahma Salie
Heather Lee Smith
Douglas J. Stone
Xavier Suarez
Michael Theodoridis
James Anthony Trentini
Mary Barbara Trentini
Pendyala Vamsikrishna
Mary Wahlstrom
Kenneth Waldie
John Wenckus
Candace Lee Williams
Christopher Rudolph Zarba

UNITED AIRLINES FLIGHT 175
BOSTON TO LOS ANGELES

Smoke billows from one of the towers of the World Trade Center and flames and debris explode from the second tower, Tuesday, Sept. 11, 2001. In one of the most horrifying attacks ever against the United States, terrorists crashed two airliners into the World Trade Center in a deadly series of blows that brought down the twin 110-story towers. (AP/WideWorld Photos)

Totally unaware of the events to unfold 30 minutes ahead, United Airlines Flight 175, also bound from Boston to Los Angeles, left its gate at Logan Airport at 7:58 a.m. Fourteen minutes later, it was in the air. The Boeing 767-22 plane carried 56 passengers, a crew of nine, and 60,000 pounds of fuel. The second terrorist missile had been launched.

At 8.47 a.m., as the plane crossed over the New York–New Jersey border in Sussex County, New Jersey, it abruptly turned south and headed towards central New Jersey. When it was roughly adjacent to the lower tip of Manhattan, it turned sharply east directly towards the World Trade Center just across the Hudson River. At 9:03 a.m. Flight 175 exploded right through the South Tower of the World Trade Center, setting it on fire. What might initially have been attributed to pilot error in the first crash was now no longer in doubt. We were at war and close to 3,000 people were going to be killed at "ground zero" before the day was over.

UNITED AIRLINES FLIGHT 175
CREW AND PASSENGER LIST

CREW:

Victor J. Saracini, captain
Michael Horrocks, first officer
Robert Fangman, flight attendant
Amy N. Jarret, flight attendant
Amy R. King, flight attendant
Kathryn L. Laborie, flight attendant
Alfred Joseph Marchand, flight attendant
Michael Tarrou, flight attendant
Alicia N. Titus, flight attendant

PASSENGERS:

Alona Avraham, *Israel*
Garnet Edward "Ace" Bailey
Mark Lawrence Bavis
Graham Andrew Berkeley
Touri Bolourchi
Klaus Bothe
Daniel R. Brandhorst
David Brandhorst
John Brett Cahill
Christoffer Mikael Carstanjen
John "Jay" Corcoran
Ana Gloria Pocasangre de Barrera, *El Salvador*
Dorothy Alma De Aranjo
Lisa Frost
Ronald Gamboa
Lynn Goodchild
The Rev. Francis E. Grogan
Carl Max Hammond
Christine Lee Hanson
Peter Hanson
Susan Kim-Hanson
Gerald F. Hardacre
Eric Samadikan Hartono
James E. Hayden
Herbert W. Homer
Robert Adirien Jalbert
Ralph Kershaw
Heinrich Kimmig, *Germany*
Brian Kinney
Robert George LeBlanc
Maclovio "Joe" Lopez, Jr.
Marianne MacFarlane
Louis Neil Mariani
Juliana Valentine McCourt
Ruth Magdalene McCourt
Wolfgang Menzel, *Germany*
Shawn M. Nassaney
Marie Pappalardo
Patrick J. Quigley
Frederick Rimmele
James M. Roux
Jesus Sanchez
Kathleen Shearer
Michael Shearer
Jane Louise Simpkin
Brian D. Sweeney
Timothy Ray Ward
William M. Weems

American Airlines Flight 77
Washington, D.C. To Los Angeles

Three unidentified rescue workers walk away from the crash site at the Pentagon in Arlington, VA, Tuesday, Sept. 11, 2001. In the most devastating terrorist onslaught ever waged against the United States, hijackers crashed two airliners into the World TradeCenter on Tuesday, toppling its twin 110-story towers. The deadly calamity was witnessed on televisions across the world as another plane slammed into the Pentagon, and a fourth crashed outside Pittsburgh. (AP/WideWorld Photos)

As the two airplane missiles launched from Boston's Logan Airport were still in the air some minutes from their targets, a third plane was being added to the mix. At 8:21 a.m. American Airlines Flight 77, a Boeing 757-200, lifted off from Dulles Airport and headed westward towards Los Angeles. There were 58 passengers and a crew of six. As with the two planes out of Logan Airport, Flight 77 carried a full complement of explosive jet fuel. Around 9:00 a.m., as the world was being alerted to the first World Trade Center attack and just minutes before the second attack, Flight 77, now over Illinois, reversed direction and headed back towards Washington, D.C.

On a collision course with the White House, our nation's symbol of pride and stability, the plane made a last-minute change in direction. With its crew, its passengers, and most of its fuel load, the plane crashed into the outside three rings of the Pentagon complex in Virginia and carved a 100-foot-wide hole in the five-story structure. Why the plane changed its course at the last instant will most likely never be known. Although many innocent people lost their lives in this terrible crash, America's pride and joy, the White House, was still standing for the whole world to see. It was 9:45 a.m. The crash set off massive fires and destroyed a portion of the huge structure that houses the nation's military headquarters. In addition to all those on the plane, some 125 people in the building were killed in this, the third terrorist attack of September 11.

American Airlines Flight 77
Crew and Passenger List

CREW:

Charles Burlingame, captain
David M. Charlebois, first officer
Michele Heidenberger, flight attendant
Jennifer Lewis, flight attendant
Kenneth Lewis, flight attendant
Renee A. May, flight attendant

PASSENGERS:

Paul Ambrose
Yeneneh Betru
Mary Jane (MJ) Booth
Bernard Curtis Brown
Suzanne Calley
William E. Caswell
Sarah Clark
Zandra Cooper
Asia Cottom
James Daniel Debeuneure
Rodney Dickens
Eddie Dillard
Charles Droz
Barbara G. Edwards
Charles S. Falkenberg
Dana Falkenberg
Zoe Falkenberg
James Joe Ferguson
Darlene "Dee" Flagg
Wilson "Bud" Flagg
Richard P. Gabriel, Sr.
Ian J. Gray
Stanley Hall
Bryan Jack
Steven D. "Jake" Jacoby
Ann Judge
Chandler Keller
Yvonne Kennedy
Norma Khan
Karen A. Kincaid
Dong Lee
Dora Menchaca
Christopher Newton
Barbara Olson
Ruben Ornedo
Robert Penniger
Robert R. Ploger III
Lisa J. Raines
Todd Reuben
John Sammartino
Diane Simmons
George Simmons
Mari-Rae Sopper
Robert Speisman
Norma Lang Steuerle
Hilda E. Taylor
Leonard Taylor
Sandra Teague
Leslie A. Whittington
John D. Yamnicky
Vicki Yancey
Shuyin Yang, *China*
Zheng Yuguang, *China*

PENTAGON

Craig Amundsen, SPC, U.S. Army
Melissa Rose Barnes, Yeoman 2nd Class, U.S. Navy
Max Beilke, Master Sgt. (Retired), U.S. Army
Kris Romeo Bishundat, Information Systems
Technician 2nd Class, U.S. Navy
Carrie Blagburn
Canfield D. Boone, Lt. Col., U.S. Army
Diana Borreo de Padro
Donna Bowen
Allen Boyle
Christopher Lee Burford,
Electronics Technician 3rd Class, U.S. Navy
Daniel Martin Caballero,
Electronics Technician 3rd Class, U.S. Navy
Jose Orlando Calderon-Olmedo,
Sgt. 1st Class, U.S. Army
Angelene C. Carter
Sharon Carver
John J. Chada
Rosa Maria (Rosemary) Chapa
Julian Cooper
Eric Allen Cranford, Lt. Cmdr., U.S. Navy
Ada M. Davis
Gerald Francis Deconto, Capt., U.S. Navy
Jerry Don Dickerson, Lt. Col., U.S. Army
Johnnie Doctor, Jr., Chief Information Systems
Technican 1st Class, U.S. Navy
Robert Edward Dolan, Capt., U.S. Navy
William Howard Donovan, Jr., Cmdr., U.S. Navy
Patrick S. Dunn, Cmdr., U.S. Navy
Edward Thomas Earhart,
Aerographer's Mate 1st Class, U.S. Navy
Robert Randolph Elseth, Lt. Cmdr., U.S. Navy
Jamie Lynn Fallon, Storekeeper 3rd Class, U.S. Navy
Amelia V. Fields
Gerald P. Fisher
Matthew Michael Flocco,
Aerographer's Mate 2nd Class, U.S. Navy
Sandra N. Foster
Lawrence Daniel Getzfred, Capt., U.S. Navy
Cortz Ghee
Brenda C. Gibson
Ron Golinski
Carolyn B. Halmon
Sheila Hein
Ronald John Hemenway,
Electronics Technican 1st Class, U.S. Navy
Wallace Cole Hogan, Jr., Maj., U.S. Army
Jimmie Ira Holley
Angela Houtz
Brady K. Howell
Peggie Hurt
Stephen Neil Hyland, Jr., Lt. Col., U.S. Army
Robert J. Hymel
Lacey B. Ivory, Sgt. Maj., U.S. Army
Dennis M. Johnson, Lt. Col., U.S. Army
Judith Jones
Brenda Kegler
Michael Scott Lamana, Lt., U.S. Navy
David W. Laychak
Samantha R. Lightbourn-Allen
Steve Long, Maj., U.S. Army
James Lynch
Terrance M. Lynch
Nehamon Lyons IV,
Operations Specialist 2nd Class, U.S. Navy
Shelley A. Marshall
Teresa M. Martin
Ada L. Mason
Dean Mattson, Lt. Col., U.S. Army
Timothy J. Maude, Lt. Col., U.S. Army
Robert J. Maxwell
Molly McKenzie
Diane Hale McKinzy
Patricia E. (Patti) Mickley
Ron Milam, Maj., U.S. Army
Gerard (Jerry) P. Moran
Odessa V. Morris
Brian Anthony Moss,
Electronics Technician 2nd Class,, U.S. Navy
Ted Moy
Patrick Jude Murphy, Lt. Col., U.S. Navy
Khang Nguyen
Michael Allen Noeth,
Illustrator/Draftsman 2nd Class, U.S. Navy
Chin Sun Pak, Spc., U.S. Army

Jonas Martin Panik, Lt., U.S. Navy
Clifford L. Patterson, Maj., U.S. Navy
Darin Howard Pontell, Lt. (j.g.), U.S. Navy
Scott Powell
Jack Punches, Capt. (Retired), U.S. Navy
Joseph John Pycior, Jr.,
Aviation Warfare Systems Operator 1st Class, U.S. Navy
Debbie Ramsaur
Rhonda Rasmussen
Marsha Dianah Ratchford,
Information Systems Technican 1st Class, U.S. Navy
Martha Reszke
Cecelia E. Richard
Edward V. Rowenhorst
Judy Rowlett
Robert E. Russell
William R. Ruth,
Chief Warrant Officer 4th Class, U.S. Army
Charles E. Sabin
Marjorie C. Salamone
Dave M. Scales, Lt. Col., U.S. Army
Robert Allan Schlegel, Cmdr., U.S. Navy
Janice Scott
Michael L. Selves
Marion Serva
Dan Frederic Shanower, Cmdr., U.S. Navy
Antoinette Sherman
Don Simmons
Cheryle D. Sincock
Gregg Harold Smallwood, Chief
Information Systems Technican, U.S. Navy
Gary F. Smith, Lt. Col. (Retired), U.S. Army
Patricia J. Statz
Edna L. Stephens
Larry Strickland, Sgt. Maj., U.S. Army
Kip P. Taylor, Maj., U.S. Army
Sandra C. Taylor
Karl W. Teepe
Tamara Thurman, Sgt., U.S. Army
Otis Vincent Tolbert, Lt. Cmdr., U.S. Navy
Willie Q. Troy
Ronald James Vauk, Lt. Cmdr., U.S. Navy
Karen Wagner, Lt. Col., U.S. Army
Meta L. Waller
Maudlyn A. White, Staff Sgt., U.S. Army
Sandra L. White
Ernest M. Willcher
David Lucian Williams, Lt. Cmdr., U.S. Navy
Dwayne Williams, Maj., U.S. Army
Marvin R. Woods
Kevin Wayne Yokum, Information Systems
Technican 2nd Class, U.S. Navy
Donald McArthur Young, Chief
Information Systems Technician, U.S. Navy
Edmond Young
Lisa L. Young

UNITED AIRLINES FLIGHT 93
NEWARK, NJ TO SAN FRANCISCO

Firefighters and emergency personnel investigate the scene of the crash of a a United Airlines Boeing 757 with at least 45 passengers Tuesday morning, Sept. 11, 2001 near Shanksville, PA, Somerset County. Radar showed the San Francisco-bound Boeing 757 from Newark, NJ, had nearly reached Cleveland when it made a sharp left turn and headed back toward Pennsylvania, crashing in a grassy field edged by woods about 80 miles southeast of Pittsburgh. (AP/WideWorld Photos)

Just minutes before Flight 77 left Dulles Airport in Washington, D.C., United Airlines Flight 93, a Boeing 757-200, took off from Newark Airport bound for San Franscisco. There were 38 passengers and seven crew members on board.

Approximately 52 minutes into the flight, at 9:35 a.m., the plane suddenly climbed to a higher altitude without ground control authorization. Alarm bells went off throughout the country that a fourth plane has been hijacked, its destination unknown.

Within a minute or two of its unauthorized altitude change, the plane, now near Cleveland, Ohio, turned around and headed east on a course that would bring it to Washington, D.C. Aware of their circumstances, several passengers on the plane made cell phone calls to loved ones. Advised of what had already taken place at the World Trade Center in New York City, four of the passengers – Todd Beamer, Mark Bingham, Tom Burnett, and Jeremy Glick – decided that they would not allow their plane to become a missile directed at some unknown target. As the plane approached Shanksville, Pennsylvania, these passengers acted. With the now famous words, "Let's Roll," they sprang into action. While we shall never know the exact methods used to retake the plane from the hijackers, we do know they were successful to the extent that the plane never reached its intended target in Washington, D.C. At 10:10 a.m., Flight 93 crashed into a field in Shanksville, Pennsylvania, killing all people on board. Though these people lost their lives on this flight, they are heroes in that they saved an untold number of other lives in Washington, D.C. and averted the probable destruction of some highly significant national treasure, be it the White House, the Capitol Building, or some other structure.

The passengers who stood up and took matters into their own hands are true American heroes. They shall not be forgotten!

United Airlines Flight 93
Crew and Passenger List

CREW:

Jason Dahl, captain
LeRoy Homer, first officer
Lorraine G. Bay, flight attendant
Sandra W. Bradshaw, flight attendant
Wanda Anita Green, flight attendant
CeeCee Lyles, flight attendant
Deborah Welsh, flight attendant

PASSENGERS:

Christian Adams
Todd Beamer
Alan Beaven
Mark K. Bingham
Deora Frances Bodley
Marion Britton
Thomas E. Burnett, Jr.
William Joseph Cashman
Georgine Rose Corrigan
Patricia Cushing
Joseph Deluca
Patrick Joseph Driscoll
Edward P. Felt
Jane C. Folger
Colleen Laura Fraser
Andrew Garcia
Jeremy Glick
Lauren Grandcolas
Donald F. Greene
Linda Gronlund
Richard Jerry Guadagno
Toshiya Kuge, *Japan*
Hilda Marcin
Waleska Martinez
Nicole Miller
Louis J. Nacke
Donald Arthur Peterson
Jean Hoadley Peterson
Mark Rothenberg
Christine Anne Snyder
John Talignani
Honor Elizabeth Wainio
Olga Kristin Gould White

World Trade Center Collapses

Firefighters are dwarfed by debris at the site of the World Trade Center in New York Tuesday, Sept. 11, 2001. Planes crashed into the upper floors of the World Trade Center towers minutes apart Tuesday morning collapsing both 110-story buildings. (AP/WideWorld Photos)

BACKGROUND

What began as an idea in the mind(s) of one or several people, in the late 1960's, became reality in 1973, when the twin towers of the World Trade Center and all of their peripheral buildings were completed and open for business. The towers were each 110 stories tall (1,362 ft.), 208 ft. x 208 ft. square and contained 4.8 million square feet of rentable space. They, along with the rest of the complex, cost $1.5 billion to construct. In a time when the world was still comfortable talking in terms of millions of dollars, $1.5 billion was a huge sum to grasp. The towers, magnificent in their simplicity, took their place as one of the wonders of the modern world.

Each building contained 130 vertical support columns made of 100% steel. These columns were connected by 100% steel trusses and each floor was made of 4" thick concrete slabs laid over the trusses. A single floor could weigh as much as 3,000 tons and could normally support the weight of three floors. The buildings were designed to withstand the strongest hurricanes imaginable and even the crash of an errant small plane, as had the Empire State Building, shortly after it had been constructed.

In the year 2001, 50,000 people worked in the World Trade Center complex and just about that many more people visited the center on any given day. There were 75,000 telephones and 19,600 miles of telephone cable to serve the needs of these people. The electric bill for the World Trade Center was roughly $3 million per day.

On a clear day, the twin towers were visible from 20 miles away. They were such an attraction that, over their 28 years of existence, three brave (or foolhardy) souls had parachuted from the top of one of the towers. More than a dozen people had scaled the exterior of the towers.

It took an individual 4.8 minutes to reach the top of the towers by elevator. It took a group of terrorists less than two hours to destroy the entire complex, taking close to 3,000 innocent lives in the process.

SEPTEMBER 11, 2001

At 8:45 a.m., American Airlines Flight 11, a Boeing 767 from Boston with approximately 60,000 pounds of highly explosive fuel and 92 people on board slammed into the North Tower at approximately 300 miles per hour. The destruction of the World Trade Center and a terrorist war on the United States of America had begun.

With the resulting inferno raging at 2,000 degrees, the steel girders and trusses, which lose 50% of their strength at 1,500 degrees, began to sag inward toward the center of the building. It was only the superb construction design and quality of the building that kept it standing as long as it did. While escape from the floors above the impact area on the 96th-105th floors was highly problematic, the remaining tenants and victims in the building had approximately one and three quarter hours to leave the building in an orderly fashion. Most were able to do so.

Eighteen minutes after the first airline crashed into the North Tower, all of the world quickly realized that the initial crash was not an accident, as United Airlines Flight 175, also from Boston, hit the South Tower at the 87th-94th floors and almost sliced through the entire structure. Mortally wounded, even more so than the North Tower, the South Tower began to crumble as thousands of people headed for the emergency stairways and safety. Unfortunately, they were given only 47 minutes before the tower came pancaking down floor upon floor upon floor in a terrible cloud of dust and debris until all that was left was a seven-story pile of death and destruction.

As those on the street and in surrounding buildings slowly recovered from the surprise collapse of the South Tower, the North Tower could no longer sustain the damage it had incurred and it too began its total collapse. Slowly, then faster and faster, floor upon floor crashed downward onto each other until the entire 110 stories was gone. The destruction of the World Trade Center which began at 8:45 a.m. was complete. The time was now 10:29 a.m. Both towers, six other surrounding structures (some as tall as fifty stories) had been destroyed and nine others damaged. Over 3,000 people have been killed and an entire country had been changed forever. It was only through the superb designs of the original building engineers and the courageous acts of the many fire, police and general volunteers that additional thousands of people were not killed that day. Everyone lost at the World Trade Center (Ground Zero) on that fateful day in September should be considered a hero. They all gave their lives in one way or another so that the rest of us might continue to live in this wonderful country called the United States of America. Let us never forget them.

New York City Fire Department

CHIEF OF DEPARTMENT:

Peter J. Ganci, Jr.

FIRST DEPUTY COMMISSIONER:

William Feehan

ASSISTANT CHIEFS:

Gerard A. Barbara, Citywide Tour Commander
Donald James Burns, Citywide Tour Commander

BATTALION CHIEFS:

Dennis Cross, Battalion 57
Thomas P. DeAngelis, Battalion 8
Dennis Lawrence Devlin, Battalion 9
Raymond M. Downey, Special Operations
John Joseph Fanning, Haz-Mat Operations
Edward F. Geraghty, Battalion 9
Joseph Grzelak, Battalion 48
Charles L. Kasper, SOC Battalion
Joseph Marchbanks, Jr., Battalion 57
William J. McGovern, Battalion 2
John Moran, Battalion 49
Orio Joseph Palmer, Battalion 7
John M. Paolillo, Battalion 11
Richard Prunty, Battalion 2
Matthew Lancelot Ryan, Battalion 1
Fred Claude Scheffold, Battalion 12
Lawrence T. Stack, Battalion 50
John Williamson, Battalion 6

CHAPLAIN:

The Rev. Mychal Judge

CAPTAINS:

James Amato, Squad 1
Daniel Brethel, Ladder 24
Patrick J. Brown, Ladder 3
Vincent Brunton, Ladder 105
William F. Burke, Jr., Engine 21
Frank Callahan, Ladder 35
James J. Corrigan, Engine 320 (Retired)
Martin Egan, Jr., Division 15
Thomas Farino, Engine 26
Joseph Farrelly, Division 1
Thomas Theodore Haskell, Jr., Division 15
Terence S. Hatton, Rescue 1
Brian Hickey, Rescue 4
Walter Hynes, Ladder 13
Frederick Ill, Jr., Ladder 2
Louis Joseph Modafferi, Rescue 5
Thomas Moody, Division 1
William O'Keefe, Division 15
Timothy Stackpole, Division 11
Patrick J. Waters, Special Operations
David T. Wooley, Ladder 4

LIEUTENANTS:

Brian Ahearn, Battalion 13
Gregg Arthur Atlas, Engine 10
Steven T. Bates, Engine 235
John Crisci, Haz-Mat Co. 1
Edward Alexander D'Atri, Squad 1
Andrew Desperito, Engine 1
Kevin Donnelly, Ladder 3
Kevin Dowdell, Rescue 4
Michael Esposito, Squad 1
John Fischer, Ladder 20
Michael N. Fodor, Ladder 21
Peter L. Freund, Engine 55
Charles William Garbarini, Battalion 9
Vincent Francis Giammona, Ladder 5
John F. Ginley, Engine 40
Geoffrey E. Guja, Battalion 43
Joseph Gullickson, Ladder 101
Vincent Halloran, Ladder 8
Harvey L. Harrell, Rescue 5
Stephen Gary Harrell, Battalion 7
Michael K. Healey, Squad 41
Timothy Higgins, Special Operations
Anthony Jovic, Battalion 47
Ronald T. Kerwin, Squad 288

Joseph Gerard Leavey, Ladder 15
Charles Joseph Margiotta, Battalion 22
Peter Martin, Rescue 2
Paul Richard Martini, Engine 201
William E. McGinn, Squad 18
Paul Thomas Mitchell, Battalion 1
Dennis Mojica, Rescue 1
Raymond E. Murphy, Ladder 16
Robert B. Nagel, Engine 58
Daniel O'Callaghan, Ladder 4
Thomas O'Hagan, Battalion 4
Glenn Perry, Battalion 12
Philip S. Petti, Battalion 7
Kevin Pfeifer, Engine 33
Kenneth Phelan, Battalion 32
Michael Quilty, Ladder 11
Robert M. Regan, Ladder 118
Vernon Richard, Ladder 7
Michael Thomas Russo, Special Operations
Christopher P. Sullivan, Ladder 111
Robert F. Wallace, Engine 205
Michael Warchola, Ladder 5
Glenn Wilkinson, Engine 238

FIRE MARSHAL:

Ronald Paul Bucca

FIREFIGHTERS:

Joseph Agnello, Ladder 118
Eric Allen, Squad 18
Richard L. Allen, Ladder 15
Calixto Anaya, Jr., Engine 4
Joseph Angelini, Rescue 1
Joseph Angelini, Jr. Ladder 4
Faustino Apostol, Jr., Battalion 2
David Arce, Engine 33
Louis Arena, Ladder 5
Carl Asaro, Battalion 9
Gerald Atwood, Ladder 21
Gerald Jean Baptiste, Ladder 9
Matthew Barnes, Ladder 25
Arthur T. Barry, Ladder 15
Carl John Bedigian, Engine 214
Stephen Elliot Belson, Ladder 24
John P. Bergin, Rescue 5
Paul Beyer, Engine 6
Peter Bielfield, Ladder 42
Brian Bilcher, Squad 1
Carl Vincent Bini, Rescue 5
Christopher Joseph Blackwell, Rescue 3
Michael L. Bocchino, Battalion 48
Frank Bonomo, Engine 230
Gary R. Box, Squad 1
Michael Boyle, Engine 33
Kevin Bracken, Engine 40
Michael Emmett Brennan, Ladder 4
Peter Brennan, Rescue 4
Andrew Brunn, Ladder 5
Greg Joseph Buck, Engine 201
John Patrick Burnside, Ladder 20
Thomas M. Butler, Squad 1
Patrick Byrne, Ladder 101
George Cain, Ladder 7
Salvatore B. Calabro, Ladder 101
Michael Cammarata, Ladder 11
Brian Cannizzaro, Ladder 101
Dennis M. Carey, Haz-Mat Company 1
Michael Carlo, Engine 230
Michael T. Carroll, Ladder 3
Peter Carroll, Squad 1
Thomas Anthony Casoria, Engine 22
Michael Joseph Cawley, Ladder 136
Vernon Paul Cherry, Ladder 118
Nicholas Chiofalo, Engine 235
John Chipura, Engine 219
Michael Clarke, Ladder 2
Steven Coakley, Engine 217
Tarel Coleman, Squad 252
John Collins, Ladder 25
Robert Cordice, Squad 1
Thomas Patrick Cullen III, Squad 41
Robert Curatolo, Ladder 16
Michael D'Auria, Engine 40
Scott Matthew Davidson, Ladder 118
Edward James Day, Ladder 11
Manuel Del Valle, Engine 5
Martin DeMeo, Haz-Mat Co. 1
David Paul Derubbio, Engine 226
Gerard Dewan, Ladder 3
George DiPasquale, Ladder 2
Gerard Duffy, Ladder 21
Michael J. Elferis, Engine 22
Francis Esposito, Engine 235
Robert Evans, Engine 33
Terrence Patrick Farrell, Rescue 4
Lee S. Fehling, Engine 235
Alan D. Feinberg, Battalion 9
Michael Fiore, Rescue 5
Andre G. Fletcher, Rescue 5
John Joseph Florio, Engine 214
Thomas Foley, Rescue 3
David Fontana, Squad 1
Robert J. Foti, Ladder 7
Andrew Fredericks, Squad 18
Thomas Gambino, Jr., Rescue 3
Thomas Gardner, Haz-Mat Co. 1
Matthew David Garvey, Squad 1
Bruce Gary, Engine 40
Gary Geidel, Rescue 1
Denis Germain, Ladder 2
James Giberson, Ladder 35
Ronnie Giles, Squad 288

Paul John Gill, Engine 54
Jeffrey Giordano, Ladder 3
John Giordano, Engine 37
Keith Glascoe, Ladder 21
James Michael Gray, Ladder 20
Jose Guadalupe, Engine 54
David Halderman, Squad 18
Robert Hamilton, Squad 41
Sean Hanley, Ladder 20
Thomas Hannifin, Ladder 5
Dana Hannon, Engine 26
Daniel Harlin, Ladder 2
Timothy Haskell, Squad 18
Michael H. Haub, Ladder 4
Philip T. Hayes, Engine 217 (Retired)
John Heffernan, Ladder 11
Ronnie Lee Henderson, Engine 279
Joseph P. Henry, Ladder 21
William Henry, Rescue 1
Thomas Hetzel, Ladder 13
Jonathan R. Hohmann, Haz-Mat Co. 1
Thomas Holohan, Engine 6
Joseph Hunter, Squad 288
Jonathan Lee Ielpi, Squad 288
William Johnston, Engine 6
Andrew Jordan, Ladder 132
Karl Henri Joseph, Engine 207
Angel Luis Juarbe, Jr., Ladder 12
Vincent D. Kane, Engine 22
Paul H. Keating, Ladder 5
Richard John Kelly, Jr., Ladder 11
Thomas Kelly, Ladder 15
Thomas Kelly, Ladder 105
Thomas J. Kennedy, Ladder 101
Michael Kiefer, Ladder 132
Robert King, Jr., Engine 33
Scott Kopytko, Ladder 15
William Krukowski, Ladder 21
Kenneth Kumpel, Ladder 25
Thomas Kuveikis, Squad 252
David LaForge, Ladder 20
William David Lake, Rescue 2
Robert T. Lane, Engine 55
Peter J. Langone, Squad 252
Scott Larsen, Ladder 15
Neil Leavy, Engine 217
Daniel F. Libretti, Rescue 2
Robert Thomas Linnane, Ladder 20
Michael F. Lynch, Engine 40
Michael F. Lynch, Ladder 4
Michael J. Lyons, Squad 41
Patrick Lyons, Squad 252
Joseph Maffeo, Ladder 101
William Mahoney, Rescue 4
Joseph E. Maloney, Ladder 3
Kenneth Joseph Marino, Rescue 1
John Marshall, Ladder 27
Joseph A. Mascali, Tactical Support 2
Keithroy Maynard, Engine 33
Brian McAleese, Engine 226
John McAvoy, Ladder 3
Thomas McCann, Battalion 8
Dennis P. McHugh, Ladder 13
Robert Dismas McMahon, Ladder 20
Robert William McPadden, Engine 23
Terence A. McShane, Ladder 101
Timothy Patrick McSweeney, Ladder 3
Martin E. McWilliams, Engine 22
Raymond Meisenheimer, Rescue 3
Charles Mendez, Ladder 7
Steve Mercado, Engine 40
Douglas C. Miller, Rescue 5
Henry Miller, Jr., Ladder 105
Robert Minara, Ladder 25
Thomas Mingione, Ladder 132
Manuel Mojica, Squad 18
Carl Molinaro, Ladder 2
Michael Montesi, Rescue 1
Vincent S. Morello, Ladder 35
Christopher Mozzillo, Engine 55
Richard Muldowney, Jr., Ladder 7
Michael D. Mullan, Ladder 12
Dennis Michael Mulligan, Ladder 2
John Napolitano, Rescue 2
Peter Allen Nelson, Rescue 4
Gerard Terence Nevins, Rescue 1
Denis Oberg, Ladder 105
Douglas Oelschlager, Ladder 15
Joseph J. Ogren, Ladder 3
Samuel Oitice, Ladder 4
Patrick O'Keefe, Rescue 1
Eric Olsen, Ladder 15
Jeffrey James Olsen, Engine 10
Steven John Olson, Ladder 3
Kevin O'Rourke, Rescue 2
Michael Otten, Ladder 35
Jeffrey Matthew Palazzo, Rescue 5
Frank A. Palombo, Ladder 105
Paul Pansini, Engine 10
James Pappageorge, Engine 23
Robert Parro, Engine 8
Durrell Pearsall, Rescue 4
Christopher Pickford, Engine 201
Shawn Edward Powell, Engine 207
Vincent Princiotta, Ladder 7
Kevin Prior, Squad 252
Lincoln Quappe, Rescue 2
Leonard Ragaglia, Engine 54
Michael Ragusa, Engine 279
Edward Rall, Rescue 2
Adam David Rand, Squad 288
Donald J. Regan, Rescue 3
Christian Regenhard, Ladder 131
Kevin Reilly, Engine 207

James Riches, Engine 4
Joseph Rivelli, Jr., Ladder 25
Michael Roberts, Ladder 35
Michael Edward Roberts, Engine 214
Anthony Rodriguez, Engine 279
Matthew Rogan, Ladder 11
Nicholas P. Rossomando, Rescue 5
Paul G. Ruback, Ladder 25
Stephen P. Russell, Engine 55
Thomas E. Sabella, Ladder 13
Christopher Santora, Engine 54
John Santore, Ladder 5
Gregory Saucedo, Ladder 5
Dennis Scauso, Haz-Mat Co. 1
John A. Schardt, Engine 201
Thomas G. Schoales, Engine 4
Gerard P. Schrang, Rescue 3
Gregory Sikorsky, Squad 41
Stephen Gerard Siller, Squad 1
Stanley S. Smagala, Jr., Engine 226
Kevin Smith, Haz-Mat Co. 1
Leon Smith, Jr., Ladder 18
Robert W. Spear, Jr., Engine 26
Joseph P. Spor, Ladder 38
Gregory M. Stajk, Ladder 13
Jeffrey Stark, Engine 230
Benjamin Suarez, Ladder 21
Daniel Suhr, Engine 216
Brian Edward Sweeney, Rescue 1
Sean Patrick Tallon, Ladder 10
Allan Tarasiewicz, Rescue 5
Paul A. Tegtmeier, Engine 4
John Patrick Tierney, Ladder 9
John J. Tipping II, Ladder 4
Hector Tirado, Jr., Engine 23
Richard Bruce VanHine, Squad 41
Peter A. Vega, Ladder 118
Lawrence Veling, Engine 235
John T. Vigiano II, Ladder 132
Sergio Villanueva, Ladder 132
Lawrence Virgilio, Squad 18
Jeffrey Patrick Walz, Ladder 9
Kenneth Watson, Engine 214
Michael Weinberg, Engine 1
David M. Weiss, Rescue 1
Timothy Welty, Squad 288
Eugene Whelan, Engine 230
Edward White, Engine 230
Mark Whitford, Engine 23
William X. Wren, Ladder 166 (Retired)
Raymond York, Engine 285

PARAMEDICS:

Carlos R. Lillo, Battalion 49
Ricardo Quinn, Battalion 57

NEW YORK CITY POLICE DEPARTMENT

DETECTIVES:

Claude D. Richards
Joseph Vincent Vigiano

SERGEANTS:

John Gerard Coughlin
Michael Curtin
Rodney Gillis
Timothy Roy

OFFICERS:

John D'Allara
Vincent G. Danz
Geronimo (Jerome) Dominguez
Stephen Patrick Driscoll
Mark Ellis
Robert Fazio
Ronald Philip Kloepfer
Thomas Langone
James Leahy
Brian G. McDonnell
John William Perry
Glen K. Pettit
Fazio Robery
Moira Smith
Ramon Suarez
Paul Talty
Santos Valentin
Walter E. Weaver

The Port Authority of New York and New Jersey

EXECUTIVE DIRECTOR:

Neil D. Levin

SUPERINTENDENT OF POLICE:

Ferdinand V. Morrone

CHIEF:

James A. Romito

INSPECTOR:

Anthony P. Infante, Jr.

LIEUTENANT:

Robert D. Cirri

SERGEANT:

Robert M. Kaulfers

OFFICERS:

Christopher C. Amoroso
Maurice Vincent Barry
Liam Callahan
Clinton Davis
Donald A. Foreman
Gregg J. Froehner
Thomas E. Gorman
Uhuru G. Houston
George Howard
Stephen Huczko
Paul W. Jurgens
Paul Laszcyzynski
David P. LeMagne
John J. Lennon
John D. Levi
James Francis Lynch
Kathy Nancy Mazza-Delosm
Donald James McIntyre
Walter Arthur McNeil
Joseph M. Navas
James Nelson
Alfonse J. Niedermeyer
James W. Parham
Dominick A. Pezzulo
Bruce A. Reynolds
Antonio J. Rodrigues
Richard Rodriguez
John P. Skala
Walwyn W. Stuart
Kenneth F. Tietjen
Nathaniel Webb
Michael T. Wholey

CIVILIAN:

Joseph Amatuccio
Jean A. Andrucki
Richard Avery Aronow
Ezra Aviles
Arlene T. Babakitis
James W. Barbella
Margaret L. Benson
Daniel D. Bergstein
Edward Calderon
Carlos S. Dacosta
Dwight Donald Darcy
Niurka Davila
Francis (Frank) Albert De Martini
William F. Fallon
Stephen J. Fiorelli
Barry H. Glick
Joseph F. Grillo
Kenneth Grouzalis
Patrick Aloysius Hoey
Prem N. Jerath
Mary S. Jones
Deborah H. Kaplan
Douglas G. Karpiloff
Franco Lalama
Margaret Susan Lewis
Robert H. Lynch
Myrna T. Maldonado
Pete Negron
David Ortiz
Pablo Ortiz
Nancy E. Perez
Eugene J. Raggio
Francis S. Riccardelli
Kalyan K. Sarkar
Anthony Savas
Edward T. Strauss
Lisa L. Trerotola
Simon Weiser

THE WORLD TRADE CENTER (CIVILIAN VICTIMS)

AP classification criteria
The victims are divided into these groups:

CONFIRMED DEAD. Includes those who have been confirmed dead by a coroner's office or the Defense Department. It also includes those for whom death certificates have been issued, even if no body has been recovered.

REPORTED DEAD. Includes those whose deaths have been reported by family, employers, mortuaries, places of worship or by the airlines that listed them as aboard one of the four flights. Includes people for whom memorial services have been held, even if their bodies have not been recovered or positively identified. (Those identified by federal authorities as the hijackers are not included in the database.)

REPORTED MISSING. People identified by family, official agencies or employers as missing.

– A –

Gordon McCannel Aamoth, 32, New York, N.Y., investment banker, Sandler O'Neill & Partners. Confirmed dead, World Trade Center, at/in building.
Edelmiro (Ed) Abad, 54, New York, N.Y., senior vice president, Fiduciary Trust International. Confirmed dead, World Trade Center, at/in building.
Maria Rose Abad, 49, Syosett, N.Y., senior vice president, Keefe, Bruyette & Woods. Confirmed dead, World Trade Center, at/in building.
Andrew Anthony Abate, 37, Melville, N.Y., bond trader, Cantor Fitzgerald. Confirmed dead, World Trade Center, at/in building.
Vincent Abate, 40, New York, N.Y., bond trader, Cantor Fitzgerald. Confirmed dead, World Trade Center, at/in building.
Laurence Abel, Cantor Fitzgerald. Reported missing, World Trade Center, at/in building.
William F. Abrahamson, 58, Cortland Manor, N.Y., business analyst, Marsh & McLennan Cos. Inc. Confirmed dead, World Trade Center, at/in building .
Richard Anthony Aceto, 42, Wantagh, N.Y., tax specialist, Marsh & McLennan Cos. Inc. Confirmed dead, World Trade Center, at/in building.
Alicia Acevedo Carranza, Teziutlan, Puebla, Mexico. Reported missing, World Trade Center, at/in building. *Mexican.*
Heinrich B. Ackermann, 38, New York, N.Y., Aon Corp. Confirmed dead, World Trade Center, at/in building.
Paul Andrew Acquaviva, 29, Glen Rock, N.J., eSpeed vice president of corporate development, Cantor Fitzgerald. Confirmed dead, World Trade Center, at/in building.
Donald L. Adams, 28, Chatham, N.J., vice president of sales of eSpeed division, Cantor Fitzgerald. Confirmed dead, World Trade Center, at/in building.
Patrick Adams, 60, New York, N.Y., security officer, Fuji Bank. Confirmed dead, World Trade Center, at/in building.
Shannon Lewis Adams, 25, New York, N.Y., fixed income accountant, Cantor Fitzgerald. Confirmed dead, World Trade Center, at/in building.
Stephen Adams, 51, New York, N.Y., beverage manager, Windows on the World. Confirmed dead, World Trade Center, at/in building.
Ignatius Adanga, 62, New York, N.Y., New York State Department of Transportation. Confirmed dead, World Trade Center, at/in building.
Christy A. Addamo, 28, New Hyde Park, N.Y., accountant, Marsh & McLennan Cos. Inc. Confirmed dead, World Trade Center, at/in building.
Terence E. Adderley, 22, Bloomfield Hills, Mich., Fred Alger Management. Reported dead, World Trade Center, at/in building.
Sophia B. Addo, 36, New York, N.Y., housekeeping, Windows on the World. Confirmed dead, World Trade Center, at/in building. *Guyanese.*
Lee Adler, 48, Springfield, N.J., computer designer, Cantor Fitzgerald. Confirmed dead, World Trade Center, at/in building.
Daniel Thomas Afflitto, 32, Manalapan, N.J., equities trader, Cantor Fitzgerald. Confirmed dead, World Trade Center, at/in building.
Emmanuel Afuakwah, 37, New York, N.Y. Confirmed dead, World Trade Center, at/in building.
Alok Agarwal, 37, Jersey City, N.J., Cantor Fitzgerald. Confirmed dead, World Trade Center, at/in building.
Mukul Agarwala, 37, New York, N.Y., software research analyst, Fiduciary Trust International. Confirmed dead, World Trade Center, at/in building.
David Agnes, 46, New York, N.Y., Cantor Fitzgerald. Confirmed dead, World Trade Center, at/in building.
Joao A.D. Aguiar, 30, Red Bank, N.J., investment banker, Keefe, Bruyette & Woods. Confirmed dead, World Trade Center, at/in building.

Jeremiah J. Ahern, 74, Cliffside Park, N.J., New York State Department of Taxation and Finance. Confirmed dead, World Trade Center, at/in building.
Joanne Ahladiotis, 27, New York, N.Y., Cantor Fitzgerald. Confirmed dead, World Trade Center, at/in building.
Shabbir Ahmed, 47, New York, N.Y., waiter, Windows on the World. Confirmed dead, World Trade Center, at/in building.
Terrance Andre Aiken, 30, New York, N.Y., computer consultant, Vital Computer Services. Confirmed dead, World Trade Center, at/in building.
Godwin Ajala, 33, New York, N.Y., security officer, Summit Security Services. Confirmed dead, World Trade Center, at/in building.
Gertrude M. Alagero, 37, New York, N.Y., senior vice president and practice leader, Marsh & McLennan Cos. Inc. Confirmed dead, World Trade Center, at/in building.
Andrew Alameno, 37, Westfield, N.J., trader, Cantor Fitzgerald. Confirmed dead, World Trade Center, at/in building.
Margaret Ann (Peggy) Jezycki Alario, 41, New York, N.Y., global products manager, Zurich American Insurance. Confirmed dead, World Trade Center, at/in building.
Gary Albero, 39, Emerson, N.J., insurance broker, Aon Corp. Confirmed dead, World Trade Center, at/in building.
Jon L. Albert, 46, Upper Nyack, N.Y., vice president of information technology, Marsh & McLennan Cos. Inc. Confirmed dead, World Trade Center, at/in building.
Peter Alderman, 25, New York, N.Y., salesman, Bloomberg Tradebook. Reported missing, World Trade Center, at/in building.
Jacquelyn Delaine Aldridge, 46, New York, N.Y., accountant, Marsh & McLennan Cos. Inc. Confirmed dead, World Trade Center, at/in building.
Grace Alegre-Cua, 40, Glen Rock, N.J., Mitsui Bank. Confirmed dead, World Trade Center, at/in building, *Filipino.*
David D. Alger, 57, New York, N.Y., executive vice president and chief financial officer, Fred Alger Management. Confirmed dead, World Trade Center, at/in building.
Boutros al-Hashim, 41. Reported dead, World Trade Center, at/in building. *Lebanese.*
Ernest Alikakos, 43, New York, N.Y., New York State Department of Taxation and Finance. Confirmed dead, World Trade Center, at/in building.
Edward L. Allegretto, 51, Colonia, N.J., convertible bonds broker, Cantor Fitzgerald. Confirmed dead, World Trade Center, at/in building.
Joseph Ryan Allen, 39, New York, N.Y., bond broker, Cantor Fitzgerald. Confirmed dead, World Trade Center, at/in building.
Richard D. Allen, 31, New York, N.Y. Confirmed dead, World Trade Center, at/in building.
Christopher Edward Allingham, 36, River Edge, N.J., municipal bond broker, Cantor Fitzgerald. Confirmed dead, World Trade Center, at/in building.
Janet M. Alonso, 41, Stony Point, N.Y., e-mail analyst, Marsh & McLennan Cos. Inc. Confirmed dead, World Trade Center, at/in building.
Anthony Alvarado, 31, New York, N.Y., food service handler, Forte Food Service. Confirmed dead, World Trade Center, at/in building.
Antonio Javier Alvarez, kitchen staff, Windows on the World. Reported missing, World Trade Center, at/in building. *Mexican.*
Juan Cisneros Alvarez, 24, New York, N.Y., bond trader, Cantor Fitzgerald. Reported dead, World Trade Center, at/in building.
Telmo Alvear, 25, New York, N.Y., waiter, Windows on the World. Confirmed dead, World Trade Center, at/in building.
Cesar A. Alviar, 60, Bloomfield, N.J., Marsh & McLennan Cos. Inc. Confirmed dead, World Trade Center, at/in building. *Filipino.*
Tariq Amanullah, 40, Metuchen, N.J., vice president, Fiduciary Trust International. Confirmed dead, World Trade Center, at/in building.
Angelo Amaranto, 60, New York, N.Y., janitorial, cleaner, ABM Industries. Confirmed dead, World Trade Center, at/in building.
Kazuhiro Anai, 42, Scarsdale, N.Y., deputy manager, New York branch, Nishi-Nippon Bank. Confirmed dead, World Trade Center, at/in building.
Joseph Peter Anchundia, 26, New York, N.Y., investment banker, Sandler O'Neill & Partners. Confirmed dead, World Trade Center, at/in building.
Kermit Charles Anderson, 57, Green Brook, N.J., systems analyst, Marsh Inc. Confirmed dead, World Trade Center, at/in building.
Yvette Anderson, 53, New York, N.Y., keyboard specialist, New York State Department of Taxation and Finance. Confirmed dead, World Trade Center, at/in building.
John Andreacchio, 52, New York, N.Y., human resources, Fuji Bank. Confirmed dead, World Trade Center, at/in building.
Michael Rourke Andrews, 34, Belle Harbor, N.Y., Cantor Fitzgerald. Confirmed dead, World Trade Center, at/in building.
Siew-Nya Ang, 37, East Brunswick, N.J., technical analyst, Marsh & McLennan Cos. Inc. Confirmed dead, World Trade Center, at/in building.
Laura Angilletta, 23, New York, N.Y., purchase and sales clerk, Cantor Fitzgerald. Confirmed dead, World Trade Center, at/in building.
Doreen J. Angrisani, 44, New York, N.Y., finance manager, Marsh & McLennan Cos. Inc. Confirmed dead, World Trade Center, at/in building.
Lorraine D. Antigua, 32, Middletown, N.J., securities lending department, Cantor Fitzgerald. Confirmed dead, World Trade Center, at/in building.

Peter Paul Apollo, 26, Hoboken, N.J., equity trader, Cantor Fitzgerald. Confirmed dead, World Trade Center, at/in building.
Frank Thomas Aquilino, 26, New York, N.Y., Cantor Fitzgerald. Confirmed dead, World Trade Center, at/in building.
Patrick Michael Aranyos, 26, New York, N.Y., bond broker, Euro Brokers Inc. Confirmed dead, World Trade Center, at/in building.
Michael G. Arczynski, 45, Little Silver, N.J., senior vice president, Aon Corp. Confirmed dead, World Trade Center, at/in building.
Adam Arias, 37, New York, N.Y., vice president of operations, Euro Brokers Inc. Confirmed dead, World Trade Center, at/in building.
Michael J. Armstrong, 34, New York, N.Y., Cantor Fitzgerald. Confirmed dead, World Trade Center, at/in building.
Jack Charles Aron, 52, Bergenfield, N.J., Marsh & McLennan Cos. Inc. Confirmed dead, World Trade Center, at/in building.
Joshua Aron, 29, New York, N.Y., Cantor Fitzgerald. Confirmed dead, World Trade Center, at/in building.
Japhet J. Aryee, 49, Spring Valley, N.Y., New York State Department of Taxation and Finance. Confirmed dead, World Trade Center, at/in building.
Michael A. Asciak, 47, Ridgefield, N.J., Carr Futures. Confirmed dead, World Trade Center, at/in building.
Michael Edward Asher, 53, Monroe, N.Y., Cantor Fitzgerald. Confirmed dead, World Trade Center, at/in building.
Janice Ashley, 25, Rockville Centre, N.Y., research associate, Fred Alger Management. Confirmed dead, World Trade Center, at/in building.
Thomas J. Ashton, 21, New York, N.Y., electrician, Denino Electric. Confirmed dead, World Trade Center, at/in building.
Manuel O. Asitimbay, 36, New York, N.Y., cook, Windows on the World. Confirmed dead, World Trade Center, at/in building.
Debbie S. Attlas-Bellows, 30, East Windsor, N.J., Cantor Fitzgerald. Confirmed dead, World Trade Center, at/in building.
James Audiffred, 38, New York, N.Y., janitorial, elevator starter, ABM Industries. Confirmed dead, World Trade Center, at/in building.
Frank Louis Aversano, 58, Manalapan, N.J., director of operations support, risk services, Aon Corp. Confirmed dead, World Trade Center, at/in building.
Samuel (Sandy) Ayala, 36, New York, N.Y., banquet steward, Windows on the World. Confirmed dead, World Trade Center, at/in building.

– B –

Eustace (Rudy) Bacchus, 48, Metuchen, N.J., independent trader, American Stock Exchange. Confirmed dead, World Trade Center, at/in building,
John James Badagliacca, 35, New York, N.Y., bond salesman, Cantor Fitzgerald. Confirmed dead, World Trade Center, at/in building.
Jane Ellen Baeszler, 43, New York, N.Y., broker, Cantor Fitzgerald. Confirmed dead, World Trade Center, at/in building.
Robert J. Baierwalter, 44, Albertson, N.Y., F.M. Global. Confirmed dead, World Trade Center, at/in building.
Andrew J. Bailey, 29, New York, N.Y., consultant, Marsh & McLennan Cos. Inc. Confirmed dead, World Trade Center, at/in building.
Brett T. Bailey, 28, Bricktown, N.J., options broker, Euro Brokers Inc. Confirmed dead, World Trade Center, at/in building.
Tatyana Bakalinskaya, 43, New York, N.Y. Confirmed dead, World Trade Center, at/in building.
Michael S. Baksh, 36, Englewood, N.J., private client services group, Marsh & McLennan Cos. Inc. Confirmed dead, World Trade Center, at/in building.
Julio Minto Balanca. Reported missing, World Trade Center, at/in building.
Sharon Balkcom, 43, White Plains, N.Y., computer systems manager, Marsh & McLennan Cos. Inc. Confirmed dead, World Trade Center, at/in building.
Michael Andrew Bane, 33, Yardley, Pa., Marsh & McLennan Cos. Inc. Confirmed dead, World Trade Center, at/in building.
Kathy Bantis, 44, Chicago, Ill., Marsh & McLennan Cos. Inc. Confirmed dead, World Trade Center, at/in building.
Walter Baran, 42, New York, N.Y., investment banker, Fiduciary Trust International. Confirmed dead, World Trade Center, at/in building.
Paul V. Barbaro, 35, Holmdel, N.J., strategic development and software engineer, Cantor Fitzgerald. Confirmed dead, World Trade Center, at/in building.
Ivan Kyrillos Fairbanks Barbosa, 30, Jersey City, N.J., Cantor Fitzgerald. Confirmed dead, World Trade Center, at/in building.
Victor Daniel Barbosa, 23, New York, N.Y., maintenance, Windows on the World. Reported missing, World Trade Center, at/in building.
Colleen Ann Barkow, 26, East Windsor, N.J., project manager, Cantor Fitzgerald. Confirmed dead, World Trade Center, at/in building.
David Michael Barkway, 34, Toronto, Ontario, Canada, managing director, BMO Nesbitt Burns. Confirmed dead, World Trade Center, at/in building. *Canadian.*
Sheila Patricia Barnes, 55, Bay Shore, N.Y., Aon Corp. Confirmed dead, World Trade Center, at/in building.
Evan J. Baron, 38, Bridgewater, N.J., energy futures specialist, Carr Futures. Confirmed dead, World Trade Center, at/in building.
Renee Barrett-Arjune, 41, Cantor Fitzgerald. Confirmed dead, World Trade Center, at/in building.

Diane G. Barry, 60, New York, N.Y., administrative assistant, Aon Corp. Confirmed dead, World Trade Center, at/in building.
Scott D. Bart, 28, Malverne, N.Y., Marsh & McLennan Cos. Inc. Confirmed dead, World Trade Center, at/in building.
Carlton W. Bartels, 44, New York, N.Y., broker, Cantor Fitzgerald. Confirmed dead, World Trade Center, at/in building.
Guy Barzvi, 29, New York, N.Y., Cantor Fitzgerald. Confirmed dead, World Trade Center, at/in building .
Inna Basina, 43, New York, N.Y., Cantor Fitzgerald. Confirmed dead, World Trade Center, at/in building.
Alysia Basmajian, 23, Bayonne, N.J., accountant, Cantor Fitzgerald. Confirmed dead, World Trade Center, at/in building.
Kenneth William Basnicki, 48, Etobicoke, Ontario, Canada, marketing director, BEA Systems. Confirmed dead, World Trade Center, at/in building. *Canadian.*
Paul James Battaglia, 22, New York, N.Y., consultant, Marsh & McLennan Cos. Inc. Confirmed dead, World Trade Center, at/in building.
W. David Bauer, 45, Rumson, N.J., head of global sales for eSpeed, Cantor Fitzgerald. Confirmed dead, World Trade Center, at/in building.
Ivhan Luis Carpio Bautista, 24, New York, N.Y., Windows on the World. Confirmed dead, World Trade Center, at/in building. *Peruvian.*
Marlyn C. Bautista, 46, Iselin, N.J., accounts payable, Marsh & McLennan Cos. Inc. Confirmed dead, World Trade Center, at/in building. *Filipino.*
Jasper Baxter, 45, Philadelphia, Pa., career consultant, Lee Hecht Harrison. Confirmed dead, World Trade Center, at/in building.
Michele (Du Berry) Beale, 37, Essex, England, director of conferences, Risk Waters Group. Confirmed dead, World Trade Center, at/in building. *British.*
Paul F. Beatini, 40, Park Ridge, N.J., Allendale Insurance. Confirmed dead, World Trade Center, at/in building.
Jane S. Beatty, 53, Belford, N.J., Marsh & McLennan Cos. Inc. Confirmed dead, World Trade Center, at/in building.
Larry I. Beck, 38, Baldwin, N.Y., mailroom clerk, Cantor Fitzgerald. Reported dead, World Trade Center, at/in building.
Manette Marie Beckles, 43, Rahway, N.J., account processor. Confirmed dead, World Trade Center, at/in building.
Michael Beekman, 39, New York, N.Y., head trade clerk, LaBranche. Confirmed dead, World Trade Center, at/in building.
Maria Behr, 41, Milford, N.J., securities trader, Cantor Fitzgerald. Confirmed dead, World Trade Center, at/in building.
Yelena Belilovsky, 38, Mamaroneck, N.Y., Fred Alger Management. Confirmed dead, World Trade Center, at/in building.
Nina Patrice Bell, 39, New York, N.Y., senior manager, Marsh & McLennan Cos. Inc. Confirmed dead, World Trade Center, at/in building.
Andrea Della Bella, 59, Jersey City, N.J. Confirmed dead, World Trade Center, at/in building.
Paul Michael Benedetti, 32, New York, N.Y., assistant director, Aon Corp. Confirmed dead, World Trade Center, at/in building.
Denise Lenore Benedetto, 40, New York, N.Y., executive assistant, Aon Corp. Confirmed dead, World Trade Center, at/in building.
Domingo Benilda, 37, Elmhurst, N.Y. Confirmed dead, World Trade Center, at/in building.
Bryan Craig Bennett, 25, New York, N.Y., Cantor Fitzgerald. Confirmed dead, World Trade Center, at/in building.
Eric L. Bennett, 29, New York, N.Y., area vice president, Alliance Consulting. Confirmed dead, World Trade Center, at/in building.
Oliver Duncan Bennett, 29, London, England, staff writer, *Risk* magazine, Risk Waters Group. Confirmed dead, World Trade Center, at/in building. *British.*
Dominick J. Berardi, 25, New York, N.Y., Cantor Fitzgerald. Confirmed dead, World Trade Center, at/in building.
James Patrick Berger, 44, Lower Makefield, Pa., senior vice president, Aon Corp. Confirmed dead, World Trade Center, at/in building.
Steven Howard Berger, 45, Manalapan, N.J., New York State Department of Taxation and Finance. Confirmed dead, World Trade Center, at/in building.
Alvin Bergsohn, 48, Baldwin Harbor, N.Y., equity trader, Cantor Fitzgerald. Confirmed dead, World Trade Center, at/in building.
Michael J. Berkeley, 38, New York, N.Y. Confirmed dead, World Trade Center, at/in building.
Donna Bernaerts-Kearns, 44, Hoboken, N.J., computer programmer, Accenture. Confirmed dead, World Trade Center, at/in building.
Dave Bernard, 57, Chelmsford, Mass., technical adviser, Internal Revenue Service. Reported dead, World Trade Center, at/in building.
William Bernstein, 44, New York, N.Y., mortgage bond broker, Cantor Fitzgerald. Confirmed dead, World Trade Center, at/in building.
David M. Berray, 39, New York, N.Y., vice president, MoneyLine. Confirmed dead, World Trade Center, at/in building.
David S. Berry, 43, New York, N.Y., chief of research, Keefe, Bruyette & Woods. Confirmed dead, World Trade Center, at/in building.
Joseph J. Berry, 55, Saddle River, N.J., chairman and CEO, Keefe, Bruyette & Woods. Confirmed dead, World Trade Center, at/in building.
William Reed Bethke, 36, Hamilton, N.J., computer programmer, Marsh USA. Confirmed dead, World Trade Center, at/in building.

Timothy D. Betterly, 42, Little Silver, N.J., bond trader, Cantor Fitzgerald. Confirmed dead, World Trade Center, at/in building.
Edward F. Beyea, 42, New York, N.Y. Confirmed dead, World Trade Center, at/in building.
Anil T. Bharvaney, 41, East Windsor, N.J., senior vice president, Instinet (Reuters). Confirmed dead, World Trade Center, at/in building.
Bella Bhukhan, 24, Union, N.J., human resources department, Cantor Fitzgerald. Confirmed dead, World Trade Center, at/in building.
Shimmy D. Biegeleisen, 42, New York, N.Y., vice president, Fiduciary Trust International. Confirmed dead, World Trade Center, at/in building.
William Biggart, 54, New York, N.Y., photographer. Confirmed dead, World Trade Center, at/in building.
Ralph Bijoux. Reported missing, World Trade Center, at/in building.
Gary Bird, 51, Tempe, Ariz., senior vice president, Marsh USA. Confirmed dead, World Trade Center, at/in building.
Joshua David Birnbaum, 24, New York, N.Y., assistant bond trader, Cantor Fitzgerald. Confirmed dead, World Trade Center, at/in building.
George Bishop, 52, Granite Springs, N.Y., vice president, Aon Corp. Confirmed dead, World Trade Center, at/in building.
Jeffrey D. Bittner, 27, New York, N.Y., research analyst, Keefe, Bruyette & Woods. Confirmed dead, World Trade Center, at/in building.
Balewa Albert Blackman, 26, New York, N.Y., junior accountant, Cantor Fitzgerald. Confirmed dead, World Trade Center, at/in building. *Jamaican.*
Susan L. Blair, 35, East Brunswick, N.J., insurance executive, Aon Corp. Confirmed dead, World Trade Center, at/in building.
Harry Blanding, 38, Blakeslee, Pa., claims analyst, Aon Corp. Confirmed dead, World Trade Center, at/in building.
Janice L. Blaney, 55, Williston Park, N.Y., consultant at Marsh & McLennan Cos. Inc. Confirmed dead, World Trade Center, at/in building.
Craig Michael Blass, 27, Greenlawn, N.Y., trader, Cantor Fitzgerald. Confirmed dead, World Trade Center, at/in building.
Rita Blau, 52, New York, N.Y., switchboard operator, Fiduciary Trust International. Confirmed dead, World Trade Center, at/in building.
Richard M. Blood, 38, Ridgewood, N.J., insurance broker, Aon Corp. Confirmed dead, World Trade Center, at/in building.
Michael A. Boccardi, 30, Bronxville, N.Y., senior vice president of institutional relations, Fred Alger Management. Confirmed dead, World Trade Center, at/in building.
John Paul Bocchi, 38, New Vernon, N.J., managing director of interest rate options, Cantor Fitzgerald. Confirmed dead, World Trade Center, at/in building.
Susan M. Bochino, 36, New York, N.Y., client specialist, Aon Corp. Confirmed dead, World Trade Center, at/in building.
Bruce Douglas (Chappy) Boehm, 49, West Hempstead, N.Y., broker, Cantor Fitzgerald. Confirmed dead, World Trade Center, at/in building.
Mary Katherine Boffa, 45, New York, N.Y., vice president of purchasing, Marsh & McLennan Cos. Inc. Confirmed dead, World Trade Center, at/in building.
Nicholas A. Bogdan, 34, Browns Mills, N.J., Marsh & McLennan Cos. Inc. Confirmed dead, World Trade Center, at/in building.
Darren C. Bohan, 34, New York, N.Y., temporary employee, Aon Corp. Confirmed dead, World Trade Center, at/in building.
Lawrence Francis Boisseau, 36, Freehold, N.J., fire safety director, OCS Security. Confirmed dead, World Trade Center, at/in building.
Vincent M. Boland, 25, Ringwood, N.J., business analyst, Marsh & McLennan Cos. Inc. Confirmed dead, World Trade Center, at/in building.
Alan Bondarenko, 53, Flemington, N.J., Washington Group International. Confirmed dead, World Trade Center, at/in building.
Andre Bonheur, 40, New York, N.Y., financial analyst, Citibank. Confirmed dead, World Trade Center, at/in building.
Colin Arthur Bonnett, 39, New York, N.Y., telecommunications programmer, Marsh & McLennan Cos. Inc. Confirmed dead, World Trade Center, at/in building.
Yvonne L. Bonomo, 30, New York, N.Y., corporate travel booker, American Express. Confirmed dead, World Trade Center, at/in building.
Sean Booker, 35, Irvington, N.J., account associate, Xerox Corp. Confirmed dead, World Trade Center, at/in building.
Juan Jose Borda Leyva, 59, New York, N.Y. Reported missing, World Trade Center, at/in building. *Colombian.*
Sherry Ann Bordeaux, 38, Jersey City, N.J. Confirmed dead, World Trade Center, at/in building.
Krystine C. Bordenabe, 33, Old Bridge, N.J., sales assistant, Keefe, Bruyette & Woods. Confirmed dead, World Trade Center, at/in building.
Martin Boryczewski, 29, Parsippany, N.J., Cantor Fitzgerald. Confirmed dead, World Trade Center, at/in building.
Richard E. Bosco, 34, Suffern, N.Y., banker, Citibank. Confirmed dead, World Trade Center, at/in building.
John Howard Boulton, 29, New York, N.Y., Euro Brokers Inc. Confirmed dead, World Trade Center, at/in building. *Venezuelan.*
Francisco Bourdier, 41, New York, N.Y., security guard, Deutsche Bank. Confirmed dead, World Trade Center, at/in building.
Thomas H. Bowden, 36, Wyckoff, N.J., equities trader, Cantor Fitzgerald. Confirmed dead, World Trade Center, at/in building.

Kimberly S. Bowers, 31, Islip, N.Y., administrative staff, Cantor Fitzgerald. Confirmed dead, World Trade Center, at/in building.
Veronique (Bonnie) Nicole Bowers, 28, New York, N.Y., credit collections manager, Windows on the World. Confirmed dead, World Trade Center, at/in building.
Larry Bowman, 46, New York, N.Y., security officer, Summit Security Services. Confirmed dead, World Trade Center, at/in building.
Shawn Edward Bowman, 28, New York, N.Y., human resources information specialist, Cantor Fitzgerald. Confirmed dead, World Trade Center, at/in building.
Kevin L. Bowser, 45, Philadelphia, Pa., computer trainer, Marsh & McLennan Cos. Inc. Confirmed dead, World Trade Center, at/in building.
Gennady Boyarsky, 34, New York, N.Y., travel agent, American Express. Confirmed dead, World Trade Center, at/in building.
Pamela Boyce, 43, New York, N.Y., assistant vice president of accounting, Carr Futures. Confirmed dead, World Trade Center, at/in building.
Alfred Braca, 54, Leonardo, N.J., bond broker for eSpeed, Cantor Fitzgerald. Confirmed dead, World Trade Center, at/in building.
Sandra Conaty Brace, 60, New York, N.Y. Confirmed dead, World Trade Center, at/in building.
David Brian Brady, 41, Summit, N.J., financial advisor, Merrill Lynch. Confirmed dead, World Trade Center, at/in building.
Alexander Braginsky, 38, Stamford, Conn., foreign exchange products manager, Reuters. Confirmed dead, World Trade Center, at/in building.
Nicholas W. Brandemarti, 21, Mantua, N.J., analyst, Keefe, Bruyette & Woods. Confirmed dead, World Trade Center, at/in building.
Michelle Renee Bratton, 23, Yonkers, N.Y., Cantor Fitzgerald. Confirmed dead, World Trade Center, at/in building.
Patrice Braut, Marsh & McLennan Cos. Inc. Reported missing, World Trade Center, at/in building, *Belgian*.
Lydia Estelle Bravo, 50, Dunellen, N.J., nurse, Marsh & McLennan Cos. Inc. Confirmed dead, World Trade Center, at/in building.
Ronald Michael Breitweiser, 39, Middletown Township, N.J., senior vice president, Fiduciary Trust International. Confirmed dead, World Trade Center, at/in building.
Edward A. Brennan, 37, New York, N.Y., Cantor Fitzgerald. Confirmed dead, World Trade Center, at/in building.
Frank H. Brennan, 50, New York, N.Y., senior vice president and limited partner, Cantor Fitzgerald. Confirmed dead, World Trade Center, at/in building.
Thomas M. Brennan, 32, Scarsdale, N.Y., investment banker, Sandler O'Neill & Partners. Confirmed dead, World Trade Center, at/in building.
Gary L. Bright, 36, Union City, N.J., insurance analyst, Aon Corp. Confirmed dead, World Trade Center, at/in building.
Jonathan Eric Briley, 43, audio technician, Windows on the World. Confirmed dead, World Trade Center, at/in building.
Mark A. Brisman, 34, Armonk, N.Y., associate, Harris Beach LLP. Confirmed dead, World Trade Center, at/in building.
Paul Gary Bristow, 27, New York, N.Y., conferences producer, Risk Waters Group. Confirmed dead, World Trade Center, at/in building.
Victoria Alvarez Brito, 38, New York, N.Y., Marsh & McLennan Cos. Inc. Confirmed dead, World Trade Center, at/in building.
Mark Francis Broderick, 42, Old Bridge, N.J., accountant, Cantor Fitzgerald. Confirmed dead, World Trade Center, at/in building.
Herman C. Broghammer, 58, North Merrick, N.Y., senior vice president, Aon Corp. Confirmed dead, World Trade Center, at/in building.
Keith Broomfield, 49, New York, N.Y., mechanical technician, Advent Corp. Confirmed dead, World Trade Center, at/in building. *Jamaican.*
Janice J. Brown, 35, New York, N.Y., accountant, Marsh & McLennan Cos. Inc. Confirmed dead, World Trade Center, at/in building.
Lloyd Brown, 28, Bronxville, N.Y., compliance officer for institutional equities, Cantor Fitzgerald. Confirmed dead, World Trade Center, at/in building.
Bettina Browne, 49, Atlantic Beach, N.Y. Confirmed dead, World Trade Center, at/in building.
Mark Bruce, 40, Summit, N.J., Sandler O'Neill & Partners. Confirmed dead, World Trade Center, at/in building.
Richard Bruehert, 38, Westbury, N.Y., Marsh & McLennan Cos. Inc. Confirmed dead, World Trade Center, at/in building.
Brandon J. Buchanan, 24, New York, N.Y., Cantor Fitzgerald. Confirmed dead, World Trade Center, at/in building.
Dennis Buckley, 38, Chatham, N.J., bond broker, Cantor Fitzgerald. Confirmed dead, World Trade Center, at/in building.
Nancy Bueche, 43, Hicksville, N.Y., Aon Corp. Confirmed dead, World Trade Center, at/in building.
Patrick Joseph Buhse, 36, Lincroft, N.J., bond trader, Cantor Fitzgerald. Confirmed dead, World Trade Center, at/in building.
John E. Bulaga, 35, Paterson, N.J., network engineer at eSpeed, Cantor Fitzgerald. Confirmed dead, World Trade Center, at/in building.
Stephen Bunin, 45, Cantor Fitzgerald. Confirmed dead, World Trade Center, at/in building.
Matthew J. Burke, 28, New York, N.Y., assistant equities trader, Cantor Fitzgerald. Confirmed dead, World Trade Center, at/in building.

Thomas Daniel Burke, 38, Bedford Hills, N.Y., managing director, Cantor Fitzgerald. Confirmed dead, World Trade Center, at/in building.
Kathleen A. Burns, 49, New York, N.Y., vice president, office automation, Fiduciary Trust International. Confirmed dead, World Trade Center, at/in building.
Keith James Burns, 39, East Rutherford, N.J., Cantor Fitzgerald. Confirmed dead, World Trade Center, at/in building.
Irina Buslo, 32, New York, N.Y. Confirmed dead, World Trade Center, at/in building.
Milton Bustillo, 37, New York, N.Y., computer network operator, Cantor Fitzgerald. Confirmed dead, World Trade Center, at/in building. *Colombian.*
Timothy G. Byrne, 36, Manhattan, N.Y., investment banker, Sandler O'Neill & Partners. Confirmed dead, World Trade Center, at/in building.

– C –

Jesus Cabezas, 66, New York, N.Y., cook, Windows on the World. Confirmed dead, World Trade Center, at/in building.
Lillian Caceres, 48, New York, N.Y., technology administrator, Marsh & McLennan Cos. Inc. Confirmed dead, World Trade Center, at/in building.
Brian Joseph Cachia, 26, New York, N.Y., Cantor Fitzgerald. Confirmed dead, World Trade Center, at/in building.
Steven Cafiero, 31, New York, N.Y., client specialist, Aon Corp. Confirmed dead, World Trade Center, at/in building.
Richard M. Caggiano, 25, New York, N.Y., Cantor Fitzgerald. Confirmed dead, World Trade Center, at/in building.
Cecile M. Caguicla, 55, Boonton, N.J., assistance vice president of finance, Marsh & McLennan Cos. Inc. Confirmed dead, World Trade Center, at/in building. *Filipino.*
Michael John Cahill, 37, East Williston, N.Y., senior claims attorney, Marsh & McLennan Cos. Inc. Confirmed dead, World Trade Center, at/in building.
Scott W. Cahill, 30, West Caldwell, N.J., municipal bond broker, Cantor Fitzgerald. Confirmed dead, World Trade Center, at/in building.
Thomas J. Cahill, 36, Franklin Lakes, N.J., securities trader, Cantor Fitzgerald. Confirmed dead, World Trade Center, at/in building.
Joseph Calandrillo, 49, Hawley, Pa., Risk Solutions International. Confirmed dead, World Trade Center, at/in building.
Philip V. Calcagno, 57, New York, N.Y. Confirmed dead, World Trade Center, at/in building.
Kenneth Marcus Caldwell, 30, New York, N.Y., senior account manager, Alliance Consulting. Confirmed dead, World Trade Center, at/in building.
Dominick E. Calia, 40, Manalapan, N.J., bond broker, Cantor Fitzgerald. Confirmed dead, World Trade Center, at/in building.
Felix (Bobby) Calixte, 38, New York, N.Y., BP Air Conditioning. Reported missing, World Trade Center, at/in building.
Luigi Calvi, 34, East Rutherford, N.J., bond trader, Cantor Fitzgerald. Confirmed dead, World Trade Center, at/in building.
Roko Camaj, 60, Manhasset, N.Y., janitorial, window cleaner, ABM Industries. Confirmed dead, World Trade Center, at/in building.
David Otey Campbell, 51, Basking Ridge, N.J., senior vice president of equity sales, Keefe, Bruyette & Woods. Confirmed dead, World Trade Center, at/in building.
Geoffrey Thomas Campbell, 31, New York, N.Y., Reuters. Confirmed dead, World Trade Center, at/in building.
Jill Marie Campbell, 31, New York, N.Y., administrative assistant, Baseline. Confirmed dead, World Trade Center, at/in building.
Robert Arthur Campbell, 25, New York, N.Y. Confirmed dead, World Trade Center, at/in building.
Sandra Patricia Campbell, 45, New York, N.Y., computer programmer, Cantor Fitzgerald. Confirmed dead, World Trade Center, at/in building.
Juan Ortega Campos, 32, New York, N.Y. Confirmed dead, World Trade Center, at/in building. *Mexican.*
Sean Canavan, 39, New York, N.Y., carpenter. Confirmed dead, World Trade Center, at/in building.
John A. Candela, 42, Glen Ridge, N.J., senior trader, Cantor Fitzgerald. Confirmed dead, World Trade Center, at/in building.
Vincent Cangelosi, 30, New York, N.Y., bond broker, Cantor Fitzgerald. Confirmed dead, World Trade Center, at/in building.
Stephen J. Cangialosi, 40, Middletown, N.J., bond trader, Cantor Fitzgerald. Reported dead, World Trade Center, at/in building.
Lisa B. Cannava, 30, New York, N.Y., supervisor, Carr Futures. Confirmed dead, World Trade Center, at/in building.
Michael R. Canty, 30, Schenectady, N.Y., broker, Carr Futures. Confirmed dead, World Trade Center, at/in building.
Louis A. Caporicci, 35, New York, N.Y., vice president, Cantor Fitzgerald. Confirmed dead, World Trade Center, at/in building.
Jonathan N. Cappello, 23, Garden City, N.Y., Cantor Fitzgerald. Confirmed dead, World Trade Center, at/in building.
James Christopher Cappers, 33, Wading River, N.Y., assistant vice president, Marsh & McLennan Cos. Inc. Confirmed dead, World Trade Center, at/in building.
Richard M. Caproni, 34, Lynbrook, N.Y., senior accounting specialist, Marsh & McLennan Cos. Inc. Confirmed dead, World Trade Center, at/in building .
Jose Cardona, 32, New York, N.Y., clerk, Carr Futures. Confirmed dead, World Trade Center, at/in building.

Edward Carlino, 46, New York, N.Y., Marsh & McLennan Cos. Inc. Confirmed dead, World Trade Center, at/in building.
David G. Carlone, 46, Randolph, N.J., account executive, FM Global. Confirmed dead, World Trade Center, at/in building.
Rosemarie C. Carlson, 40, New York, N.Y. Confirmed dead, World Trade Center, at/in building.
Mark Stephen Carney, 41, Rahway, N.J., recruiter, Association of Independent Recruiters. Confirmed dead, World Trade Center, at/in building.
Joyce Ann Carpeneto, 40, New York, N.Y., call records management assistant, General Telecom. Confirmed dead, World Trade Center, at/in building.
Jeremy M. Carrington, 34, New York, N.Y., swaps trader, Cantor Fitzgerald. Confirmed dead, World Trade Center, at/in building.
James J. Carson, 32, Massapequa, N.Y.,computer network administrator, Cantor Fitzgerald. Confirmed dead, World Trade Center, at/in building.
Christopher Newton Carter, 52, Middletown, N.J., associate director in charge of information technology, Sandler O'Neill & Partners. Reported dead, World Trade Center, at/in building.
James Marcel Cartier, 26, New York, N.Y., electrician, Aon Corp. Confirmed dead, World Trade Center, at/in building.
Joel Cartridge. Reported missing, World Trade Center, at/in building.
Vivian Casalduc, 45, New York, N.Y., microfiche clerk, Empire Blue Cross/Blue Shield. Confirmed dead, World Trade Center, at/in building.
John F. Casazza, 38, Colts Neck, N.J., Cantor Fitzgerald. Confirmed dead, World Trade Center, at/in building.
Paul Cascio, 23, Manhasset, N.Y., Euro Brokers Inc. Confirmed dead, World Trade Center, at/in building.
Margarito Casillas, Guadalajara, Jalisco, Mexico. Reported missing, World Trade Center, at/in building. *Mexican.*
William Otto Caspar, 57, Eatontown, N.J., data processing specialist, Marsh & McLennan Cos. Inc. Confirmed dead, World Trade Center, at/in building.
Alejandro Castano, 35, Edgewater, N.J., delivery man, Empire Distribution. Reported missing, World Trade Center, at/in building. *Colombian.*
Arcelia Castillo, 49, Elizabeth, N.J., junior accountant, Marsh & McLennan Cos. Inc. Confirmed dead, World Trade Center, at/in building.
German Castillo Galicia, Ozumba, Mexico. Reported missing, World Trade Center, at/in building. *Mexican.*
Leonard M. Castrianno, 30, New York, N.Y., broker, Cantor Fitzgerald. Confirmed dead, World Trade Center, at/in building.
Jose Ramon Castro, 37, New York, N.Y., food service handler, Forte Food Service. Confirmed dead, World Trade Center, at/in building.
Richard G. Catarelli, 47, New York, N.Y. Confirmed dead, World Trade Center, at/in building.
Christopher Sean Caton, 34, New York, N.Y., bond broker, Cantor Fitzgerald. Confirmed dead, World Trade Center, at/in building.
Robert J. Caufield, 49, Valley Stream, N.Y., electrician, Denino Electric. Confirmed dead, World Trade Center, at/in building.
Mary Teresa Caulfield, 58, New York, N.Y. Confirmed dead, World Trade Center, at/in building.
Judson Cavalier, 26, Huntington, N.Y., investment banker, Sandler O'Neill & Partners. Confirmed dead, World Trade Center, at/in building.
Jason D. Cayne, 32, Morganville, N.J., municipal bond broker and partner, Cantor Fitzgerald. Confirmed dead, World Trade Center, at/in building.
Juan Armando Ceballos, 47, New York, N.Y., mail carrier. Confirmed dead, World Trade Center, at/in building.
Marcia G. Cecil-Carter, 34, New York, N.Y., Carr Futures. Confirmed dead, World Trade Center, at/in building.
Jason Cefalu, 30, West Hempstead, N.Y., Cantor Fitzgerald. Confirmed dead, World Trade Center, at/in building.
Thomas J. Celic, 43, New York, N.Y., senior vice president, Marsh & McLennan Cos. Inc. Confirmed dead, World Trade Center, at/in building.
Ana M. Centeno, 38, Bayonne, N.J., accountant, Marsh & McLennan Cos. Inc. Confirmed dead, World Trade Center, at/in building.
Jeffrey M. Chairnoff, 35, West Windsor, N.J., Sandler O'Neill & Partners. Confirmed dead, World Trade Center, at/in building.
Swarna Chalasini, 33, Jersey City, N.J., Fiduciary Trust International. Confirmed dead, World Trade Center, at/in building.
William Chalcoff, 41, Roslyn, N.Y. Confirmed dead, World Trade Center, at/in building.
Eli Chalouh, 23, New York, N.Y., New York State Department of Taxation and Finance. Reported missing, World Trade Center, at/in building.
Charles Lawrence (Chip) Chan, 23, New York, N.Y., currency broker, Cantor Fitzgerald. Confirmed dead, World Trade Center, at/in building.
Mandy Chang, 40, New York, N.Y. Confirmed dead, World Trade Center, at/in building.
Mark L. Charette, 38, Millburn, N.J., senior vice president, Marsh Inc. Confirmed dead, World Trade Center, at/in building.
Gregorio Manuel Chavez, 48, New York, N.Y., Windows on the World. Confirmed dead, World Trade Center, at/in building.
Pedro Francisco Checo, 35, Fiduciary Trust International. Reported missing, World Trade Center, at/in building. *Colombian.*
Douglas MacMillan Cherry, 38, Maplewood, N.J., vice president of professional services group, Aon Corp. Confirmed dead, World Trade Center, at/in building.
Stephen Patrick Cherry, 41, Stamford, Conn., partner, Cantor Fitzgerald. Confirmed dead, World Trade Center, at/in building.

Nestor Chevalier, 30, New York, N.Y., Cantor Fitzgerald. Confirmed dead, World Trade Center, at/in building.
Swede Joseph Chevalier, 26, Locust, N.J., equities trader, Cantor Fitzgerald. Confirmed dead, World Trade Center, at/in building.
Alexander H. Chiang, 51, New York, N.Y., Marsh & McLennan Cos. Inc. Confirmed dead, World Trade Center, at/in building.
Dorothy J. Chiarchiaro, 61, Glenwood, N.Y., Fred Alger Management. Confirmed dead, World Trade Center, at/in building.
Luis Alfonso Chimbo, 39, New York, N.Y., receiving attendant, Windows on the World. Confirmed dead, World Trade Center, at/in building.
Robert Chin, 33, New York, N.Y., account associate, Xerox Corp. Confirmed dead, World Trade Center, at/in building.
Wing Wai (Eddie) Ching, 29, Union, N.J., client support administrator, UmeVoice. Confirmed dead, World Trade Center, at/in building.
Peter A. Chirchirillo, 47, Langhorne, Pa., Marsh & McLennan Cos. Inc. Confirmed dead, World Trade Center, at/in building.
Catherine E. Chirls, 47, Princeton, N.J., eSpeed/banker, Cantor Fitzgerald. Confirmed dead, World Trade Center, at/in building.
Kyung (Kaccy) Cho, 30, N.J., Marsh & McLennan Cos. Inc. Reported missing, World Trade Center, at/in building.
Abdul K. Chowdhury, 30, New York, N.Y., senior assistant analyst, Cantor Fitzgerald. Confirmed dead, World Trade Center, at/in building.
Mohammed Salahuddin Chowdhury, 38, New York, N.Y., waiter, Windows on the World. Confirmed dead, World Trade Center, at/in building.
Kirsten L. Christophe, 39, Maplewood, N.J., vice president of risk services, Aon Corp. Confirmed dead, World Trade Center, at/in building.
Pamela Chu, 31, New York, N.Y., Cantor Fitzgerald. Confirmed dead, World Trade Center, at/in building.
Steven Paul Chucknick, 44, Cliffwood Beach, N.J., vice president of communications and facilities, Euro Brokers Inc. Reported dead, World Trade Center, at/in building.
Wai-ching Chung, 36, New York, N.Y., division vice president, UBS PaineWebber. Confirmed dead, World Trade Center, at/in building.
Christopher Ciafardini, 30, New York, N.Y., vice president and financial analyst, Fred Alger Management. Confirmed dead, World Trade Center, at/in building.
Alex F. Ciccone, 38, New Rochelle, N.Y., assistant vice president, Marsh & McLennan Cos. Inc. Confirmed dead, World Trade Center, at/in building.
Frances Ann Cilente, 26, New York, N.Y., administrative assistant, Cantor Fitzgerald. Confirmed dead, World Trade Center, at/in building.
Elaine Cillo, 40, New York, N.Y., vice president, Marsh & McLennan Cos. Inc. Confirmed dead, World Trade Center, at/in building.
Edna Cintron, 46, New York, N.Y., administrative assistant, Marsh & McLennan Cos. Inc. Confirmed dead, World Trade Center, at/in building.
Nestor Andre Cintron, 26, New York, N.Y., broker, Cantor Fitzgerald. Confirmed dead, World Trade Center, at/in building.
Benjamin Keefe Clark, 39, New York, N.Y., chef, Sodexho. Confirmed dead, World Trade Center, at/in building.
Eugene Clark, 47, New York, N.Y., administrative assistant, Aon Corp. Confirmed dead, World Trade Center, at/in building.
Gregory A. Clark, 40, Teaneck, N.J., computer technician, Cantor Fitzgerald. Confirmed dead, World Trade Center, at/in building.
Mannie Leroy Clark, 54, New York, N.Y. Confirmed dead, World Trade Center, at/in building.
Thomas R. Clark, 37, Summit, N.J., equity sales trader, Sandler O'Neill & Partners. Confirmed dead, World Trade Center, at/in building.
Christopher Robert Clarke, 34, Philadelphia, Pa., trader, Sandler O'Neill & Partners. Confirmed dead, World Trade Center, at/in building.
Donna Clarke, 39, New York, N.Y., Marsh & McLennan Cos. Inc. Confirmed dead, World Trade Center, at/in building.
Suria R.E. Clarke, 30, New York, N.Y., vice president for media relations at eSpeed, Cantor Fitzgerald. Confirmed dead, World Trade Center, at/in building.
Kevin Francis Cleary, 38, New York, N.Y., broker, Euro Brokers Inc. Confirmed dead, World Trade Center, at/in building.
James D. Cleere, 55, Newton, Iowa, assistant vice president, telecommunications, Seabury & Smith Co. Confirmed dead, World Trade Center, at/in building.
Geoffrey W. Cloud, 36, Stamford, Conn., lawyer, Cantor Fitzgerald. Confirmed dead, World Trade Center, at/in building.
Susan M. Clyne, 42, Lindenhurst, N.Y., Marsh & McLennan Cos. Inc. Confirmed dead, World Trade Center, at/in building.
Jeffrey Coale, 31, Souderton, Pa., assistant wine master, Windows on the World. Confirmed dead, World Trade Center, at/in building.
Patricia A. Cody, 46, Brigantine, N.J. Confirmed dead, World Trade Center, at/in building.
Daniel Michael Coffey, 54, Newburgh, N.Y., senior vice president, Guy Carpenter. Confirmed dead, World Trade Center, at/in building.
Jason Matthew Coffey, 25, Newburgh, N.Y., accountant, Marsh & McLennan Cos. Inc. Confirmed dead, World Trade Center, at/in building.
Florence Cohen, 62, New York, N.Y., secretary, New York State Department of Taxation and Finance. Confirmed dead, World Trade Center, at/in building.
Kevin Sanford Cohen, 28, Metuchen, N.J., eSpeed desktop support person, Cantor Fitzgerald. Confirmed dead, World Trade Center, at/in building.

Anthony Joseph Coladonato, 47, New York, N.Y., vice president, Cantor Fitzgerald. Confirmed dead, World Trade Center, at/in building.
Mark J. Colaio, 34, New York, N.Y., senior managing director, Cantor Fitzgerald. Confirmed dead, World Trade Center, at/in building.
Stephen J. Colaio, 32, Montauk, N.Y., senior managing director, Cantor Fitzgerald. Confirmed dead, World Trade Center, at/in building.
Christopher M. Colasanti, 33, Hoboken, N.J., bond trader, Cantor Fitzgerald. Confirmed dead, World Trade Center, at/in building.
Kevin Nathaniel Colbert, 25, New York, N.Y., Keefe, Bruyette & Woods. Confirmed dead, World Trade Center, at/in building.
Michel Paris Colbert, 39, West New York, N.J., bond trader, Cantor Fitzgerald. Confirmed dead, World Trade Center, at/in building.
Keith Eugene Coleman, 34, Warren, N.J., senior vice president and partner, Cantor Fitzgerald. Confirmed dead, World Trade Center, at/in building.
Scott Thomas Coleman, 31, New York, N.Y., Cantor Fitzgerald. Confirmed dead, World Trade Center, at/in building.
Liam Joseph Colhoun, 34. Confirmed dead, World Trade Center, at/in building.
Robert D. Colin, 49, West Babylon, N.Y., Aon Corp. Confirmed dead, World Trade Center, at/in building.
Robert J. Coll, 35, Glen Ridge, N.J., senior vice president of financial markets, Euro Brokers Inc. Confirmed dead, World Trade Center, at/in building.
Jean Marie Collin, 42, New York, N.Y., risk manager, Pfizer Inc. Confirmed dead, World Trade Center, at/in building.
Michael L. Collins, 38, Montclair, N.J., Cantor Fitzgerald. Confirmed dead, World Trade Center, at/in building.
Thomas J. Collins, 36, New York, N.Y., managing director, Sandler O'Neill & Partners. Confirmed dead, World Trade Center, at/in building.
Joseph Collison, Kidder Peabody-Paine Webber. Reported missing, World Trade Center, at/in building.
Patricia Malia Colodner, 39, New York, N.Y., secretary, Marsh & McLennan Cos. Inc. Confirmed dead, World Trade Center, at/in building.
Linda M. Colon, 46, Perrineville, N.J., senior vice president for facilities management, Marsh & McLennan Cos. Inc. Confirmed dead, World Trade Center, at/in building.
Soledi Colon, 39, New York, N.Y., Aon Corp. Confirmed dead, World Trade Center, at/in building.
Ronald Comer, 56, Northport, N.Y., insurance executive, Marsh & McLennan Cos. Inc. Confirmed dead, World Trade Center, at/in building.
Jaime Concepcion, 46, New York, N.Y., Windows on the World. Confirmed dead, World Trade Center, at/in building.
Albert Conde, 62, Englishtown, N.J., insurance underwriter, AGI. Confirmed dead, World Trade Center, at/in building.
Denease Conley, 44, New York, N.Y., security officer, Summit Security Services. Confirmed dead, World Trade Center, at/in building.
Susan Clancy Conlon, 41, New York, N.Y., supervisor, Bank of America. Confirmed dead, World Trade Center, at/in building.
Margaret Mary Conner, 57, New York, N.Y., receptionist, Cantor Fitzgerald. Confirmed dead, World Trade Center, at/in building.
Cynthia L. Connolly, 40, Metuchen, N.J. Confirmed dead, World Trade Center, at/in building.
John E. Connolly, 46, Allenwood, N.J., assistant vice president, Euro Brokers Inc. Confirmed dead, World Trade Center, at/in building.
James Lee Connor, 38, Summit, N.J., partner, Sandler O'Neill & Partners. Confirmed dead, World Trade Center, at/in building.
Jonathan (J.C.) Connors, 55, Old Brookville, N.Y., senior vice president, Cantor Fitzgerald. Confirmed dead, World Trade Center, at/in building.
Kevin P. Connors, 55, Greenwich, Conn., senior vice president, Euro Brokers Inc. Confirmed dead, World Trade Center, at/in building.
Kevin Francis Conroy, 47, New York, N.Y., vice president of corporate accounting, Marsh & McLennan Cos. Inc. Confirmed dead, World Trade Center, at/in building.
Brenda E. Conway, 40, New York, N.Y., Marsh & McLennan Cos. Inc. Confirmed dead, World Trade Center, at/in building.
Dennis Michael Cook, 33, Colts Neck, N.J., assistant trader, Cantor Fitzgerald. Confirmed dead, World Trade Center, at/in building.
Helen D. Cook, 24, New York, N.Y., customer service account representative, General Telecom. Confirmed dead, World Trade Center, at/in building.
James L. Cooper, 46, Wall, N.J. Reported missing, World Trade Center, at/in building.
John A. Cooper, 40, Bayonne, N.J., account manager, SunGard Trading Systems/BRASS. Confirmed dead, World Trade Center, at/in building.
Joseph J. Coppo, 47, New Canaan, Conn., municipal bond trader, Cantor Fitzgerald. Confirmed dead, World Trade Center, at/in building.
Gerard J. Coppola, 46, New Providence, N.J., broadcast engineer, WNET-TV. Confirmed dead, World Trade Center, at/in building.
Joseph Albert Corbett, 28, Islip, N.Y., securities trader, Cantor Fitzgerald. Confirmed dead, World Trade Center, at/in building.
Alejandro Cordero, 23, Marsh & McLennan Cos. Inc. Confirmed dead, World Trade Center, at/in building.
Davids Vargas Cordoba, manager, T&T. Reported missing, World Trade Center, at/in building.

Danny A. Correa-Gutierrez, 25, Fairview, N.J., Marsh & McLennan Cos. Inc. Confirmed dead, World Trade Center, at/in building.
James Corrigan, 60, New York, N.Y., fire and safety operations. Reported dead, World Trade Center, at/in building.
Carlos Cortes, 57, New York, N.Y., Washington Group International. Confirmed dead, World Trade Center, at/in building.
Kevin M. Cosgrove, 46, West Islip, N.Y., claims vice president, Aon Corp. Confirmed dead, World Trade Center, at/in building.
Dolores Marie Costa, 53, Middletown, N.J., vice president, Fred Alger Management. Confirmed dead, World Trade Center, at/in building.
Digna Alexandra Rivera Costanza, 25, New York, N.Y., Marsh & McLennan Cos. Inc. Reported dead, World Trade Center, at/in building.
Charles G. Costello, 46, Old Bridge, N.J., elevator technician, Thyssen Kropp. Confirmed dead, World Trade Center, at/in building.
Michael S. Costello, 27, Hoboken, N.J., Cantor Fitzgerald. Confirmed dead, World Trade Center, at/in building.
Conrod K.H. Cottoy, 51, New York, N.Y., Carr Futures. Confirmed dead, World Trade Center, at/in building.
Martin Coughlan, 54, County Tipperary, Ireland, carpenter. Confirmed dead, World Trade Center, at/in building. *Irish.*
Timothy John Coughlin, 42, New York, N.Y., senior managing director, Cantor Fitzgerald. Confirmed dead, World Trade Center, at/in building.
James E. Cove, 48, Rockville Centre, N.Y., Aon Corp. Confirmed dead, World Trade Center, at/in building.
Andre Cox, 29, New York, N.Y., food service handler, Forte Food Service. Confirmed dead, World Trade Center, at/in building.
Frederick John Cox, 27, New York, N.Y., investment banker, Sandler O'Neill & Partners. Confirmed dead, World Trade Center, at/in building.
Michelle Coyle-Eulau, 38, Garden City, N.Y., systems analyst/management consultant, Marsh & McLennan Cos. Inc. Confirmed dead, World Trade Center, at/in building.
Anne M. Cramer, 47, New York, N.Y., tax specialist, Fiduciary Trust International. Confirmed dead, World Trade Center, at/in building.
Christopher S. Cramer, 34, Manahawkin, N.J., assistant vice president for tax operations, Fiduciary Trust International. Confirmed dead, World Trade Center, at/in building.
Denise Crant, 46, Hackensack, N.J. Confirmed dead, World Trade Center, at/in building.
James L. Crawford, 33, Madison, N.J., Cantor Fitzgerald. Confirmed dead, World Trade Center, at/in building.
Joanne Mary Cregan, 32, New York, N.Y., Cantor Fitzgerald. Confirmed dead, World Trade Center, at/in building.
Lucia Crifasi, 51, Glendale, N.Y., travel coordinator assigned to Marsh & McLennan Cos. Inc., American Express. Confirmed dead, World Trade Center, at/in building.
Daniel Hal Crisman, 25, New York, N.Y., training coordinator, Marsh & McLennan Cos. Inc. Confirmed dead, World Trade Center, at/in building.
Helen Crossin-Kittle, 34, Larchmont, N.Y., networking specialist, Cantor Fitzgerald. Confirmed dead, World Trade Center, at/in building.
Kevin Raymond Crotty, 43, Summit, N.J., managing director, Sandler O'Neill & Partners. Confirmed dead, World Trade Center, at/in building.
Thomas G. Crotty, 42, Rockville Centre, N.Y., bond trader, Sandler O'Neill & Partners. Confirmed dead, World Trade Center, at/in building.
John Crowe, 57, Rutherford, N.J., Aon Corp. Confirmed dead, World Trade Center, at/in building.
Welles Remy Crowther, 24, Upper Nyack, N.Y., equities trader, Sandler O'Neill & Partners. Confirmed dead, World Trade Center, at/in building.
Robert L. Cruikshank, 64, New York, N.Y., executive vice president, Carr Futures. Confirmed dead, World Trade Center, at/in building.
Francisco Cruz, 47, New York, N.Y., security officer, Summit Security Services. Confirmed dead, World Trade Center, at/in building.
John Robert Cruz, 32, Jersey City, N.J., Cantor Fitzgerald. Confirmed dead, World Trade Center, at/in building.
Kenneth John Cubas, 48, Woodstock, N.Y., vice president, Fiduciary Trust International. Confirmed dead, World Trade Center, at/in building.
Francisco C. Cubero, 47, New York, N.Y. Confirmed dead, World Trade Center, at/in building.
Richard Joseph Cudina, 46, Glen Gardner, N.J., bond broker, Cantor Fitzgerald. Confirmed dead, World Trade Center, at/in building.
Neil James Cudmore, 38, Port Washington, N.Y., sales director, *Waters* magazine, Risk Waters Group. Confirmed dead, World Trade Center, at/in building.
Joan McConnell Cullinan, 47, Scarsdale, N.Y., assistant to the president, Cantor Fitzgerald. Confirmed dead, World Trade Center, at/in building.
Joyce Cummings, 65. Confirmed dead, World Trade Center, at/in building.
Brian Thomas Cummins, 38, Manasquan, N.J., partner, Cantor Fitzgerald. Confirmed dead, World Trade Center, at/in building.
Nilton Albuquerque Fernao Cunha, 41. Reported missing, World Trade Center, at/in building.
Michael J. Cunningham, 39, West Windsor, N.J., securities broker, Euro Brokers Inc. Reported dead, World Trade Center, at/in building.
Laurence Curia, 41, Garden City, N.Y., broker, Cantor Fitzgerald. Confirmed dead, World Trade Center, at/in building.

Paul Dario Curioli, 53, Norwalk, Conn., vice president, FM Global. Confirmed dead, World Trade Center, at/in building.
Beverly Curry, 41, New York, N.Y., operations manager, Cantor Fitzgerald. Confirmed dead, World Trade Center, at/in building.
Gavin Cushny, 47, Hoboken, N.J., computer programmer in eSpeed division, Cantor Fitzgerald. Confirmed dead, World Trade Center, at/in building.

– D –

Manuel Da Mota, 43, Valley Stream, N.Y., millwork foreman, Bronx Builders. Confirmed dead, World Trade Center, at/in building.
Caleb Arron Dack, 39, Montclair, N.J., vice president and director of global sales and alliances, Encompys. Confirmed dead, World Trade Center, at/in building.
Vincent D'Amadeo, 36, East Patchouge, N.Y., Cantor Fitzgerald. Confirmed dead, World Trade Center, at/in building.
Thomas A. Damaskinos, 33, Matawan, N.J., vice president for operations, Cantor Fitzgerald. Confirmed dead, World Trade Center, at/in building.
Jack L. D'Ambrosi, 45, Woodcliff Lake, N.J., vice president of operations, Cantor Fitzgerald. Confirmed dead, World Trade Center, at/in building.
Jeannine Marie Damiani-Jones, 28, New York, N.Y., bond broker, Cantor Fitzgerald. Confirmed dead, World Trade Center, at/in building.
Patrick W. Danahy, 35, Yorktown Heights, N.Y., portfolio manager, Fiduciary Trust International. Confirmed dead, World Trade Center, at/in building.
Mary D'Antonio, 55, New York, N.Y., Marsh & McLennan Cos. Inc. Confirmed dead, World Trade Center, at/in building.
Elizabeth Ann Darling, 28, Newark, N.J., Marsh & McLennan Cos. Inc. Confirmed dead, World Trade Center, at/in building.
Annette Andrea Dataram, 25, New York, N.Y., accountant, Windows on the World. Confirmed dead, World Trade Center, at/in building.
Lawrence Davidson, 51, New York, N.Y., broker, Aon Corp. Confirmed dead, World Trade Center, at/in building.
Michael Allen Davidson, 27, Westfield, N.J., Cantor Fitzgerald. Confirmed dead, World Trade Center, at/in building.
Wayne Terrial Davis, 29, Fort Meade, Md., Callixa. Confirmed dead, World Trade Center, at/in building.
Anthony Richard Dawson, 32, Southampton, Hampshire, England. Confirmed dead, World Trade Center, at/in building. *British.*
Calvin Dawson, 46, New York, N.Y., Euro Brokers Inc. Confirmed dead, World Trade Center, at/in building.
Jayceryll M. de Chavez, 24, Carteret, N.J., portfolio analyst, Fiduciary Trust International. Confirmed dead, World Trade Center, at/in building. *Filipino.*
Nataly de la Cruz, New York, N.Y. Reported missing, World Trade Center, at/in building. *Venezuelan.*
Emerita (Emy) De La Pena, 32, New York, N.Y., administrative assistant, Fiduciary Trust International. Confirmed dead, World Trade Center, at/in building.
Azucena de la Torre, 50, New York, N.Y., Cantor Fitzgerald. Reported dead, World Trade Center, at/in building.
Cristina de Laura. Reported missing, World Trade Center, at/in building. *Colombian.*
Oscar de Laura. Reported missing, World Trade Center, at/in building. *Colombian.*
William T. Dean, 35, Floral Park, N.Y., Marsh & McLennan Cos. Inc. Confirmed dead, World Trade Center, at/in building.
Robert J. DeAngelis, 48, West Hempstead, N.Y., project manager, Washington Group International. Confirmed dead, World Trade Center, at/in building.
Tara Debek, 35, Babylon, N.Y., assistant vice president, Marsh & McLennan Cos. Inc. Confirmed dead, World Trade Center, at/in building.
Anna Debin, 30, East Farmingdale, N.Y., Cantor Fitzgerald. Confirmed dead, World Trade Center, at/in building.
James V. DeBlase, 45, Manalapan, N.J., bond broker, Cantor Fitzgerald. Confirmed dead, World Trade Center, at/in building.
Paul DeCola, 39, Ridgewood, N.Y., Cantor Fitzgerald. Confirmed dead, World Trade Center, at/in building.
Simon Dedvukaj, 26, Mohegan Lake, N.Y., janitorial, foreman, ABM Industries. Confirmed dead, World Trade Center, at/in building.
Jason DeFazio, 29, New York, N.Y., bond broker, Cantor Fitzgerald. Reported dead, World Trade Center, at/in building.
David A. Defeo, 37, New York, N.Y., Sandler O'Neill & Partners. Confirmed dead, World Trade Center, at/in building.
Jennifer DeJesus, 23, New York, N.Y., data entry worker, Morgan Stanley. Confirmed dead, World Trade Center, at/in building.
Monique E. DeJesus, 28, New York, N.Y., Cantor Fitzgerald. Confirmed dead, World Trade Center, at/in building.
Nereida DeJesus, 30, New York, N.Y., claims adjuster, Aon Corp. Confirmed dead, World Trade Center, at/in building.
Donald A. Delapenha, 37, Allendale, N.J., Keefe, Bruyette & Woods. Confirmed dead, World Trade Center, at/in building.
Vito Joseph Deleo, 41, New York, N.Y., engineering, tenant man, ABM Industries. Confirmed dead, World Trade Center, at/in building.
Danielle Delie, 47, New York, N.Y. Confirmed dead, World Trade Center, at/in building.
Joseph Della Pietra, 24, New York, N.Y., Cantor Fitzgerald. Reported dead, World Trade Center, at/in building.

Palmina Delli Gatti, 33, New York, N.Y., Marsh & McLennan Cos. Inc. Confirmed dead, World Trade Center, at/in building.
Colleen Ann Deloughery, 41, Bayonne, N.J., reinsurance specialist, Aon Corp. Confirmed dead, World Trade Center, at/in building.
Anthony Demas, 61, New York, N.Y., managing director, Aon Corp. Confirmed dead, World Trade Center, at/in building.
Francis X. Deming, 47, Franklin Lakes, N.J., practice director, Oracle Corp. Confirmed dead, World Trade Center, at/in building.
Carol K. Demitz, 49, New York, N.Y., senior vice president, chief corporate counsel, and secretary, Fiduciary Trust International. Confirmed dead, World Trade Center, at/in building.
Kevin Dennis, 43, Peapack, N.J., Cantor Fitzgerald. Confirmed dead, World Trade Center, at/in building.
Thomas F. Dennis, 43, Setauket, N.Y., Cantor Fitzgerald. Confirmed dead, World Trade Center, at/in building.
Jean C. DePalma, 42, Newfoundland, N.J., vice president of C.A.P.S. division, Marsh USA. Confirmed dead, World Trade Center, at/in building.
Jose Nicholas Depena, 42, New York, N.Y. Confirmed dead, World Trade Center, at/in building.
Robert J. Deraney, 43, New York, N.Y., financial consultant. Confirmed dead, World Trade Center, at/in building.
Michael DeRienzo, 37, Hoboken, N.J., broker, Cantor Fitzgerald. Confirmed dead, World Trade Center, at/in building.
Jermal Legesse DeSantis, 28, Jersey City, N.J. Confirmed dead, World Trade Center, at/in building.
Christian D. DeSimone, 23, Ringwood, N.J., accountant, Marsh & McLennan Cos. Inc. Confirmed dead, World Trade Center, at/in building.
Edward DeSimone, 36, Atlantic Highlands, N.J., vice president, Cantor Fitzgerald. Confirmed dead, World Trade Center, at/in building.
Michael Jude D'Esposito, 32, Morganville, N.J., computer programming consultant at Marsh & McLennan Cos. Inc. Confirmed dead, World Trade Center, at/in building.
Cindy Ann Deuel, 28, New York, N.Y., executive assistant, Carr Futures. Confirmed dead, World Trade Center, at/in building.
Melanie Louise DeVere, 30, Portsmouth, England, publisher of Waters Reference Products, Risk Waters Group. Confirmed dead, World Trade Center, at/in building. *British.*
Jerry DeVito, 66, New York, N.Y., Fred Alger Management. Confirmed dead, World Trade Center, at/in building.
Robert P. Devitt, 36, Plainsboro, N.J., Cantor Fitzgerald. Confirmed dead, World Trade Center, at/in building.
Simon Dhanani, 63, Hartsdale, N.Y., vice president, Aon Corp. Reported missing, World Trade Center, at/in building.
Michael L. DiAgostino, 41, Garden City, N.Y., Cantor Fitzgerald. Confirmed dead, World Trade Center, at/in building.
Lourdes Galleti Diaz, 32, New York, N.Y., executive secretary, Cantor Fitzgerald. Confirmed dead, World Trade Center, at/in building.
Matthew Diaz, 33, New York, N.Y., carpenter. Confirmed dead, World Trade Center, at/in building.
Nancy Diaz, 28, New York, N.Y., kitchen assistant, Windows on the World. Confirmed dead, World Trade Center, at/in building.
Obdulio Ruiz Diaz, 44, New York, N.Y., Bronx Builders. Confirmed dead, World Trade Center, at/in building.
Michael Diaz-Piedra, 49, vice president in charge of money planning, Bank of New York. Confirmed dead, World Trade Center, at/in building.
Judith Berquis Diaz-Sierra, 32, Bay Shore, N.Y., administrative assistant, Fiduciary Trust International. Confirmed dead, World Trade Center, at/in building.
Patricia F. DiChiaro, 63, New York, N.Y., Marsh & McLennan Cos. Inc. Confirmed dead, World Trade Center, at/in building.
Joseph Dermot Dickey, 50, Manhasset, N.Y., managing director, Cantor Fitzgerald. Confirmed dead, World Trade Center, at/in building.
Lawrence Patrick Dickinson, 35, Morganville, N.J., broker, Harvey Young Yurman Inc. Confirmed dead, World Trade Center, at/in building.
Michael D. Diehl, 48, Brick, N.J., vice president, Fiduciary Trust International. Confirmed dead, World Trade Center, at/in building.
John DiFato, 39, New York, N.Y., securities controller, Cantor Fitzgerald. Confirmed dead, World Trade Center, at/in building.
Vincent F. DiFazio, 43, Hampton, N.J., Cantor Fitzgerald. Reported dead, World Trade Center, at/in building.
Carl DiFranco, 27, New York, N.Y., assistant vice president, Marsh & McLennan Cos. Inc. Confirmed dead, World Trade Center, at/in building.
Donald J. DiFranco, 43, New York, N.Y., broadcast engineer, WABC-TV. Confirmed dead, World Trade Center, at/in building.
Alexandra Costanza Digna, 25, New York, N.Y. Confirmed dead, World Trade Center, at/in building.
Debra Ann DiMartino, 36, New York, N.Y., assistant trader, Keefe, Bruyette & Woods. Confirmed dead, World Trade Center, at/in building.
Stephen P. Dimino, 48, Basking Ridge, N.J., partner, Cantor Fitzgerald. Confirmed dead, World Trade Center, at/in building.
William J. Dimmling, 47, Garden City, N.Y., senior vice president financial system, Marsh Inc. Confirmed dead, World Trade Center, at/in building.
Christopher Dincuff, 31, Jersey City, N.J., assistant trader, Carr Futures. Confirmed dead, World Trade Center, at/in building.

Jeffrey M. Dingle, 32, New York, N.Y., Encompys. Confirmed dead, World Trade Center, at/in building.
Anthony DiOnisio, 38, Glen Rock, N.J., vice president of operations, Cantor Fitzgerald. Confirmed dead, World Trade Center, at/in building.
Joseph DiPilato, 57, New York, N.Y., electrician, Petrocelli Electric. Confirmed dead, World Trade Center, at/in building.
Douglas Frank DiStefano, 24, Hoboken, N.J., Cantor Fitzgerald. Confirmed dead, World Trade Center, at/in building.
Ramzi A. Doany, 35, Bayonne, N.J., auditor, Marsh & McLennan Cos. Inc. Confirmed dead, World Trade Center, at/in building.
John J. Doherty, 58, Hartsdale, N.Y., vice president, Aon Corp. Confirmed dead, World Trade Center, at/in building.
Melissa C. Doi, 32, New York, N.Y., IQ Financial Systems. Confirmed dead, World Trade Center, at/in building.
Brendan Dolan, 37, Glen Rock, N.J., broker, Carr Futures. Confirmed dead, World Trade Center, at/in building.
Neil Dollard, 28, Hoboken, N.J., bond broker, Cantor Fitzgerald. Confirmed dead, World Trade Center, at/in building.
James Domanico, 56, New York, N.Y., New York State Department of Taxation and Finance. Confirmed dead, World Trade Center, at/in building.
Benilda P. Domingo, 38, New York, N.Y., janitorial, cleaner, ABM Industries. Reported missing, World Trade Center, at/in building. *Filipino.*
Charles Dominguez, Marsh & McLennan Cos. Inc. Reported missing, World Trade Center, at/in building.
Jacqueline Donovan, 34, New York, N.Y., secretary, Keefe, Bruyette & Woods. Confirmed dead, World Trade Center, at/in building.
Stephen Dorf, 39, New Milford, N.J., maintenance and commications worker, Euro Brokers Inc. Confirmed dead, World Trade Center, at/in building.
Thomas Dowd, 37, Monroe, N.Y., bond broker, Cantor Fitzgerald. Confirmed dead, World Trade Center, at/in building.
Mary Yolanda Dowling, 46, New York, N.Y., Aon Corp. Confirmed dead, World Trade Center, at/in building.
Frank Joseph Doyle, 39, Englewood, N.J., head of equity trading, Keefe, Bruyette & Woods. Confirmed dead, World Trade Center, at/in building.
Joseph M. Doyle, 25, New York, N.Y., government bond supervisor, Cantor Fitzgerald. Confirmed dead, World Trade Center, at/in building.
Randy Drake, 37, Lee's Summit, Mo., network integration manager, Siemens. Reported dead, World Trade Center, at/in building.
Mirna A. Duarte, 31, New York, N.Y. Confirmed dead, World Trade Center, at/in building.
Luke A. Dudek, 50, Livingston, N.J., food and beverage controller, Windows on the World. Confirmed dead, World Trade Center, at/in building.
Christopher Michael Duffy, 23, New York, N.Y., assistant trader, Keefe, Bruyette & Woods. Reported dead, World Trade Center, at/in building.
Michael Joseph Duffy, 29, Northport, N.Y., bond salesman, Keefe, Bruyette & Woods. Confirmed dead, World Trade Center, at/in building.
Thomas W. Duffy, 52, Pittsford, N.Y., Marsh & McLennan Cos. Inc. Confirmed dead, World Trade Center, at/in building.
Antoinette Duger, 44, Belleville, N.J., operations associate, Wachovia Corp. Confirmed dead, World Trade Center, at/in building.
Sareve Dukat, 53, New York, N.Y., tax conferee, New York State Department of Taxation and Finance. Confirmed dead, World Trade Center, at/in building.
Christopher Joseph Dunne, 28, Mineola, N.Y. Confirmed dead, World Trade Center, at/in building.
Richard A. Dunstan, 54, New Providence, N.J., Aon Corp. Confirmed dead, World Trade Center, at/in building.
Patrick Thomas Dwyer, 37, Nissequogue, N.Y., Cantor Fitzgerald. Confirmed dead, World Trade Center, at/in building.

– E –

Joseph Anthony Eacobacci, 26, New York, N.Y., Cantor Fitzgerald. Confirmed dead, World Trade Center, at/in building.
John Bruce Eagleson, 53, Middlefield, Conn., vice president, East Coast, The Westfield Group. Confirmed dead, World Trade Center, at/in building.
Robert D. Eaton, 37, Manhasset, N.Y., broker, Cantor Fitzgerald. Confirmed dead, World Trade Center, at/in building.
Dean P. Eberling, 44, Cranford, N.J., securities analyst, Keefe, Bruyette & Woods. Confirmed dead, World Trade Center, at/in building.
Margaret Ruth Echtermann, 33, Hoboken, N.J., leasing representative, Regus. Confirmed dead, World Trade Center, at/in building.
Paul Robert Eckna, 28, West New York, N.J., Cantor Fitzgerald. Confirmed dead, World Trade Center, at/in building.
Constantine (Gus) Economos, 41, New York, N.Y., partner, Sandler O'Neill & Partners. Confirmed dead, World Trade Center, at/in building.
Dennis Michael Edwards, 35, Huntington, N.Y., partner, Cantor Fitzgerald. Confirmed dead, World Trade Center, at/in building.
Michael Hardy Edwards, 33, New York, N.Y., managing director, Sandler O'Neill & Partners. Reported dead, World Trade Center, at/in building.
Christine Egan, 55, Winnipeg, Manitoba, Canada, nurse epidemiologist, Health Canada. Confirmed dead, World Trade Center, at/in building. *Canadian.*
Lisa Egan, 31, Cliffside Park, N.J., human resources manager, Cantor Fitzgerald. Confirmed dead, World Trade Center, at/in building.

Michael Egan, 51, Middletown, N.J., Aon Corp. Confirmed dead, World Trade Center, at/in building.
Samantha Egan, 24, Jersey City, N.J., Cantor Fitzgerald. Confirmed dead, World Trade Center, at/in building.
Carole Eggert, 60, New York, N.Y., assistant vice president and supervisor in finance department, Marsh & McLennan Cos. Inc. Reported dead, World Trade Center, at/in building.
Lisa Caren Weinstein Ehrlich, 36, New York, N.Y., relationship manager, Aon Corp. Confirmed dead, World Trade Center, at/in building.
John Ernst (Jack) Eichler, 69, Cedar Grove, N.J., retired director of administration, Cadwalader, Wickersham & Taft. Confirmed dead, World Trade Center, at/in building.
Eric Adam Eisenberg, 32, Commack, N.Y., Aon Corp. Confirmed dead, World Trade Center, at/in building.
Daphne F. Elder, 36, Newark, N.J., business analyst, Marsh & McLennan Cos. Inc. Confirmed dead, World Trade Center, at/in building.
Valerie Silver Ellis, 46, New York, N.Y., equities trader, Cantor Fitzgerald. Confirmed dead, World Trade Center, at/in building.
Albert Alfy William Elmarry, 30, North Brunswick, N.J., computer technician, Cantor Fitzgerald. Confirmed dead, World Trade Center, at/in building.
Edgar H. Emery, 45, Clifton, N.J., Fiduciary Trust International. Confirmed dead, World Trade Center, at/in building.
Doris Suk-Yuen Eng, 30, New York, N.Y., club manager, Windows on the World. Confirmed dead, World Trade Center, at/in building.
Christopher S. Epps, 29, accountant, Marsh & McLennan Cos. Inc. Reported missing, World Trade Center, at/in building.
Ulf Ramm Ericson, 79, Greenwich, Conn., civil engineer, Washington Group International. Confirmed dead, World Trade Center, at/in building.
Erwin L. Erker, 41, Farmingdale, N.Y., vice president, Marsh & McLennan Cos. Inc. Confirmed dead, World Trade Center, at/in building.
William J. Erwin, 30, Verona, N.J., broker, Cantor Fitzgerald. Confirmed dead, World Trade Center, at/in building.
Robert Martinez Escanel, 24, Long Island City, N.Y., security officer, Summit Security Services. Reported missing, World Trade Center, at/in building. *Peruvian.*
Sarah (Ali) Escarcega, 35, Balham, England, freelance marketing consultant, Risk Waters Group. Reported missing, World Trade Center, at/in building. *British.*
Jose Espinal, 31. Confirmed dead, World Trade Center, at/in building.
Fanny M. Espinoza, 29, Teaneck, N.J., compliance officer, Cantor Fitzgerald. Confirmed dead, World Trade Center, at/in building.
Brigette Ann Esposito, 34, New York, N.Y., consultant at Marsh & McLennan Cos. Inc. Confirmed dead, World Trade Center, at/in building.
William Esposito, 51, Bellmore, N.Y., partner, Cantor Fitzgerald. Confirmed dead, World Trade Center, at/in building.
Ruben Esquilin, 35, New York, N.Y., maintenance employee, Fiduciary Trust International. Confirmed dead, World Trade Center, at/in building.
Sadie Ette, 36, New York, N.Y., accountant, Windows on the World. Confirmed dead, World Trade Center, at/in building.
Barbara G. Etzold, 43, Jersey City, N.J., receptionist, Fred Alger Management. Confirmed dead, World Trade Center, at/in building.
Eric Brian Evans, 31, Weehawken, N.J., Aon Corp. Confirmed dead, World Trade Center, at/in building.
Meredith Emily June Ewart, 29, Hoboken, N.J., Aon Corp. Confirmed dead, World Trade Center, at/in building.

– F –

Catherine K. Fagan, 58, New York, N.Y. Confirmed dead, World Trade Center, at/in building.
Patricia M. Fagan, 55, Toms River, N.J., insurance adjuster, Aon Corp. Confirmed dead, World Trade Center, at/in building.
Keith G. Fairben, 24, Floral Park, N.Y., paramedic, New York Presbyterian Hospital. Confirmed dead, World Trade Center, at/in building.
William Fallon, 38, Coram, N.Y., Cantor Fitzgerald. Confirmed dead, World Trade Center, at/in building.
Anthony J. Fallone, 39, New York, N.Y., bond broker, Cantor Fitzgerald. Confirmed dead, World Trade Center, at/in building.
Dolores B. Fanelli, 38, Farmingville, N.Y., Marsh & McLennan Cos. Inc. Confirmed dead, World Trade Center, at/in building.
Kathleen (Kit) Faragher, 33, Denver, Colo., systems consultant, Janus Capital Corp. Confirmed dead, World Trade Center, at/in building.
Nancy Carole Farley, 45, Jersey City, N.J., claims negotiator, Reinsurance Solutions Inc. Confirmed dead, World Trade Center, at/in building.
Elizabeth Ann (Betty) Farmer, 62, New York, N.Y., executive assistant contractor at Cantor Fitzgerald. Confirmed dead, World Trade Center, at/in building.
Douglas Farnum, 33, New York, N.Y., Marsh & McLennan Cos. Inc. Confirmed dead, World Trade Center, at/in building.
John G. Farrell, 32, New York, N.Y., Cantor Fitzgerald. Confirmed dead, World Trade Center, at/in building.
John W. Farrell, 41, Basking Ridge, N.J., trader, Sandler O'Neill & Partners. Confirmed dead, World Trade Center, at/in building.
Thomas P. Farrelly, 54, East Northport, N.Y. Confirmed dead, World Trade Center, at/in building.
Syed Abdul Fatha, 54, Newark, N.J., customer service associate, Pitney Bowes. Confirmed dead, World Trade Center, at/in building.

Christopher Faughnan, 37, South Orange, N.J., bond trader, Cantor Fitzgerald. Confirmed dead, World Trade Center, at/in building.
Wendy R. Faulkner, 47, Mason, Ohio, vice president, Aon Corp. Confirmed dead, World Trade Center, at/in building.
Shannon M. Fava, 30, New York, N.Y., assistant broker, Cantor Fitzgerald. Confirmed dead, World Trade Center, at/in building.
Bernard D. Favuzza, 52, Suffern, N.Y., broker, Cantor Fitzgerald. Confirmed dead, World Trade Center, at/in building.
Ronald C. Fazio, 57, Closter, N.J., accountant, Aon Corp. Confirmed dead, World Trade Center, at/in building.
Francis J. (Frank) Feely, 41, Middletown, N.Y., vice president, Marsh & McLennan Cos. Inc. Confirmed dead, World Trade Center, at/in building.
Garth E. Feeney, 28, New York, N.Y., corporate development director, Data Synapse. Confirmed dead, World Trade Center, at/in building.
Sean B. Fegan, 34, New York, N.Y., broker, Fred Alger Management. Confirmed dead, World Trade Center, at/in building.
Peter Feidelberg, 34, Hoboken, N.J., Aon Corp. Confirmed dead, World Trade Center, at/in building.
Rosa M. Feliciano, 30, New York, N.Y., Marsh & McLennan Cos. Inc. Confirmed dead, World Trade Center, at/in building.
Edward T. Fergus, 40, Wilton, Conn., Cantor Fitzgerald. Confirmed dead, World Trade Center, at/in building.
George Ferguson, 54, Teaneck, N.J. Confirmed dead, World Trade Center, at/in building.
Henry Fernandez, 23, New York, N.Y., pastry maker, Windows on the World. Confirmed dead, World Trade Center, at/in building.
Jose Manuel Contreras Fernandez, El Aguacate, Jalisco, Mexico. Reported missing, World Trade Center, at/in building. *Mexican.*
Judy H. Fernandez, 27, Parlin, N.J., eSpeed, Cantor Fitzgerald. Confirmed dead, World Trade Center, at/in building.
Elisa Giselle Ferraina, 27, London, England, senior conferences sponsorship coordinator, Risk Waters Group. Confirmed dead, World Trade Center, at/in building. *British.*
Anne Marie Sallerin Ferreira, 29, Jersey City, N.J., Cantor Fitzgerald. Confirmed dead, World Trade Center, at/in building.
Robert John Ferris, 63, Garden City, N.Y., Aon Corp. Confirmed dead, World Trade Center, at/in building.
David Francis Ferrugio, 46, Middletown, N.J., Cantor Fitzgerald. Confirmed dead, World Trade Center, at/in building.
Louis V. Fersini, 38, Basking Ridge, N.J., bond trader, Cantor Fitzgerald. Confirmed dead, World Trade Center, at/in building.
Mike Ferugio, New York, N.Y., insurance broker, Aon Corp. Reported dead, World Trade Center, at/in building.
Bradley James Fetchet, 24, New York, N.Y., Keefe, Bruyette & Woods. Confirmed dead, World Trade Center, at/in building.
Jennifer Louise Fialko, 29, Teaneck, N.J., client services, Aon Corp. Confirmed dead, World Trade Center, at/in building.
Kristen Fiedel, 27, New York, N.Y., Marsh & McLennan Cos. Inc. Confirmed dead, World Trade Center, at/in building.
Samuel Fields, 36, New York, N.Y., security officer, Summit Security Services. Confirmed dead, World Trade Center, at/in building.
Michael Bradley Finnegan, 37, Basking Ridge, N.J., currency broker, Cantor Fitzgerald. Confirmed dead, World Trade Center, at/in building.
Timothy J. Finnerty, 33, Glen Rock, N.J., broker, Cantor Fitzgerald. Confirmed dead, World Trade Center, at/in building.
Paul M. Fiori, 31, Yorktown Heights, N.Y., Cantor Fitzgerald. Confirmed dead, World Trade Center, at/in building.
John Fiorito, 40, Stamford, Conn., broker, Cantor Fitzgerald. Confirmed dead, World Trade Center, at/in building.
Andrew Fisher, 42, New York, N.Y., director of internet sales, Imagine Software Inc. Confirmed dead, World Trade Center, at/in building.
Bennett Lawson Fisher, 58, Stamford, Conn., senior vice president, Fiduciary Trust International. Confirmed dead, World Trade Center, at/in building.
John Roger Fisher, 46, Bayonne, N.J., security consultant, NanoTek. Confirmed dead, World Trade Center, at/in building.
Thomas J. Fisher, 36, Union, N.J., vice president for operations, Fiduciary Trust International. Confirmed dead, World Trade Center, at/in building.
Lucy Fishman, 37, New York, N.Y., executive secretary, Aon Corp. Confirmed dead, World Trade Center, at/in building.
Ryan D. Fitzgerald, 26, New York, N.Y., foreign currency trader, Fiduciary Trust International. Confirmed dead, World Trade Center, at/in building.
Thomas Fitzpatrick, 35, Tuckahoe, N.Y., bond salesman financial adviser, Sandler O'Neill & Partners. Confirmed dead, World Trade Center, at/in building.
Richard P. Fitzsimons, 57, Lynbrook, N.Y., fire safety director, OCS Security. Confirmed dead, World Trade Center, at/in building.
Salvatore A. Fiumefreddo, 47, Manalapan, N.J., phone technician, IPC Kleinknect Electric Co. Confirmed dead, World Trade Center, at/in building.
Christina Donovan Flannery, 26, New York, N.Y., Sandler O'Neill & Partners. Confirmed dead, World Trade Center, at/in building.
Eileen Flecha, 33, New York, N.Y., junior trader, Fiduciary Trust International. Confirmed dead, World Trade Center, at/in building.

Carl Flickinger, 38, Conyers, N.Y., bond broker, Cantor Fitzgerald. Confirmed dead, World Trade Center, at/in building.
Joseph W. Flounders, 46, East Stroudsburg, Pa., money market broker, Euro Brokers Inc. Confirmed dead, World Trade Center, at/in building.
David Fodor, 38, Garrison, N.Y., accountant and volunteer fire marshal, Fiduciary Trust International. Confirmed dead, World Trade Center, at/in building.
Steven Mark Fogel, 40, Westfield, N.Y., Cantor Fitzgerald. Confirmed dead, World Trade Center, at/in building.
Chih Min (Dennis) Foo, 40, Holmdel, N.J. Confirmed dead, World Trade Center, at/in building.
Bobby Forbes, 37, N.J. Reported missing, World Trade Center, at/in building.
Del Rose Forbes-Cheatham, 48, New York, N.Y., Cantor Fitzgerald. Confirmed dead, World Trade Center, at/in building. *Jamaican.*
Godwin Forde, 39, New York, N.Y., Confirmed dead, World Trade Center, at/in building.
Christopher Hugh Forsythe, 44, Basking Ridge, N.J., foreign exchange money broker, Cantor Fitzgerald. Confirmed dead, World Trade Center, at/in building.
Claudia Alicia Martinez Foster, 26, New York, N.Y., broker assistant, Cantor Fitzgerald. Confirmed dead, World Trade Center, at/in building.
Noel J. Foster, 40, Bridgewater, N.J., vice president and producing broker, Aon Corp. Confirmed dead, World Trade Center, at/in building.
Ana Fosteris, 58, Coram, N.Y. Confirmed dead, World Trade Center, at/in building.
Yolette Fouchet. Reported missing, World Trade Center, at/in building.
Jeffrey L. Fox, 40, Cranbury, N.J., Keefe, Bruyette & Woods. Confirmed dead, World Trade Center, at/in building.
Virginia Fox, 58, New York, N.Y., Marsh & McLennan Cos. Inc. Confirmed dead, World Trade Center, at/in building.
Joan Francis. Reported missing, World Trade Center, at/in building.
Pauline Francis, 57, New York, N.Y., food service handler, Forte Food Service. Confirmed dead, World Trade Center, at/in building.
Virgin (Lucy) Francis, 62, New York, N.Y., housekeeping staff, Windows on the World. Confirmed dead, World Trade Center, at/in building.
Gary J. Frank, 35, South Amboy, N.J., director of document control, Aon Corp. Confirmed dead, World Trade Center, at/in building.
Morton Frank, 31, New York, N.Y., institutional sales desk, Cantor Fitzgerald. Confirmed dead, World Trade Center, at/in building.
Peter Christopher Frank, 29, New York, N.Y., financial analyst, Fred Alger Management. Confirmed dead, World Trade Center, at/in building.
Richard K. Fraser, 32, New York, N.Y., Aon Corp. Confirmed dead, World Trade Center, at/in building.
Kevin Joseph Frawley, 34, Bronxville, N.Y., trader, Euro Brokers Inc. Confirmed dead, World Trade Center, at/in building.
Clyde Frazier, 41, New York, N.Y., tax investigator, New York State Department of Taxation and Finance. Confirmed dead, World Trade Center, at/in building.
Lillian I. Frederick, 46, Teaneck, N.J. Confirmed dead, World Trade Center, at/in building.
Jamitha Freemen, 35, New York, N.Y., Aon Corp. Confirmed dead, World Trade Center, at/in building.
Brett O. Freiman, 29, Roslyn, N.Y. Confirmed dead, World Trade Center, at/in building.
Arlene E. Fried, 49, Roslyn Heights, N.Y., vice president and assistant general counsel, Cantor Fitzgerald. Confirmed dead, World Trade Center, at/in building.
Alan Wayne Friedlander, 52, Yorktown Heights, N.Y., Aon Corp. Confirmed dead, World Trade Center, at/in building.
Andrew K. Friedman, 44, Woodbury, N.Y., vice president for institutional equities, Carr Futures. Confirmed dead, World Trade Center, at/in building.
Peter Christian Fry, 36, Walton, Conn., vice president of international money markets, Euro Brokers Inc. Confirmed dead, World Trade Center, at/in building.
Clement Fumando, 59, New York, N.Y., foreign exchange operations manager, Cantor Fitzgerald. Confirmed dead, World Trade Center, at/in building.
Steven Elliot Furman, 40, Wesley Hills, N.Y., electricity options broker, Cantor Fitzgerald. Confirmed dead, World Trade Center, at/in building.
Paul James Furmato, 37, Colts Neck, N.J., vice president and institutional sales trader, Cantor Fitzgerald. Reported dead, World Trade Center, at/in building.

– G –

Fredric Gabler, 30, New York, N.Y., institutional equities trader, Cantor Fitzgerald. Confirmed dead, World Trade Center, at/in building.
Richard S. Gabrielle, 50, West Haven, Conn., insurance broker, Aon Corp. Confirmed dead, World Trade Center, at/in building.
James Andrew Gadiel, 23, New York, N.Y., Cantor Fitzgerald. Confirmed dead, World Trade Center, at/in building.
Pamela Gaff, 51, Robinsville, N.J., Aon Corp. Confirmed dead, World Trade Center, at/in building.
Ervin Vincent Gailliard, 42, New York, N.Y., security officer, Summit Security Services. Confirmed dead, World Trade Center, at/in building.
Deanna L. Galante, 32, New York, N.Y., personal assistant for eSpeed, Cantor Fitzgerald. Confirmed dead, World Trade Center, at/in building.
Grace Galante, 29, New York, N.Y., broker assistant, Cantor Fitzgerald. Confirmed dead, World Trade Center, at/in building.
Anthony Edward Gallagher, 41, New York, N.Y., energy broker, Cantor Fitzgerald. Confirmed dead, World Trade Center, at/in building.

Daniel James Gallagher, 23, Red Bank, N.J., Cantor Fitzgerald. Confirmed dead, World Trade Center, at/in building.
John Patrick Gallagher, 31, Yonkers, N.Y., electricity trader, Cantor Fitzgerald. Confirmed dead, World Trade Center, at/in building.
Tomas Gallegos Linares, Queretaro, Mexico. Reported missing, World Trade Center, at/in building. *Mexican.*
Lourdes Galletti, 33, New York, N.Y., executive assistant, Cantor Fitzgerald. Confirmed dead, World Trade Center, at/in building.
Cono E. Gallo, 30, Maspeth, N.Y., Carr Futures. Confirmed dead, World Trade Center, at/in building.
Vincenzo Gallucci, 36, Monroe, N.J., senior vice president, Marsh & McLennan Cos. Inc. Confirmed dead, World Trade Center, at/in building.
Thomas Edward Galvin, 32, New York, N.Y., senior vice president and corporate bond broker, Cantor Fitzgerald. Confirmed dead, World Trade Center, at/in building.
Giovanna (Genni) Gambale, 27, New York, N.Y., vice president in communications and media events, Cantor Fitzgerald. Confirmed dead, World Trade Center, at/in building.
Giann F. Gamboa, 26, New York, N.Y., manager, Top of the World Cafe. Confirmed dead, World Trade Center, at/in building.
Ladkat K. Ganesh, 27, N.J. Confirmed dead, World Trade Center, at/in building.
Claude Michael Gann, 41, Roswell, Ga., sales executive, Algorithmics. Confirmed dead, World Trade Center, at/in building.
Cesar Garcia, 36, New York, N.Y., Marsh & McLennan Cos. Inc. Reported missing, World Trade Center, at/in building.
David Garcia, 40, Freeport, N.Y., consultant, Marsh & McLennan Cos. Inc. Confirmed dead, World Trade Center, at/in building.
Jorge Luis Morron Garcia, 38, New York, N.Y., security officer, Summit Security Services. Confirmed dead, World Trade Center, at/in building. *Colombian.*
Juan Garcia, 50, New York, N.Y., food service handler, Forte Food Service. Confirmed dead, World Trade Center, at/in building.
Marlyn C. Garcia, 21, New York, N.Y., Marsh & McLennan Cos. Inc. Confirmed dead, World Trade Center, at/in building.
Christopher Gardner, 36, Darien, Conn., Aon Corp. Confirmed dead, World Trade Center, at/in building.
Douglas B. Gardner, 39, New York, N.Y., vice chairman of eSpeed, Cantor Fitzgerald. Confirmed dead, World Trade Center, at/in building.
Harvey J. Gardner, 35, Lakewood, N.J., call records management supervisor, General Telecom. Confirmed dead, World Trade Center, at/in building.
Jeffrey B. Gardner, 36, Hoboken, N.J., environmental insurance broker, Marsh & McLennan Cos. Inc. Confirmed dead, World Trade Center, at/in building.
William Arthur Gardner, 45, Lynbrook, N.Y., Cantor Fitzgerald. Confirmed dead, World Trade Center, at/in building.
Francesco Garfi, 29, New York, N.Y., trader, Cantor Fitzgerald. Confirmed dead, World Trade Center, at/in building.
Rocco Gargano, 28, Bayside, N.Y., Cantor Fitzgerald. Confirmed dead, World Trade Center, at/in building.
James M. Gartenberg, 36, New York, N.Y., associate director, Julien J. Studley Inc. Confirmed dead, World Trade Center, at/in building.
Boyd A. Gatton, 38, Jersey City, N.J. Confirmed dead, World Trade Center, at/in building. *Bermudan.*
Donald Richard Gavagan, 35, New York, N.Y., Cantor Fitzgerald. Confirmed dead, World Trade Center, at/in building.
Terence D. Gazzani, 24, New York, N.Y., worked on repo desk, Cantor Fitzgerald. Confirmed dead, World Trade Center, at/in building.
Paul Hamilton Geier, 36, Farmingdale, N.Y., Cantor Fitzgerald. Confirmed dead, World Trade Center, at/in building.
Julie M. Geis, 44, Lees Summit, Mo., senior vice president, Aon Corp. Confirmed dead, World Trade Center, at/in building.
Peter Gelinas, 34, New York, N.Y., partner, Cantor Fitzgerald. Confirmed dead, World Trade Center, at/in building.
Steven Paul Geller, 52, New York, N.Y., institutional trader, Cantor Fitzgerald. Confirmed dead, World Trade Center, at/in building.
Howard G. Gelling, 28, New York, N.Y., managing director, Sandler O'Neill & Partners. Reported dead, World Trade Center, at/in building.
Peter Victor Genco, 36, Rockville Centre, N.Y., bond trader, Cantor Fitzgerald. Confirmed dead, World Trade Center, at/in building.
Steven Gregory Genovese, 37, Basking Ridge, N.J., trader, Cantor Fitzgerald. Confirmed dead, World Trade Center, at/in building.
Alayne F. Gentul, 44, Mountain Lakes, N.J., director of human resources, Fiduciary Trust International. Confirmed dead, World Trade Center, at/in building.
Suzanne Geraty, 30, New York, N.Y., system support worker, Cantor Fitzgerald. Confirmed dead, World Trade Center, at/in building.
Ralph Gerhardt, 33, New York, N.Y., vice president, Cantor Fitzgerald. Confirmed dead, World Trade Center, at/in building.
Robert J. Gerlich, 56, Monroe, Conn., accountant and consultant, Reinsurance Solutions Inc. Confirmed dead, World Trade Center, at/in building.
Marina R. Gertsberg, 25, New York, N.Y., junior manager, Cantor Fitzgerald. Confirmed dead, World Trade Center, at/in building.
Susan M. Getzendanner, 57, New York, N.Y., vice president, Fiduciary Trust International. Confirmed dead, World Trade Center, at/in building.

James Gerard Geyer, 41, Rockville Centre, N.Y., Cantor Fitzgerald. Confirmed dead, World Trade Center, at/in building.
Joseph M. Giaconne, 43, Monroe, N.J., head of telecommunications, eSpeed, Cantor Fitzgerald. Reported dead, World Trade Center, at/in building.
Debra L. Gibbon, 43, Hackettstown, N.J., senior vice president, Aon Corp. Confirmed dead, World Trade Center, at/in building.
Craig Neil Gibson, 37, New York, N.Y., reinsurance broker, Marsh & McLennan Cos. Inc. Confirmed dead, World Trade Center, at/in building.
Laura A. Giglio, 35, Oceanside, N.Y., executive assistant, Alliance Consulting. Confirmed dead, World Trade Center, at/in building.
Andrew Clive Gilbert, 39, Califon, N.J., Cantor Fitzgerald. Confirmed dead, World Trade Center, at/in building.
Timothy Paul Gilbert, 35, Lebanon, N.J., Cantor Fitzgerald. Confirmed dead, World Trade Center, at/in building.
Paul Stuart Gilbey, 39, Chatham, N.J., Euro Brokers Inc. Confirmed dead, World Trade Center, at/in building. *British.*
Mark Y. Gilles, 33, New York, N.Y. Confirmed dead, World Trade Center, at/in building.
Evan H. Gillette, 40, New York, N.Y., vice president, Sandler O'Neill & Partners. Confirmed dead, World Trade Center, at/in building.
Ronald Gilligan, 43, Norwalk, Conn., Cantor Fitzgerald. Confirmed dead, World Trade Center, at/in building. *British.*
Laura Gilly, 32, New York, N.Y., technical support, Cantor Fitzgerald. Confirmed dead, World Trade Center, at/in building.
Donna Marie Giordano, 44, Parlin, N.J., broker, Aon Corp. Confirmed dead, World Trade Center, at/in building.
Steven A. Giorgetti, 43, Manhasset, N.Y., senior vice president, Marsh & McLennan Cos. Inc. Confirmed dead, World Trade Center, at/in building.
Martin Giovinazzo, 34, New York, N.Y., maintenance worker, Marsh & McLennan Cos. Inc. Confirmed dead, World Trade Center, at/in building.
Jinny Lady Giraldo, 27. Reported missing, World Trade Center, at/in building. *Colombian.*
Kum-Kum Girolamo, 41, New York, N.Y., Aon Corp. Confirmed dead, World Trade Center, at/in building.
Salvatore Gitto, 44, Manalapan, N.J., Marsh & McLennan Cos. Inc. Confirmed dead, World Trade Center, at/in building.
Cynthia Giugliano, 46, Nesconset, N.Y., chief technical specialist, Empire Blue Cross/Blue Shield. Confirmed dead, World Trade Center, at/in building.
Mon Gjonbalaj, 65, New York, N.Y., janitorial, porter, ABM Industries. Confirmed dead, World Trade Center, at/in building.
Dianne Gladstone, 55, New York, N.Y., section head, New York State Department of Taxation and Finance. Confirmed dead, World Trade Center, at/in building.
Thomas I. Glasser, 40, Summit, N.J., partner, Sandler O'Neill & Partners. Confirmed dead, World Trade Center, at/in building.
Harry Glenn, 38, Piscataway, N.J., assistant vice president, global technology, Marsh & McLennan Cos. Inc. Confirmed dead, World Trade Center, at/in building.
Steven Lawrence Glick, 42, Greenwich, Conn., financial consultant, Credit Suisse First Boston. Confirmed dead, World Trade Center, at/in building.
John T. Gnazzo, 32, New York, N.Y., vice president of operations, Cantor Fitzgerald. Confirmed dead, World Trade Center, at/in building.
William (Bill) Robert Godshalk, 35, New York, N.Y., vice president, institutional equity sales, Keefe, Bruyette & Woods. Confirmed dead, World Trade Center, at/in building.
Michael Gogliormella, 43, New Providence, N.J., Cantor Fitzgerald. Confirmed dead, World Trade Center, at/in building.
Brian Fredric Goldberg, 26, Union, N.J., Fiduciary Trust International. Confirmed dead, World Trade Center, at/in building.
Jeffrey Grant Goldflam, 48, Melville, N.Y., Cantor Fitzgerald. Confirmed dead, World Trade Center, at/in building.
Michelle Herman Goldstein, 31, New York, N.Y., brokerage services, Aon Corp. Reported dead, World Trade Center, at/in building.
Monica Goldstein, 25, New York, N.Y., Cantor Fitzgerald. Confirmed dead, World Trade Center, at/in building.
Steven Goldstein, 35, Princeton, N.J., computer analyst, Cantor Fitzgerald. Confirmed dead, World Trade Center, at/in building.
Andrew H. Golkin, 30, New York, N.Y., vice president, Cantor Fitzgerald. Confirmed dead, World Trade Center, at/in building.
Dennis James Gomes, 40, New York, N.Y., Fiduciary Trust International. Confirmed dead, World Trade Center, at/in building.
Enrique Antonio Gomez, 42, New York, N.Y., kitchen worker, Windows on the World. Confirmed dead, World Trade Center, at/in building.
Jose Bienvenido Gomez, 45, New York, N.Y., kitchen worker, Windows on the World. Confirmed dead, World Trade Center, at/in building.
Manuel Gomez, 42, New York, N.Y., vice president, Fuji Bank. Confirmed dead, World Trade Center, at/in building.
Max Gomez. Reported missing, World Trade Center, at/in building.
Wilder Gomez, 38, New York, N.Y., waiter and bartender, Windows on the World. Reported missing, World Trade Center, at/in building. *Colombian.*

Ana Irene Medina Gonzalez. Reported missing, World Trade Center, at/in building.
Jenine Gonzalez, 27, New York, N.Y., secretary, Aon Corp. Confirmed dead, World Trade Center, at/in building.
Joel Guevara Gonzalez, Aguascalientes, Aguascalientes, Mexico. Reported missing, World Trade Center, at/in building. *Mexican.*
Mauricio Gonzalez, 27, New York, N.Y., carpenter. Confirmed dead, World Trade Center, at/in building.
Rosa J. Gonzalez, 32, Jersey City, N.J., secretary, McKeon-Grano. Confirmed dead, World Trade Center, at/in building.
Calvin J. Gooding, 38, Riverside, N.Y., financial trader, Cantor Fitzgerald. Confirmed dead, World Trade Center, at/in building.
Harry Goody, 50, New York, N.Y., New York State Department of Taxation and Finance. Confirmed dead, World Trade Center, at/in building.
Kiran Reddy Gopu, 24, Bridgeport, Conn., graduate student in computer science, University of Bridgeport (Conn.) and Marsh USA. Confirmed dead, World Trade Center, at/in building.
Catherine Carmen Gorayeb, 41, New York, N.Y. Confirmed dead, World Trade Center, at/in building.
Kerene Gordon, 43, New York, N.Y., food service handler, Forte Food Service. Confirmed dead, World Trade Center, at/in building. *Jamaican.*
Sebastian Gorki, 27, New York, N.Y., global equities division, Deutsche Bank. Confirmed dead, World Trade Center, at/in building.
Kieran Gorman, 35, Yonkers, N.Y., mason tender, Structure Tone. Confirmed dead, World Trade Center, at/in building.
Michael Edward Gould, 29, Hoboken, N.J., NASDAQ trader, Cantor Fitzgerald. Confirmed dead, World Trade Center, at/in building.
Douglas A. Gowell, 52, Methuen, Mass., director of new market development, Avid Technologies. Confirmed dead, World Trade Center, at/in building.
Yuji Goya, 42, Rye, N.Y., vice president, Mizuho Capital Markets Corp. Confirmed dead, World Trade Center, at/in building. *Japanese.*
Jon Grabowski, 33, New York, N.Y., vice president for technology information, Marsh & McLennan Cos. Inc. Confirmed dead, World Trade Center, at/in building.
Christopher Michael Grady, 39, Cranford, N.J., Cantor Fitzgerald. Confirmed dead, World Trade Center, at/in building.
Edwin John Graf, 48, Rowayton, Conn., vice president, Cantor Fitzgerald. Confirmed dead, World Trade Center, at/in building.
David M. Graifman, 40, New York, N.Y., vice president, Keefe, Bruyette & Woods. Confirmed dead, World Trade Center, at/in building.
Gilbert Granados, 51, Hicksville, N.Y., Aon Corp. Confirmed dead, World Trade Center, at/in building.
Elvira Granitto, 43, New York, N.Y. Confirmed dead, World Trade Center, at/in building.
Winston A. Grant, 59, West Hempstead, N.Y. Confirmed dead, World Trade Center, at/in building.
Christopher Stewart Gray, 32, Weehawken, N.J., foreign exchange broker, Cantor Fitzgerald. Confirmed dead, World Trade Center, at/in building.
Linda Mair Grayling, 44, New York, N.Y., receptionist, Marsh & McLennan Cos. Inc. Confirmed dead, World Trade Center, at/in building.
John Michael Grazioso, 41, Middletown, N.J., eSpeed salesman, Cantor Fitzgerald. Confirmed dead, World Trade Center, at/in building.
Timothy Grazioso, 42, Gulf Stream, Fla., trader, Cantor Fitzgerald. Confirmed dead, World Trade Center, at/in building.
Derrick Arthur Green, 44, New York, N.Y., drywall worker. Confirmed dead, World Trade Center, at/in building.
Wade Brian Green, 42, Westbury, N.Y., Thomson Financial Services. Confirmed dead, World Trade Center, at/in building.
Elaine Myra Greenberg, 56, New York, N.Y. Confirmed dead, World Trade Center, at/in building.
Gayle R. Greene, 51, Montville, N.J., vice president of professional resource group, Marsh & McLennan Cos. Inc. Confirmed dead, World Trade Center, at/in building.
James Arthur Greenleaf, 32, New York, N.Y., foreign exchange trader, Carr Futures. Confirmed dead, World Trade Center, at/in building.
Eileen Marsha Greenstein, 52, Morris Plains, N.J., Aon Corp. Confirmed dead, World Trade Center, at/in building.
Elizabeth (Lisa) Martin Gregg, 52, New York, N.Y., senior vice president, Fred Alger Management. Confirmed dead, World Trade Center, at/in building.
Denise Gregory, 39, New York, N.Y., Carr Futures. Confirmed dead, World Trade Center, at/in building, *Jamaican.*
Donald H. Gregory, 62, Ramsey, N.J., bond broker, Cantor Fitzgerald. Confirmed dead, World Trade Center, at/in building.
Florence M. Gregory, 38, New York, N.Y., marine insurance specialist, Aon Corp. Confirmed dead, World Trade Center, at/in building.
Pedro (David) Grehan, 35, Hoboken, N.J., Cantor Fitzgerald. Confirmed dead, World Trade Center, at/in building.
John M. Griffin, 38, Waldwick, N.J., Silverstein Properties. Confirmed dead, World Trade Center, at/in building.
Tawanna Griffin, 30, New York, N.Y., food service handler, Forte Food Service. Confirmed dead, World Trade Center, at/in building.
Joan D. Griffith, 39, Willingboro, N.J., office manager, Fiduciary Trust International. Confirmed dead, World Trade Center, at/in building.
Warren Grifka, 54, New York, N.Y., Marsh & McLennan Cos. Inc. Confirmed dead, World Trade Center, at/in building.

Ramon Grijalvo, 58, Morgan Stanley. Confirmed dead, World Trade Center, at/in building. *Filipino.*
David Grimner, 51, Merrick, N.Y., Marsh & McLennan Cos. Inc. Confirmed dead, World Trade Center, at/in building.
Matthew J. Grzymalski, 34, New Hyde Park, N.Y., bond broker, Cantor Fitzgerald. Confirmed dead, World Trade Center, at/in building.
Robert Joseph Gschaar, 55, Spring Valley, N.Y., Aon Corp. Confirmed dead, World Trade Center, at/in building.
Liming (Michael) Gu, 34, Piscataway, N.J., Marsh & McLennan Cos. Inc. Confirmed dead, World Trade Center, at/in building.
Yan Z. (Cindy) Guan, 25, New York, N.Y., New York State Department of Taxation and Finance. Confirmed dead, World Trade Center, at/in building.
Babita Guman, 33, New York, N.Y., computer specialist, Fiduciary Trust International. Confirmed dead, World Trade Center, at/in building.
Douglas B. Gurian, 38, Tenafly, N.J., Radianz. Confirmed dead, World Trade Center, at/in building.
Janet H. Gustafson, 48, New York, N.Y. Confirmed dead, World Trade Center, at/in building.
Philip T. Guza, 54, Sea Bright, N.J., client specialist, Aon Corp. Confirmed dead, World Trade Center, at/in building.
Sabita Guzman. Reported missing, World Trade Center, at/in building.
Barbara Guzzardo, 49, Glendale, N.Y., insurance underwriter, Aon Corp. Confirmed dead, World Trade Center, at/in building.
Peter Gyulavary, 44, Warwick, N.Y., environmental engineer, Washington Group International. Confirmed dead, World Trade Center, at/in building.

– H –

Gary Robert Haag, 36, Ossining, N.Y., claims department vice president, Marsh & McLennan Cos. Inc. Confirmed dead, World Trade Center, at/in building.
Andrea Lyn Haberman, 25, Chicago, Ill., Carr Futures. Confirmed dead, World Trade Center, at/in building.
Barbara M. Habib, 49, New York, N.Y., vice president, Marsh & McLennan Cos. Inc. Confirmed dead, World Trade Center, at/in building.
Philip Haentzler, 49, New York, N.Y., legal administrative officer, Kidder Peabody-Paine Webber. Confirmed dead, World Trade Center, at/in building.
Nizam A. Hafiz, 32, New York, N.Y., computer analyst, Marsh & McLennan Cos. Inc. Confirmed dead, World Trade Center, at/in building. *Guyanese.*
Karen Hagerty, 34, New York, N.Y., senior vice president, Aon Corp. Confirmed dead, World Trade Center, at/in building.
Steven Hagis, 31, New York, N.Y., vice president, Cantor Fitzgerald. Confirmed dead, World Trade Center, at/in building.
Mary Lou Hague, 26, New York, N.Y., financial analyst, Keefe, Bruyette & Woods. Confirmed dead, World Trade Center, at/in building.
Maile Rachel Hale, 26, Cambridge, Mass., vice president of operations, Boston Investor Services. Confirmed dead, World Trade Center, at/in building.
Richard Hall, 49, Purchase, N.Y., senior vice president, Aon Corp. Confirmed dead, World Trade Center, at/in building.
Vaswald George Hall, 50, New York, N.Y., courier. Confirmed dead, World Trade Center, at/in building. *Jamaican.*
Robert John Halligan, 59, Basking Ridge, N.J., reinsurance broker, Aon Corp. Confirmed dead, World Trade Center, at/in building. *British.*
James D. Halvorson, 56, Greenwich, Conn., head of Global Infrastructure Group, Marsh & McLennan Cos. Inc. Confirmed dead, World Trade Center, at/in building.
Mohammed Salman Hamdani, 23, New York, N.Y., research technician, Howard Hughes Medical Institute at Rockefeller University. Reported missing, World Trade Center, at/in building.
Felicia Hamilton, 62, New York, N.Y., Fiduciary Trust International. Confirmed dead, World Trade Center, at/in building.
Frederic Kim Han, 45, Marlboro, N.J., senior vice president, Cantor Fitzgerald. Confirmed dead, World Trade Center, at/in building.
Christopher James Hanley, 34, New York, N.Y., manager of business development, Radianz. Confirmed dead, World Trade Center, at/in building.
Valerie Joan Hanna, 57, Freeville, N.Y., senior vice president, Marsh & McLennan Cos. Inc. Confirmed dead, World Trade Center, at/in building.
Kevin James Hannaford, 32, Basking Ridge, N.J., commodities broker, Cantor Fitzgerald. Confirmed dead, World Trade Center, at/in building.
Michael L. Hannan, 34, Lynbrook, N.Y., Marsh & McLennan Cos. Inc. Confirmed dead, World Trade Center, at/in building.
Vassilios G. Haramis, 56, New York, N.Y., mechanical engineer, Washington Group International. Confirmed dead, World Trade Center, at/in building.
James A. Haran, 41, Malverne, N.Y., Cantor Fitzgerald. Confirmed dead, World Trade Center, at/in building.
Jeffrey P. Hardy, 46, New York, N.Y., executive chef, Forte Food Service. Confirmed dead, World Trade Center, at/in building.
Timothy John Hargrave, 38, Readington, N.J., vice president, Cantor Fitzgerald. Confirmed dead, World Trade Center, at/in building.
Frances Haros, 76, New York, N.Y., Keefe, Bruyette & Woods. Confirmed dead, World Trade Center, at/in building.
Aisha Harris, 22, New York, N.Y., switch operations technician, General Telecom. Confirmed dead, World Trade Center, at/in building.
Stewart D. Harris, 52, Marlboro, N.J., chief credit officer, Cantor Fitzgerald. Confirmed dead, World Trade Center, at/in building.
John Patrick Hart, 38, Danville, Calif., director of global operations, Franklin Templeton Investments. Reported missing, World Trade Center, at/in building.

John Clinton Hartz, 64, Basking Ridge, N.J., senior vice president, Fiduciary Trust International. Confirmed dead, World Trade Center, at/in building.
Emeric J. Harvey, 56, Montclair, N.J., president, Harvey Young Yurman Inc. Confirmed dead, World Trade Center, at/in building.
Joseph John Hasson, 34, New York, N.Y., Cantor Fitzgerald. Confirmed dead, World Trade Center, at/in building.
Leonard William Hatton, 45, Ridgefield Park, N.J., special agent, Federal Bureau of Investigation. Confirmed dead, World Trade Center, at/in building.
Timothy Aaron Haviland, 41, Oceanside, N.Y., software developer/computer programmer, Marsh & McLennan Cos. Inc. Confirmed dead, World Trade Center, at/in building.
Donald G. Havlish, 53, Yardley, Pa., senior vice president, Aon Corp. Confirmed dead, World Trade Center, at/in building.
Anthony Hawkins, 30, New York, N.Y., maintenance worker, Cantor Fitzgerald. Reported missing, World Trade Center, at/in building.
Nobuhiro Hayatsu, 36, Scarsdale, N.Y., Chuo Mitsui Trust and Banking Co. Confirmed dead, World Trade Center, at/in building.
Philip Hayes, 67, Northport, N.Y., fire safety director, OCS Security. Confirmed dead, World Trade Center, at/in building.
William Ward Haynes, 35, Rye, N.Y., derivatives broker, Cantor Fitzgerald. Confirmed dead, World Trade Center, at/in building.
Scott Hazelcorn, 29, Hoboken, N.J., bond trader, Cantor Fitzgerald. Confirmed dead, World Trade Center, at/in building.
Roberta Bernstein Heber, 60, New York, N.Y., systems analyst, Marsh & McLennan Cos. Inc. Confirmed dead, World Trade Center, at/in building.
Charles Francis Xavier Heeran, 23, Belle Harbor, N.Y., institutional equities trader, Cantor Fitzgerald. Confirmed dead, World Trade Center, at/in building.
Howard Joseph Heller, 37, Ridgefield, Conn., managed funds expert, Carr Futures. Confirmed dead, World Trade Center, at/in building.
JoAnn L. Heltibridle, 46, Springfield, N.J., senior vice president, Marsh & McLennan Cos. Inc. Confirmed dead, World Trade Center, at/in building.
Mark F. Hemschoot, 45, Red Bank, N.J., senior vice president, Aon Corp. Confirmed dead, World Trade Center, at/in building.
Janet Hendricks, Aon Corp. Reported dead, World Trade Center, at/in building.
Brian Hennessey, 35, Ringoes, N.J., Cantor Fitzgerald. Confirmed dead, World Trade Center, at/in building.
Michelle Marie Henrique, 27, New York, N.Y., administrative assistant, Fiduciary Trust International. Confirmed dead, World Trade Center, at/in building.
John Henwood, 35, New York, N.Y., broker, Cantor Fitzgerald. Confirmed dead, World Trade Center, at/in building.
Robert Allan Hepburn, 39, Union, N.J., office service manager, Marsh & McLennan Cos. Inc. Confirmed dead, World Trade Center, at/in building.
Mary (Molly) Herencia, 47, New York, N.Y., insurance broker, Aon Corp. Confirmed dead, World Trade Center, at/in building.
Lindsay Coates Herkness, 58, New York, N.Y., senior vice president, Morgan Stanley. Confirmed dead, World Trade Center, at/in building.
Harvey Robert Hermer, 59, wire person, Forest Electric Corp. Confirmed dead, World Trade Center, at/in building.
Anabel Hernandez, 41. Chase Manhattan Bank. Reported missing, World Trade Center, at/in building. *Venezuelan.*
Claribel Hernandez, 31, New York, N.Y., administrative assistant, Sybase. Confirmed dead, World Trade Center, at/in building.
Eduardo Hernandez, 40, Chase Manhattan Bank. Reported missing, World Trade Center, at/in building. *Venezuelan.*
Norberto Hernandez, 42, New York, N.Y., pastry sous chef, Windows on the World. Confirmed dead, World Trade Center, at/in building.
Raul Hernandez, 51, New York, N.Y., maintenance supervisor, Cantor Fitzgerald. Reported missing, World Trade Center, at/in building.
Gary Herold, 44, Farmingdale, N.Y., risk management insurance, Aon Corp. Confirmed dead, World Trade Center, at/in building.
Jeffrey A. Hersch, 53, New York, N.Y., Cantor Fitzgerald. Confirmed dead, World Trade Center, at/in building.
Ysidro Hidalgo-Tejada, Dominican Republic, Windows on the World. Reported missing, World Trade Center, at/in building. *Dominican.*
Robert D. Higley, 29, New Fairfield, Conn., client services, Aon Corp. Confirmed dead, World Trade Center, at/in building.
Todd Russell Hill, 34, Boston, Mass., account executive, QRS Corp. Confirmed dead, World Trade Center, at/in building.
Clara Victorine Hinds, 52, New York, N.Y., seamstress, Windows on the World. Confirmed dead, World Trade Center, at/in building.
Neal Hinds, 28, New York, N.Y., personal banker, Bank of New York. Confirmed dead, World Trade Center, at/in building. *Jamaican.*
Mark D. Hindy, 28, New York, N.Y., Cantor Fitzgerald. Confirmed dead, World Trade Center, at/in building.
Katsuyuki Hirai, 32, Hartsdale, N.Y. Confirmed dead, World Trade Center, at/in building.
Heather Malia Ho, 32, New York, N.Y., executive pastry chef, Windows on the World. Confirmed dead, World Trade Center, at/in building.
Tara Yvette Hobbs, 31, New York, N.Y., employee in insurance division, Aon Corp. Confirmed dead, World Trade Center, at/in building.
Thomas A. Hobbs, 41, Baldwin, N.Y., Cantor Fitzgerald. Confirmed dead, World Trade Center, at/in building.

James L. Hobin, 47, Marlborough, Conn., vice president, Marsh & McLennan Cos. Inc. Confirmed dead, World Trade Center, at/in building.
Robert Wayne Hobson, 36, New Providence, N.J., broker, Cantor Fitzgerald. Confirmed dead, World Trade Center, at/in building.
DaJuan Hodges, 29, New York, N.Y., management services, Marsh & McLennan Cos. Inc. Confirmed dead, World Trade Center, at/in building.
Ronald George Hoerner, 58, Massapequa Park, N.Y., security manager, Summit Security Services. Confirmed dead, World Trade Center, at/in building.
Frederick J. Hoffman, 53, N.J., Cantor Fitzgerald. Reported dead, World Trade Center, at/in building.
Joseph Hoffman, 43. Confirmed dead, World Trade Center, at/in building.
Marcia Hoffman, 52, New York, N.Y., Cantor Fitzgerald. Confirmed dead, World Trade Center, at/in building.
Michele L. Hoffman, 27, Freehold, N.J., Cantor Fitzgerald. Confirmed dead, World Trade Center, at/in building.
Stephen G. Hoffman, 36, Long Beach, N.Y., bond broker, Cantor Fitzgerald. Confirmed dead, World Trade Center, at/in building.
Judith Florence Hofmiller, 53, Brookfield, Conn., senior software consultant, Marsh & McLennan Cos. Inc. Confirmed dead, World Trade Center, at/in building.
Thomas Warren Hohlweck, 57, Harrison, N.Y., senior vice president, Aon Corp. Confirmed dead, World Trade Center, at/in building.
John Holland, 30, Windows on the World. Confirmed dead, World Trade Center, at/in building.
Joseph Francis Holland, 32, Glen Rock, N.J., broker, Carr Futures. Confirmed dead, World Trade Center, at/in building.
Elizabeth Holmes, 42, New York, N.Y., communications, Euro Brokers Inc. Confirmed dead, World Trade Center, at/in building.
Bradley Hoorn, 22, Richland, Mich., Fred Alger Management. Reported missing, World Trade Center, at/in building.
James P. Hopper, 51, Farmingdale, N.Y., Cantor Fitzgerald. Reported dead, World Trade Center, at/in building.
Montgomery McCullough Hord, 46, Pelham, N.Y., vice president, Cantor Fitzgerald. Confirmed dead, World Trade Center, at/in building.
Michael Horn, 27, Lynbrook, N.Y., Cantor Fitzgerald. Reported dead, World Trade Center, at/in building.
Matthew D. Horning, 26, Hoboken, N.J., Marsh & McLennan Cos. Inc. Confirmed dead, World Trade Center, at/in building.
Robert L. Horohoe, 31, New York, N.Y., vice president, corporate bonds, Cantor Fitzgerald. Confirmed dead, World Trade Center, at/in building.
Aaron Horwitz, 24, New York, N.Y., bond broker, Cantor Fitzgerald. Confirmed dead, World Trade Center, at/in building.
Malverse Houscal, N.J. Reported missing, World Trade Center, at/in building.
Charles J. Houston, 42, New York, N.Y., Euro Brokers Inc. Confirmed dead, World Trade Center, at/in building.
Michael C. Howell, 60, New York, N.Y., information services manager, Fred Alger Management. Confirmed dead, World Trade Center, at/in building.
Steven L. Howell, 36, New York, N.Y., desktop support manager, Marsh & McLennan Cos. Inc. Confirmed dead, World Trade Center, at/in building.
Jennifer L. Howley, 34, New Hyde Park, N.Y., Aon Corp. Confirmed dead, World Trade Center, at/in building.
Milagros Hromada, 35, New York, N.Y., Aon Corp. Confirmed dead, World Trade Center, at/in building.
Marian Hrycak, 56, New York, N.Y., New York State Department of Taxation and Finance. Confirmed dead, World Trade Center, at/in building.
Kris R. Hughes, 30, Nesconset, N.Y., securities trader, Keefe, Bruyette & Woods. Confirmed dead, World Trade Center, at/in building.
Melissa Harrington Hughes, 31, San Francisco, Calif., director of business development, Slam Dunk Networks. Confirmed dead, World Trade Center, at/in building.
Paul R. Hughes, 38, Stamford, Conn., data systems manager, Marsh USA. Confirmed dead, World Trade Center, at/in building.
Robert T. "Bobby" Hughes, 23, Sayreville, N.J., margins clerk, Bank of America. Confirmed dead, World Trade Center, at/in building.
Thomas F. Hughes, 46, Spring Lake Heights, N.J., owner, Colonial Art Decorators. Confirmed dead, World Trade Center, at/in building.
Timothy Robert Hughes, 43, Madison, N.J., Cantor Fitzgerald. Confirmed dead, World Trade Center, at/in building.
Susan Huie, 43, Fair Lawn, N.J., Compaq. Confirmed dead, World Trade Center, at/in building.
Mychal Lamar Hulse, 30, New York, N.Y. Confirmed dead, World Trade Center, at/in building.
Kathleen (Casey) Hunt, 43, Middletown, N.J., employee on equity trading desk, Sandler O'Neill & Partners. Confirmed dead, World Trade Center, at/in building.
William C. Hunt, 32, Norwalk, Conn., bond trader, Euro Brokers Inc. Confirmed dead, World Trade Center, at/in building.
Robert Hussa, 51, Roslyn, N.Y., senior vice president, Carr Futures. Confirmed dead, World Trade Center, at/in building.
Thomas E. Hynes, 28, Norwalk, Conn., account manager, Vestek division of Thomson Financial. Reported dead, World Trade Center, at/in building.

– I –

Joseph Anthony Ianelli, 28, Hoboken, N.J., accountant, Marsh & McLennan Cos. Inc. Confirmed dead, World Trade Center, at/in building.
Zuhtu Ibis, 25, Clifton, N.J., Cantor Fitzgerald. Confirmed dead, World Trade Center, at/in building.
Michael Patrick Iken, 37, New York, N.Y., bond trader, Euro Brokers Inc. Confirmed dead, World Trade Center, at/in building.
Daniel Ilkanayev, 36, New York, N.Y., Cantor Fitzgerald. Confirmed dead, World Trade Center, at/in building.
Abraham Nethanel Ilowitz, 51, New York, N.Y., financial services representative, Metropolitan Life Insurance Co. Confirmed dead, World Trade Center, at/in building.
Louis S. Inghilterra, 45, New Castle, N.Y., Fiduciary Trust International. Confirmed dead, World Trade Center, at/in building.
Christopher N. Ingrassia, 28, Watchung, N.J., equity options trader, Cantor Fitzgerald. Confirmed dead, World Trade Center, at/in building.
Paul Innella, 33, East Brunswick, N.J., systems analyst, Cantor Fitzgerald. Confirmed dead, World Trade Center, at/in building.
Stephanie V. Irby, 38, New York, N.Y., accountant, Marsh & McLennan Cos. Inc. Confirmed dead, World Trade Center, at/in building.
Douglas Irgang, 32, New York, N.Y., Sandler O'Neill & Partners. Confirmed dead, World Trade Center, at/in building.
Kristin A. Irvine-Ryan, 30, New York, N.Y., trader, Sandler O'Neill & Partners. Confirmed dead, World Trade Center, at/in building.
Todd A. Isaac, 29, New York, N.Y., Cantor Fitzgerald. Confirmed dead, World Trade Center, at/in building.
Erik Hans Isbrandtsen, 30, New York, N.Y., industrial sales trader, Cantor Fitzgerald. Confirmed dead, World Trade Center, at/in building.
William Iselepis, 33. Confirmed dead, World Trade Center, at/in building.
Taizo Ishikawa, 50. New York branch general manager, Fuji Bank. Confirmed dead, World Trade Center, at/in building. *Japanese.*
Aram Iskenderian, 41, Merrick, N.Y., Cantor Fitzgerald. Confirmed dead, World Trade Center, at/in building.
John Iskyan, 41, Wilton, Conn., financial analyst, Cantor Fitzgerald. Confirmed dead, World Trade Center, at/in building.
Kazushige Ito, 35, New York, N.Y., manager, Fuji Bank. Confirmed dead, World Trade Center, at/in building. *Japanese.*
Aleksandr Valeryerich Ivantsov, 23, New York, N.Y., computer engineer for eSpeed division, Cantor Fitzgerald. Confirmed dead, World Trade Center, at/in building. *Russian.*

– J –

Virginia Jablonski, 49, Matawan, N.J., assistant vice president, Marsh & McLennan Cos. Inc. Confirmed dead, World Trade Center, at/in building.
Brooke Alexandra Jackman, 23, New York, N.Y., assistant bond trader, Cantor Fitzgerald. Confirmed dead, World Trade Center, at/in building.
Aaron Jacobs, 27, New York, N.Y., vice president and partner, international trading desk, Cantor Fitzgerald. Confirmed dead, World Trade Center, at/in building.
Ariel Louis Jacobs, 29, Briarcliff Manor, N.Y., executive vice president, Caplin Systems. Confirmed dead, World Trade Center, at/in building.
Jason Kyle Jacobs, 32, Mendham, N.J., business partner, Fiduciary Trust International. Confirmed dead, World Trade Center, at/in building.
Michael Grady Jacobs, 54, Danbury, Conn., accountant/vice president for tax operations, Fiduciary Trust International. Confirmed dead, World Trade Center, at/in building.
Steven A. Jacobson, 53, New York, N.Y., transmitter engineer, WPIX-TV. Confirmed dead, World Trade Center, at/in building.
Ricknauth Jaggernauth, 58, New York, N.Y., construction worker, NTX Interiors. Confirmed dead, World Trade Center, at/in building.
Jake Denis Jagoda, 24, trader for TradeSpark, Cantor Fitzgerald. Confirmed dead, World Trade Center, at/in building.
Yudh V.S. Jain, 54, New City, N.Y., senior project manager at eSpeed, Cantor Fitzgerald. Confirmed dead, World Trade Center, at/in building.
Maria Jakubiak, 41, Ridgewood, N.Y., Marsh & McLennan Cos. Inc. Confirmed dead, World Trade Center, at/in building.
Ernest James, 40, New York, N.Y., Marsh & McLennan Cos. Inc. Reported missing, World Trade Center, at/in building.
Gricelda E. James, 44, Willingboro, N.J. Confirmed dead, World Trade Center, at/in building.
Mark Jardin, 39, New York, N.Y. Confirmed dead, World Trade Center, at/in building.
Mohammed Jawara, 30, New York, N.Y., MAS Security. Confirmed dead, World Trade Center, at/in building.
Francois Jean-Pierre, 58, New York, N.Y., Windows on the World. Confirmed dead, World Trade Center, at/in building.
Paul E. Jeffers, 39, New York, N.Y., Cantor Fitzgerald. Confirmed dead, World Trade Center, at/in building.
Joseph Jenkins, 47, New York, N.Y. Confirmed dead, World Trade Center, at/in building.
Alan K. Jensen, 49, Wyckoff, N.J. Confirmed dead, World Trade Center, at/in building.
Farah Jeudy, 32, Spring Valley, N.Y., administrative assistant, Aon Corp. Confirmed dead, World Trade Center, at/in building.
Hweidar Jian, 42, East Brunswick, N.J., senior programmer analyst, Cantor Fitzgerald. Confirmed dead, World Trade Center, at/in building.

Eliezer Jimenez, 38, New York, N.Y., chef's assistant, Windows on the World. Confirmed dead, World Trade Center, at/in building.
Luis Jimenez, 25, New York, N.Y., accountant, Marsh & McLennan Cos. Inc. Confirmed dead, World Trade Center, at/in building.
Fernando Jimenez Molina, Oaxaca, Mexico. Reported missing, World Trade Center, at/in building. *Mexican.*
Charles Gregory John, 44, security officer, Royston and Zamani. Confirmed dead, World Trade Center, at/in building.
Nicholas John, 42, New York, N.Y. Confirmed dead, World Trade Center, at/in building.
LaShawana Johnson, 27, New York, N.Y., customer service manager, General Telecom. Confirmed dead, World Trade Center, at/in building.
Scott M. Johnson, 26, New York, N.Y., securities analyst, Keefe, Bruyette & Woods. Confirmed dead, World Trade Center, at/in building.
Allison Horstmann Jones, 31, New York, N.Y., Sandler O'Neill & Partners. Confirmed dead, World Trade Center, at/in building.
Arthur Joseph Jones, 37, Ossining, N.Y., Carr Futures. Confirmed dead, World Trade Center, at/in building.
Brian L. Jones, 44, New York, N.Y., systems administrator, IBM Global. Confirmed dead, World Trade Center, at/in building.
Christopher D. Jones, 53, Huntington, N.Y., partner, Cantor Fitzgerald. Reported dead, World Trade Center, at/in building.
Donald T. Jones, 39, Livingston, N.J., executive vice president, municipal bonds, Cantor Fitzgerald. Confirmed dead, World Trade Center, at/in building.
Donald W. Jones, 43, Fairless Hills, Pa., bond broker, Cantor Fitzgerald. Confirmed dead, World Trade Center, at/in building.
Linda Jones, 50, New York, N.Y., Aon Corp. Confirmed dead, World Trade Center, at/in building.
Robert Thomas Jordan, 34, Williston, N.Y., bond trader, Cantor Fitzgerald. Confirmed dead, World Trade Center, at/in building.
Albert Joseph, 79, maintenance worker, Morgan Stanley. Confirmed dead, World Trade Center, at/in building.
Ingeborg Joseph, 60, Germany, import manager, Rohde & Liesenfeld shipping agency. Confirmed dead, World Trade Center, at/in building. *German.*
Stephen Joseph, 39, Franklin Park, N.J., Fiduciary Trust International. Confirmed dead, World Trade Center, at/in building.
Jane Eileen Josiah, 47, Bellmore, N.Y., Fiduciary Trust International. Confirmed dead, World Trade Center, at/in building.
Karen Susan Juday, 52, New York, N.Y., administrative assistant, Cantor Fitzgerald. Confirmed dead, World Trade Center, at/in building.
Thomas Edward Jurgens, 26, Lawrence, N.Y., court officer, New York State Supreme Court. Confirmed dead, World Trade Center, at/in building.

– K –

Shashi Kiran L. Kadaba, 26, Hackensack, N.J., software designer, Wipro Technologies. Reported missing, World Trade Center, at/in building.
Gavkharoy Mukhometovna Kamardinova, 26, New York, N.Y. Confirmed dead, World Trade Center, at/in building. *Uzbek.*
Shari Kandell, 27, Wyckoff, N.J., trader, Cantor Fitzgerald. Confirmed dead, World Trade Center, at/in building.
Howard Lee Kane, 40, Hazlet, N.J., comptroller, Windows on the World. Confirmed dead, World Trade Center, at/in building.
Jennifer Lynn Kane, 26, Fair Lawn, N.J., accountant, Marsh & McLennan Cos. Inc. Confirmed dead, World Trade Center, at/in building.
Joon Koo Kang, 34, Riverdale, N.J., systems analyst, Cantor Fitzgerald. Confirmed dead, World Trade Center, at/in building.
Sheldon R. Kanter, 53, Edison, N.J., systems vice president, Cantor Fitzgerald. Confirmed dead, World Trade Center, at/in building.
Alvin Peter Kappelmann, 57, Green Brook, N.J., insurance executive, Royal & SunAlliance. Confirmed dead, World Trade Center, at/in building.
Charles Karczewski, 34, Union, N.J., benefits consultant, Aon Corp. Confirmed dead, World Trade Center, at/in building.
William A. Karnes, 37, New York, N.Y., technology trainer, Marsh & McLennan Cos. Inc. Confirmed dead, World Trade Center, at/in building.
Andrew Kates, 37, New York, N.Y., senior managing director, Cantor Fitzgerald. Confirmed dead, World Trade Center, at/in building.
John Katsimatides, 31, East Marion, N.Y., financial trader, Cantor Fitzgerald. Confirmed dead, World Trade Center, at/in building.
Don Jerome Kauth, 51, Saratoga Springs, N.Y., bank analyst, Keefe, Bruyette & Woods. Confirmed dead, World Trade Center, at/in building.
Hideya Kawauchi, 36, Fort Lee, N.J., manager, Fuji Bank. Confirmed dead, World Trade Center, at/in building. *Japanese.*
Edward T. Keane, 66, West Caldwell, N.J., engineer, Hill International. Confirmed dead, World Trade Center, at/in building.
Richard M. Keane, 54, Wethersfield, Conn., senior vice president, Marsh Inc. Confirmed dead, World Trade Center, at/in building.
Lisa Kearney-Griffin, 35, Jamaica, N.Y., American Express Corporate Travel, Marsh & McLennan Cos. Inc. Confirmed dead, World Trade Center, at/in building.
Karol Ann Keasler, 42, New York, N.Y., event planner, Keefe, Bruyette & Woods. Confirmed dead, World Trade Center, at/in building.
Leo Russell Keene, 34, Westfield, N.J., financial analyst, Keefe, Bruyette & Woods. Confirmed dead, World Trade Center, at/in building.

Joseph J. Keller, 31, Park Ridge, N.J., department head, Marriott World Trade Center Hotel. Confirmed dead, World Trade Center, at/in building.
Peter Rodney Kellerman, 35, New York, N.Y., partner, Cantor Fitzgerald. Confirmed dead, World Trade Center, at/in building.
Joseph P. Kellett, 37, Riverdale, N.Y., commodities trader, Carr Futures. Confirmed dead, World Trade Center, at/in building.
Frederick H. Kelley, 57, Huntington, N.Y., municipal bonds, Cantor Fitzgerald. Confirmed dead, World Trade Center, at/in building.
James Joseph Kelly, 39, Oceanside, N.Y., bond broker, Cantor Fitzgerald. Confirmed dead, World Trade Center, at/in building.
Joseph A. Kelly, 40, Oyster Bay, N.Y., broker, Cantor Fitzgerald. Confirmed dead, World Trade Center, at/in building.
Maurice Patrick Kelly, 41, New York, N.Y., carpenter/ foreman, National Acoustics Inc. Confirmed dead, World Trade Center, at/in building.
Thomas Michael Kelly, 41, Wykoff, N.J., Euro Brokers Inc. Confirmed dead, World Trade Center, at/in building.
Timothy C. Kelly, 37, Port Washington, N.Y., municipal bond trader, Cantor Fitzgerald. Confirmed dead, World Trade Center, at/in building.
William Hill Kelly, 30, New York, N.Y., salesman, Bloomberg L.P. Confirmed dead, World Trade Center, at/in building.
Robert C. (Bob) Kennedy, 55, Toms River, N.J., senior vice president, Marsh & McLennan Cos. Inc. Confirmed dead, World Trade Center, at/in building.
John Keohane, 41, Jersey City, N.J., assistant general counsel, Zurich American Insurance. Confirmed dead, World Trade Center, at/in building.
Howard L. Kestenbaum, 56, Montclair, N.J., senior vice president, Aon Corp. Confirmed dead, World Trade Center, at/in building.
Douglas D. Ketcham, 27, New York, N.Y., stockbroker, Cantor Fitzgerald. Confirmed dead, World Trade Center, at/in building.
Ruth E. Ketler, 42, New York, N.Y., director of research, Fiduciary Trust International. Confirmed dead, World Trade Center, at/in building.
Boris Khalif, 30, New York, N.Y., computer consultant, Marsh & McLennan Cos. Inc. Confirmed dead, World Trade Center, at/in building.
Sarah Khan, 32, New York, N.Y., food service handler, Forte Food Service. Confirmed dead, World Trade Center, at/in building.
Taimour Firaz Khan, 29, New York, N.Y., trader, Carr Futures. Confirmed dead, World Trade Center, at/in building.
Rajesh Khandelwal, 33, South Plainfield, N.J., Marsh & McLennan Cos. Inc. Confirmed dead, World Trade Center, at/in building.
Bhowanie Devi Khemraj, Jersey City, N.J., restaurant worker. Reported missing, World Trade Center, at/in building.
SeiLai Khoo, 38, Jersey City, N.J., Fred Alger Management. Confirmed dead, World Trade Center, at/in building.
Satoshi Kikuchihara, 43, Scarsdale, N.Y. Confirmed dead, World Trade Center, at/in building.
Andrew Jay-Hoon Kim, 26, Leonia, N.J., ceritified financial analyst, Fred Alger Management. Confirmed dead, World Trade Center, at/in building.
Don Kim, 34, Marsh & McLennan Cos. Inc. Reported missing, World Trade Center, at/in building.
Lawrence Don Kim, 31, Blue Bell, Pa., Marsh & McLennan Cos. Inc. Confirmed dead, World Trade Center, at/in building.
Mary Jo Kimelman, 34, New York, N.Y., volume control clerk, Cantor Fitzgerald. Confirmed dead, World Trade Center, at/in building.
Andrew Marshall King, 42, Princeton, N.J., trader, Cantor Fitzgerald. Confirmed dead, World Trade Center, at/in building.
Lucille T. King, 59, Ridgewood, N.J., Aon Corp. Confirmed dead, World Trade Center, at/in building.
Lisa M. King-Johnson, 34, New York, N.Y., Keefe, Bruyette & Woods. Confirmed dead, World Trade Center, at/in building.
Takashi Kinoshita, 46, president, Mizuho Capital Markets Corp. Reported missing, World Trade Center, at/in building. *Japanese*.
Chris Michael Kirby, 21, New York, N.Y., carpenter. Confirmed dead, World Trade Center, at/in building.
Howard (Barry) Kirschbaum, 53, New York, N.Y., Marsh & McLennan Cos. Inc. Confirmed dead, World Trade Center, at/in building.
Glenn Davis Kirwin, 40, Scarsdale, N.Y., senior vice president of eSpeed, Cantor Fitzgerald. Confirmed dead, World Trade Center, at/in building.
Richard J. Klares, 59, Somers, N.Y., risk management, Marsh & McLennan Cos. Inc. Confirmed dead, World Trade Center, at/in building.
Peter A. Klein, 35, Weehawken, N.J., consultant, Marsh & McLennan Cos. Inc. Confirmed dead, World Trade Center, at/in building.
Alan D. Kleinberg, 39, East Brunswick, N.J., securities trader, Cantor Fitzgerald. Confirmed dead, World Trade Center, at/in building.
Karen J. Klitzman, 38, New York, N.Y., eSpeed, Cantor Fitzgerald. Confirmed dead, World Trade Center, at/in building.
Andrew Knox, 30, Adelaide, Australia, Cantor Fitzgerald. Confirmed dead, World Trade Center, at/in building. *Australian*.
Thomas Patrick Knox, 31, Hoboken, N.J., Cantor Fitzgerald. Confirmed dead, World Trade Center, at/in building.
Yevgeny Knyazev, 46, New York, N.Y., Windows on the World. Confirmed dead, World Trade Center, at/in building.
Rebecca Lee Koborie, 48, Guttenberg, N.J., executive secretary, Marsh & McLennan Cos. Inc. Confirmed dead, World Trade Center, at/in building.

Deborah Kobus, 36, New York, N.Y., assistant vice president, Chuo Mitsui Trust and Banking Company. Confirmed dead, World Trade Center, at/in building.
Gary Edward Koecheler, 57, Harrison, N.Y., government bond broker, Euro Brokers Inc. Confirmed dead, World Trade Center, at/in building.
Frank J. Koestner, 48, New York, N.Y., trader, Cantor Fitzgerald. Confirmed dead, World Trade Center, at/in building.
Ryan Kohart, 26, New York, N.Y., trader, Cantor Fitzgerald. Confirmed dead, World Trade Center, at/in building.
Vanessa Lynn Kolpak, 21, financial researcher, Keefe, Bruyette & Woods. Reported dead, World Trade Center, at/in building.
Irina Kolpakova, 37, New York, N.Y., file clerk, Harris Beach LLP. Confirmed dead, World Trade Center, at/in building.
Suzanne Kondratenko, 27, Chicago, Ill., senior consultant, Keane Consulting Group. Reported missing, World Trade Center, at/in building.
Abdoulaye Kone, 37, New York, N.Y., Windows on the World. Confirmed dead, World Trade Center, at/in building.
Bon-seok Koo, 32, River Edge, N.J., LG Insurance Co. Reported missing, World Trade Center, at/in building.
Dorota Kopiczko, 26, Nutley, N.J., Marsh & McLennan Cos. Inc. Confirmed dead, World Trade Center, at/in building.
Bojan Kostic, 34, New York, N.Y., Cantor Fitzgerald. Confirmed dead, World Trade Center, at/in building.
Danielle Kousoulis, 29, New York, N.Y., vice president, Cantor Fitzgerald. Confirmed dead, World Trade Center, at/in building.
John J. Kren, 52. Confirmed dead, World Trade Center, at/in building.
Lyudmila Ksido, 46, New York, N.Y., consultant, Accenture. Confirmed dead, World Trade Center, at/in building.
Shekhar Kumar, 30, New York, N.Y., Cantor Fitzgerald. Confirmed dead, World Trade Center, at/in building.
Frederick Kuo, 53, Great Neck, N.Y., engineer, Washington Group International. Confirmed dead, World Trade Center, at/in building. *Filipino.*
Patricia Kuras, 42, New York, N.Y., Marsh & McLennan Cos. Inc. Confirmed dead, World Trade Center, at/in building.
Nauka Kushitani, 44, New York, N.Y., FiduciaryTrust International. Confirmed dead, World Trade Center, at/in building.
Victor Kwarkye, 35, New York, N.Y., Windows on the World. Confirmed dead, World Trade Center, at/in building.
Kui Fai Kwok, 31, New York, N.Y., Cantor Fitzgerald. Confirmed dead, World Trade Center, at/in building.
Angela R. Kyte, 49, Boonton, N.J., managing director, Marsh USA. Confirmed dead, World Trade Center, at/in building.

– L –

Amarnauth Lachhman, 42, Valley Stream, N.Y., PM Contracting. Confirmed dead, World Trade Center, at/in building.
Andrew LaCorte, 61, Jersey City, N.J., trader, Carr Futures. Confirmed dead, World Trade Center, at/in building.
Ganesh Ladkat, 27, Somerset, N.J., eSpeed, Cantor Fitzgerald. Reported missing, World Trade Center, at/in building.
James P. Ladley, 41, Colts Neck, N.J., partner and corporate bond broker, Cantor Fitzgerald. Confirmed dead, World Trade Center, at/in building.
Joseph A. Lafalce, 54, New York, N.Y., Cantor Fitzgerald. Confirmed dead, World Trade Center, at/in building.
Jeanette LaFond-Menichino, 49, New York, N.Y. Confirmed dead, World Trade Center, at/in building.
Michael Patrick LaForte, 39, Holmdel, N.J., vice president, Cantor Fitzgerald. Confirmed dead, World Trade Center, at/in building.
Alan Lafranco, 43, freelance audio video technician, Windows on the World. Reported missing, World Trade Center, at/in building.
Juan Lafuente, 61, Poughkeepsie, N.Y., computer analyst, Citibank. Reported missing, World Trade Center, at/in building.
Neil K. Lai, 59, East Windsor, N.J., New York State Department of Taxation and Finance. Confirmed dead, World Trade Center, at/in building.
Vincent A. Laieta, 31, Edison, N.J., vice president of operations, Aon Corp. Confirmed dead, World Trade Center, at/in building.
Chow Kwan Lam, 48, Maywood, N.J., New York State Department of Taxation and Finance. Confirmed dead, World Trade Center, at/in building.
Stephen LaMantia, 38, Darien, Conn., securities trader, Cantor Fitzgerald. Confirmed dead, World Trade Center, at/in building.
Amy Hope Lamonsoff, 29, New York, N.Y., events manager, North America, Risk Waters Group. Confirmed dead, World Trade Center, at/in building.
Brendan M. Lang, 30, Red Bank, N.J., project manager, Structure Tone. Confirmed dead, World Trade Center, at/in building.
Rosanne P. Lang, 42, Middletown, N.J., equities trader, Cantor Fitzgerald. Confirmed dead, World Trade Center, at/in building.
Vanessa Langer, 29, Yonkers, N.Y., office manager, Regus. Confirmed dead, World Trade Center, at/in building.
Mary Lou Langley, 53, New York, N.Y., Aon Corp. Confirmed dead, World Trade Center, at/in building.
Michele B. Lanza, 36, New York, N.Y., administrative assistant, Fiduciary Trust International. Confirmed dead, World Trade Center, at/in building.
Ruth Sheila Lapin, 53, East Windsor, N.J., senior business analyst, Baseline Financial Services. Confirmed dead, World Trade Center, at/in building.

Carol Ann LaPlante, 59, New York, N.Y., Marsh & McLennan Cos. Inc. Confirmed dead, World Trade Center, at/in building.
Ingeborg Astrid Desiree Lariby, 42, New York, N.Y., center manager, Regus. Confirmed dead, World Trade Center, at/in building.
Robin Larkey, 48, Chatham, N.J., currency broker, Cantor Fitzgerald. Confirmed dead, World Trade Center, at/in building.
Christopher Randall Larrabee, 26, New York, N.Y., Cantor Fitzgerald. Confirmed dead, World Trade Center, at/in building.
Hamidou S. Larry, 37, New York, N.Y., Marsh & McLennan Cos. Inc. Confirmed dead, World Trade Center, at/in building.
John Adam Larson, 37, Colonia, N.J., senior vice president, Aon Corp. Confirmed dead, World Trade Center, at/in building.
Gary E. Lasko, 49, Memphis, Tenn., Marsh & McLennan Cos. Inc. Confirmed dead, World Trade Center, at/in building.
Nicholas C. Lassman, 28, Cliffside Park, N.J., computer programming department, Cantor Fitzgerald. Confirmed dead, World Trade Center, at/in building.
Jeffrey Latouche, 49, Windows on the World. Confirmed dead, World Trade Center, at/in building.
Charles Laurencin, 61, New York, N.Y., security guard, Morgan Stanley. Confirmed dead, World Trade Center, at/in building.
Stephen James Lauria, 39, New York, N.Y., project manager, Marsh & McLennan Cos. Inc. Confirmed dead, World Trade Center, at/in building.
Maria Lavache, 60, New York, N.Y., receptionist, Marsh & McLennan Cos. Inc. Confirmed dead, World Trade Center, at/in building.
Denis F. Lavelle, 42, Yonkers, N.Y., accountant, Syncorp. Confirmed dead, World Trade Center, at/in building.
Jeannine M. LaVerde, 36, New York, N.Y., new accountants administrator, Keefe, Bruyette & Woods. Confirmed dead, World Trade Center, at/in building.
Anna A. Laverty, 52, Middletown, N.J., Fiduciary Trust International. Confirmed dead, World Trade Center, at/in building.
Steven Lawn, 28, West Windsor, N.J. Confirmed dead, World Trade Center, at/in building.
Robert A. Lawrence, 41, Summit, N.J., mortgage-backed securities specialist, Sandler O'Neill & Partners. Confirmed dead, World Trade Center, at/in building.
Nathaniel Lawson, 61, New York, N.Y., food service handler, Forte Food Service. Confirmed dead, World Trade Center, at/in building.
Eugene Lazar, 27, New York, N.Y., programmer for eSpeed, Cantor Fitzgerald. Confirmed dead, World Trade Center, at/in building.
Leon Lebor, 51, Jersey City, N.J., janitorial, cleaner, ABM Industries. Confirmed dead, World Trade Center, at/in building.
Kenneth Charles Ledee, 38, Monmouth, N.J., Marsh & McLennan Cos. Inc. Confirmed dead, World Trade Center, at/in building.
Alan J. Lederman, 43, New York, N.Y., senior client specialist, Aon Corp. Confirmed dead, World Trade Center, at/in building.
Elena Ledesma, 36, New York, N.Y., maintenance coordinator, Marsh & McLennan Cos. Inc. Confirmed dead, World Trade Center, at/in building.
Alexis Leduc, 45, New York, N.Y., maintenance supervisor. Confirmed dead, World Trade Center, at/in building.
David S. Lee, 37, West Orange, N.J., senior vice president, Fiduciary Trust International. Confirmed dead, World Trade Center, at/in building.
Gary H. Lee, 62, Lindenhurst, N.Y., senior vice president, Cantor Fitzgerald. Confirmed dead, World Trade Center, at/in building.
Hyun-joon (Paul) Lee, 32, New York, N.Y., New York State Department of Taxation and Finance. Confirmed dead, World Trade Center, at/in building.
Jong-min Lee. Reported missing, World Trade Center, at/in building.
Juanita Lee, 44, New York, N.Y., Aon Corp. Confirmed dead, World Trade Center, at/in building.
Kathryn Blair Lee, 55, New York, N.Y., Web page designer, Marsh & McLennan Cos. Inc. Confirmed dead, World Trade Center, at/in building.
Linda C. Lee, 34, New York, N.Y., senior associate, Jennison Associates. Confirmed dead, World Trade Center, at/in building.
Lorraine Lee, 37, New York, N.Y., administrative assistant, Aon Corp. Confirmed dead, World Trade Center, at/in building.
Myung-woo Lee, 41, Lyndhurst, N.J., tax auditor, New York State Department of Taxation and Finance. Confirmed dead, World Trade Center, at/in building.
Richard Y.C. Lee, 34, Great Neck, N.Y., managing director of equities, Cantor Fitzgerald. Confirmed dead, World Trade Center, at/in building.
Stuart (Soo-Jin) Lee, 30, New York, N.Y., vice president of integrated services, Data Synapse. Confirmed dead, World Trade Center, at/in building.
Yang Der Lee, 63, New York, N.Y., delivery clerk, Windows on the World. Confirmed dead, World Trade Center, at/in building.
Stephen Lefkowitz, 50, Belle Harbor, N.Y., mediator, New York State Department of Taxation and Finance. Confirmed dead, World Trade Center, at/in building.
Adriana Legro, 32, New York, N.Y., broker, Carr Futures. Confirmed dead, World Trade Center, at/in building. *Colombian.*
Edward J. Lehman, 41, Glen Cove, N.Y., risk services, Aon Corp. Confirmed dead, World Trade Center, at/in building.
Eric Andrew Lehrfeld, 32, New York, N.Y., director of business development, Random Walk Computing. Confirmed dead, World Trade Center, at/in building.
David Ralph Leistman, 43, Garden City, N.Y., bond trader and partner, Cantor Fitzgerald. Confirmed dead, World Trade Center, at/in building.

Joseph A. Lenihan, 41, Greenwich, Conn., executive vice president, Keefe, Bruyette & Woods. Confirmed dead, World Trade Center, at/in building.
John Robinson Lenoir, 38, Locust Valley, N.Y., vice president, Sandler O'Neill & Partners. Reported dead, World Trade Center, at/in building.
Jorge Luis Leon, 43, Union City, N.J., Cantor Fitzgerald. Confirmed dead, World Trade Center, at/in building.
Matthew Gerard Leonard, 38, New York, N.Y., attorney, Cantor Fitzgerald. Confirmed dead, World Trade Center, at/in building.
Michael Lepore, 39, New York, N.Y., technical services employee, Marsh & McLennan Cos. Inc. Confirmed dead, World Trade Center, at/in building.
Charles Antoine Lesperance, 55, New York State Department of Transportation. Confirmed dead, World Trade Center, at/in building.
Jeffrey Earle LeVeen, 55, Manhasset, N.Y., senior vice president of equity sales, Cantor Fitzgerald. Reported dead, World Trade Center, at/in building.
Alisha Caren Levin, 33, New York, N.Y., vice president for human resources, Fuji Bank. Confirmed dead, World Trade Center, at/in building.
Robert Levine, 56, West Babylon, N.Y., Cantor Fitzgerald. Confirmed dead, World Trade Center, at/in building.
Robert M. Levine, 66, Edgewater, N.J. Confirmed dead, World Trade Center, at/in building.
Shai Levinhar, 29, New York, N.Y., Cantor Fitzgerald. Confirmed dead, World Trade Center, at/in building. *Israeli.*
Adam J. Lewis, 36, Fairfield, Conn., senior trader, Keefe, Bruyette & Woods. Confirmed dead, World Trade Center, at/in building.
Ye Wei Liang, 27, New York, N.Y., technology information specialist, Marsh & McLennan Cos. Inc. Confirmed dead, World Trade Center, at/in building.
Orasri Liangthanasarn, 26, Bayonne, N.J., Windows on the World. Confirmed dead, World Trade Center, at/in building.
Ralph M. Licciardi, 30, West Hempstead, N.Y., electrician, P.E. Stone Inc. Confirmed dead, World Trade Center, at/in building.
Edward Lichtschein, 35, New York, N.Y., software designer, Cantor Fitzgerald. Confirmed dead, World Trade Center, at/in building.
Steven B. Lillianthal, 38, Millburn, N.J., Cantor Fitzgerald. Confirmed dead, World Trade Center, at/in building.
Craig Damian Lilore, 30, Lyndhurst, N.J., institutional stock trader, Cantor Fitzgerald. Confirmed dead, World Trade Center, at/in building.
Arnold A. Lim, 28, Fiduciary Trust International. Confirmed dead, World Trade Center, at/in building. *Filipino.*
Darya Lin, 32, Chicago, Ill., senior manager, Keane Consulting Group. Confirmed dead, World Trade Center, at/in building.
Wei Rong Lin, 31, Jersey City, N.J., president, Frank W. Lin & Co. Confirmed dead, World Trade Center, at/in building.
Nickie L. Lindo, 31, New York, N.Y. Confirmed dead, World Trade Center, at/in building.
Thomas V. Linehan, 39, Montville, N.J., senior vice president, Marsh & McLennan Cos. Inc. Confirmed dead, World Trade Center, at/in building.
Alan Linton, 26, Jersey City, N.J., Sandler O'Neill & Partners. Confirmed dead, World Trade Center, at/in building.
Diane Theresa Lipari, 42, New York, N.Y., commodities trader, Carr Futures. Confirmed dead, World Trade Center, at/in building.
Kenneth P. Lira, 28, Paterson, N.J., Genuity. Reported missing, World Trade Center, at/in building. *Peruvian.*
Francisco Alberto Liriano, 33, New York, N.Y. Confirmed dead, World Trade Center, at/in building.
Lorraine Lisi, 44, New York, N.Y., Fiduciary Trust International. Confirmed dead, World Trade Center, at/in building. *Italian.*
Paul Lisson, 45, New York, N.Y., clerk, Pitney Bowes. Confirmed dead, World Trade Center, at/in building.
Vincent Litto, 52, New York, N.Y., vice president, Cantor Fitzgerald. Confirmed dead, World Trade Center, at/in building.
Ming-Hao Liu, 41, Livingston, N.J., engineer, Washington Group International. Confirmed dead, World Trade Center, at/in building.
Joseph Livera, 67. Confirmed dead, World Trade Center, at/in building.
Nancy Liz, 39, New York, N.Y., Aon Corp. Confirmed dead, World Trade Center, at/in building.
Harold Lizcano, 31, East Elmhurst, N.Y., accountant, Carr Futures. Confirmed dead, World Trade Center, at/in building.
Martin Lizzul, 31, New York, N.Y., account executive, Krestrel Technologies. Confirmed dead, World Trade Center, at/in building.
George A. Llanes, 33, New York, N.Y., clerk, Carr Futures. Confirmed dead, World Trade Center, at/in building.
Elizabeth Claire Logler, 31, Rockville Centre, N.Y., employee of eSpeed division, Cantor Fitzgerald. Confirmed dead, World Trade Center, at/in building.
Catherine Lisa Loguidice, 30, New York, N.Y., assistant bond trader, Cantor Fitzgerald. Confirmed dead, World Trade Center, at/in building.
Jerome Robert Lohez, 30, Jersey City, N.J., software architect at NexxtHealth subsidiary, Empire Blue Cross and Blue Shield. Confirmed dead, World Trade Center, at/in building.
Michael W. Lomax, 37, New York, N.Y., Aon Corp. Confirmed dead, World Trade Center, at/in building.
Laura M. Longing, 35, Pearl River, N.Y., assistant vice president, Marsh USA. Confirmed dead, World Trade Center, at/in building.
Salvatore Lopes, 40, Franklin Square, N.Y., travel consultant at Sandler O'Neil & Partners. Reported missing, World Trade Center, at/in building.

Daniel Lopez, 39, Greenpoint, N.Y., Carr Futures. Confirmed dead, World Trade Center, at/in building.
George Lopez, 40, Stroudsburg, Pa., Fiduciary Trust International. Confirmed dead, World Trade Center, at/in building.
Luis Lopez, 38, New York, N.Y. Confirmed dead, World Trade Center, at/in building.
Manuel L. Lopez, 54, Jersey City, N.J., tax accountant, Marsh & McLennan Cos. Inc. Confirmed dead, World Trade Center, at/in building. *Filipino.*
Joseph Lostrangio, 48, Langhorne, Pa. Confirmed dead, World Trade Center, at/in building.
Chet Louie, 45, New York, N.Y., Cantor Fitzgerald. Confirmed dead, World Trade Center, at/in building.
Stuart Seid Louis, 43, East Brunswick, N.J., Sandler O'Neill & Partners. Confirmed dead, World Trade Center, at/in building.
Joseph Lovero, 60, Jersey City, N.J., dispatcher, Jersey City Fire Department. Reported dead, World Trade Center, at/in building.
Michael W. Lowe, 48, New York, N.Y., electrical worker, Liberty Electrical Supply Inc. Confirmed dead, World Trade Center, at/in building.
Garry Lozier, 47, Darien, Conn., managing director, Sandler O'Neill & Partners. Confirmed dead, World Trade Center, at/in building.
John Peter Lozowsky, 45, New York, N.Y. Confirmed dead, World Trade Center, at/in building.
Charles Peter Lucania, 34, East Atlantic Beach, N.Y., electrician, P.E. Stone Inc. Confirmed dead, World Trade Center, at/in building.
Edward (Ted) H. Luckett, 40, Fair Haven, N.J., partner, Cantor Fitzgerald. Confirmed dead, World Trade Center, at/in building.
Mark G. Ludvigsen, 32, New York, N.Y., Keefe, Bruyette & Woods. Confirmed dead, World Trade Center, at/in building.
Lee Charles Ludwig, 49, New York, N.Y., vice president of international investment management, Fiduciary Trust International. Confirmed dead, World Trade Center, at/in building.
Sean Thomas Lugano, 28, New York, N.Y., Keefe, Bruyette & Woods. Confirmed dead, World Trade Center, at/in building.
Daniel Lugo, 45, New York, N.Y., security officer, Summit Security Services. Confirmed dead, World Trade Center, at/in building.
Jin Lui, 34, Piscataway, N.J. Confirmed dead, World Trade Center, at/in building.
Marie Lukas, 32, New York, N.Y., securities broker at eSpeed, Cantor Fitzgerald. Confirmed dead, World Trade Center, at/in building.
William Lum, 45, New York, N.Y., senior claims specialist, Marsh & McLennan Cos. Inc. Confirmed dead, World Trade Center, at/in building.
Michael P. Lunden, 37, New York, N.Y., partner and vice president of TradeSpark, Cantor Fitzgerald. Confirmed dead, World Trade Center, at/in building.
Christopher Lunder, 34, Wall, N.J., broker, Cantor Fitzgerald. Reported dead, World Trade Center, at/in building.
Anthony Luparello, 62, New York, N.Y., janitorial, cleaner, ABM Industries. Confirmed dead, World Trade Center, at/in building.
Gary Lutnick, 36, New York, N.Y., partner, trader on U.S. agency desk, Cantor Fitzgerald. Confirmed dead, World Trade Center, at/in building.
Linda Luzzicone, 33, New York, N.Y., trader, Cantor Fitzgerald. Confirmed dead, World Trade Center, at/in building.
Alexander Lygin, 28, New York, N.Y., programmer, Cantor Fitzgerald. Confirmed dead, World Trade Center, at/in building.
Farrell Peter Lynch, 39, Centerport, N.Y., trader, Cantor Fitzgerald. Confirmed dead, World Trade Center, at/in building.
Louise A. Lynch, 58, Amityville, N.Y., Marsh & McLennan Cos. Inc. Confirmed dead, World Trade Center, at/in building.
Michael Lynch, 34, Cantor Fitzgerald. Confirmed dead, World Trade Center, at/in building.
Richard Dennis Lynch, 30, Bedford Hills, N.Y., bond trader, Euro Brokers Inc. Confirmed dead, World Trade Center, at/in building.
Sean Lynch, 34, New York, N.Y., senior vice president of equity trading, Cantor Fitzgerald. Confirmed dead, World Trade Center, at/in building.
Sean Patrick Lynch, 36, Morristown, N.J., broker, Cantor Fitzgerald. Confirmed dead, World Trade Center, at/in building.
Monica Lyons, 51, New York, N.Y., Marsh & McLennan Cos. Inc. Confirmed dead, World Trade Center, at/in building.

– M –

Robert Francis Mace, 43, New York, N.Y., assistant counsel, Cantor Fitzgerald. Confirmed dead, World Trade Center, at/in building.
Jan Maciejewski, 37, New York, N.Y., waiter/computer consultant, Windows on the World/Julien J. Studley Inc. Confirmed dead, World Trade Center, at/in building.
Catherine Fairfax MacRea, 23, New York, N.Y., stock analyst, Fred Alger Management. Confirmed dead, World Trade Center, at/in building.
Richard B. Madden, 35, Westfield, N.J., Aon Corp. Confirmed dead, World Trade Center, at/in building.
Simon Maddison, 40, Florham Park, N.J., contractor at Cantor Fitzgerald. Confirmed dead, World Trade Center, at/in building. *British.*
Noell Maerz, 29, Long Beach, N.Y., bond trader, Euro Brokers Inc. Confirmed dead, World Trade Center, at/in building.
Jeannieann Maffeo, 40, New York, N.Y., senior associate in systems development, UBS PaineWebber. Confirmed dead, World Trade Center, at/in building.
Jay Robert Magazine, 48, New York, N.Y., catering sales manager, Windows on the World. Confirmed dead, World Trade Center, at/in building.
Brian Magee, 52, Floral Park, N.J. Confirmed dead, World Trade Center, at/in building.

Charles Wilson Magee, 51, Wantagh, N.Y., chief engineer, Silverstein Properties. Confirmed dead, World Trade Center, at/in building.
Joseph Maggitti, 47, Abingdon, Md., Marsh & McLennan Cos. Inc. Confirmed dead, World Trade Center, at/in building.
Ronald E. Magnuson, 57, Park Ridge, N.J., contractor at Cantor Fitzgerald. Confirmed dead, World Trade Center, at/in building.
Daniel L. Maher, 50, Hamilton, N.J., Marsh & McLennan Cos. Inc. Confirmed dead, World Trade Center, at/in building.
Thomas Anthony Mahon, 37, East Norwich, N.Y., broker, Cantor Fitzgerald. Confirmed dead, World Trade Center, at/in building.
Joseph Maio, 32, Roslyn Harbor, N.Y., director of equity derivatives, Cantor Fitzgerald. Confirmed dead, World Trade Center, at/in building.
Takashi Makimoto, 49, general manager, Fuji Bank. Confirmed dead, World Trade Center, at/in building. *Japanese.*
Abdu Malahi, 37, New York, N.Y. Confirmed dead, World Trade Center, at/in building.
Debora Maldonado, 47, New York, N.Y., executive secretary, Marsh & McLennan Cos. Inc. Confirmed dead, World Trade Center, at/in building.
Alfred R. Maler, 39, Convent Station, N.J., bond broker, Governments Zero Desk, Cantor Fitzgerald. Confirmed dead, World Trade Center, at/in building.
Gregory James Malone, 42, Hoboken, N.J., bond broker, Euro Brokers Inc. Confirmed dead, World Trade Center, at/in building.
Edward Francis (Teddy) Maloney, 32, Darien, Conn., account manager at Tradespark division, Cantor Fitzgerald. Confirmed dead, World Trade Center, at/in building.
Gene E. Maloy, 41, New York, N.Y., analyst, Marsh & McLennan Cos. Inc. Confirmed dead, World Trade Center, at/in building.
Christian Maltby, 37, Chatham, N.J., vice president, Cantor Fitzgerald. Confirmed dead, World Trade Center, at/in building.
Francisco Miguel (Frank) Mancini, 26, New York, N.Y., subcontractor, Bronx Builders. Confirmed dead, World Trade Center, at/in building.
Joseph Mangano, 53, Jackson, N.J., software analyst, Marsh & McLennan Cos. Inc. Confirmed dead, World Trade Center, at/in building.
Sara Elizabeth Manley, 31, New York, N.Y., vice president and senior security analyst, Fred Alger Management. Confirmed dead, World Trade Center, at/in building.
Debra M. Mannetta, 31, Islip, N.Y., Carr Futures. Confirmed dead, World Trade Center, at/in building.
Marion Victoria (Vickie) Manning, 27, Rochdale, N.Y., executive secretary, Marsh & McLennan Cos. Inc. Confirmed dead, World Trade Center, at/in building.
Terence J. Manning, 36, Rockville Centre, N.Y., computer consultant, ARC Partners. Confirmed dead, World Trade Center, at/in building.
James Maounis, 42, New York, N.Y. Confirmed dead, World Trade Center, at/in building.
Peter Edward Mardikian, 29, New York, N.Y., sales manager, Imagine Software Inc. Confirmed dead, World Trade Center, at/in building.
Edward Joseph Mardovich, 42, Lloyd Harbor, N.Y., president, Euro Brokers Inc. Confirmed dead, World Trade Center, at/in building.
Lester Vincent Marino, 57, Massapequa, N.Y., electrician, Forest Electric Corp. Confirmed dead, World Trade Center, at/in building.
Vita Marino, 49, New York, N.Y., Sandler O'Neill & Partners. Confirmed dead, World Trade Center, at/in building.
Kevin D. Marlo, 28, New York, N.Y., associate director, Sandler O'Neill & Partners. Confirmed dead, World Trade Center, at/in building.
Jose J. Marrero, 32, Old Bridge, N.J., facilities manager, Euro Brokers Inc. Confirmed dead, World Trade Center, at/in building.
James Martello, 41, Rumson, N.J., equity sales trader, Cantor Fitzgerald. Confirmed dead, World Trade Center, at/in building.
Michael A. Marti, 26, Glendale, N.Y., bond trader, Cantor Fitzgerald. Confirmed dead, World Trade Center, at/in building.
William J. Martin, 35, Rockaway, N.J., Cantor Fitzgerald. Confirmed dead, World Trade Center, at/in building.
Brian E. Martineau, 37, Edison, N.J., benefits consultant, Aon Corp. Confirmed dead, World Trade Center, at/in building.
Betsy Martinez, 33, New York, N.Y., Cantor Fitzgerald. Confirmed dead, World Trade Center, at/in building.
Edward J. Martinez, 60, New York, N.Y., operations manager, Cantor Fitzgerald. Confirmed dead, World Trade Center, at/in building.
Jose Martinez, 49, Hauppauge, N.Y., electrical worker, Forest Electric Corp. Confirmed dead, World Trade Center, at/in building.
Robert Gabriel Martinez, 24, New York, N.Y., security officer, Summit Security Services. Confirmed dead, World Trade Center, at/in building. *Peruvian.*
Lizie Martinez-Calderon, 32, New York, N.Y., secretary, Aon Corp. Confirmed dead, World Trade Center, at/in building.
Bernard Mascarenhas, 54, Newmarket, Ontario, Canada, Marsh & McLennan Cos. Inc. Confirmed dead, World Trade Center, at/in building. *Canadian.*
Stephen F. Masi, 55, New York, N.Y., Cantor Fitzgerald. Confirmed dead, World Trade Center, at/in building.
Nicholas G. Massa, 65, New York, N.Y., senior vice president, Aon Corp. Confirmed dead, World Trade Center, at/in building.
Patricia A. Massari, 25, Glendale, N.Y., Marsh & McLennan Cos. Inc. Confirmed dead, World Trade Center, at/in building.

Michael Massaroli, 38, New York, N.Y., vice president, Cantor Fitzgerald. Confirmed dead, World Trade Center, at/in building.
Philip W. Mastrandrea, 42, Chatham, N.J., Cantor Fitzgerald. Confirmed dead, World Trade Center, at/in building.
Rudolph Mastrocinque, 43, Kings Park, N.Y., property claims representative, Marsh & McLennan Cos. Inc. Confirmed dead, World Trade Center, at/in building.
Joseph Mathai, 49, Arlington, Mass., managing partner, Cambridge Technology Partners. Confirmed dead, World Trade Center, at/in building.
Charles William Mathers, 61, Sea Girt, N.J., managing director, Marsh & McLennan Cos. Inc. Confirmed dead, World Trade Center, at/in building.
William A. Mathesen, 40, Morristown, N.J., vice president, Euro Brokers Inc. Confirmed dead, World Trade Center, at/in building.
Marcello Matricciano, 31, New York, N.Y., Cantor Fitzgerald. Confirmed dead, World Trade Center, at/in building.
Margaret Elaine Mattic, 51, New York, N.Y., customer service account representative, General Telecom. Confirmed dead, World Trade Center, at/in building.
Robert D. Mattson, 54, Green Pond, N.J., banking executive, Fiduciary Trust International. Confirmed dead, World Trade Center, at/in building.
Walter Matuza, 39, New York, N.Y., analyst, Carr Futures. Confirmed dead, World Trade Center, at/in building.
Charles A. (Chuck) Mauro, 65, New York, N.Y., senior client specialist, Aon Corp. Confirmed dead, World Trade Center, at/in building.
Charles J. Mauro, 38, New York, N.Y., director of purchasing, Windows on the World. Confirmed dead, World Trade Center, at/in building.
Dorothy Mauro, 55, New York, N.Y., state tax clerk, Marsh & McLennan Cos. Inc. Confirmed dead, World Trade Center, at/in building.
Nancy T. Mauro, 51, New York, N.Y., insurance broker, Marsh & McLennan Cos. Inc. Confirmed dead, World Trade Center, at/in building.
Tyrone May, 44, Rahway, N.J., New York State Department of Taxation and Finance. Confirmed dead, World Trade Center, at/in building.
Robert J. Mayo, 46, Morganville, N.J., fire safety director, OCS Security. Confirmed dead, World Trade Center, at/in building.
Edward Mazzella, 62, Monroe, N.Y., senior vice president, Cantor Fitzgerald. Confirmed dead, World Trade Center, at/in building.
Jennifer Mazzotta, 23, New York, N.Y., trader, Cantor Fitzgerald. Confirmed dead, World Trade Center, at/in building.
Kaaria Mbaya, 39, Edison, N.J., senior computer analyst, Cantor Fitzgerald. Confirmed dead, World Trade Center, at/in building.
James J. McAlary, 42, Spring Lake Heights, N.J., heating-oil trader, Carr Futures. Confirmed dead, World Trade Center, at/in building.
Patricia A. McAneney, 50, Pomona, N.Y., Marsh & McLennan Cos. Inc. Confirmed dead, World Trade Center, at/in building.
Colin Richard McArthur, 52, Howell, N.J., Aon Corp. Reported dead, World Trade Center, at/in building.
Kenneth M. McBrayer, 49, New York, N.Y., Sandler O'Neill & Partners. Confirmed dead, World Trade Center, at/in building.
Brendan McCabe, 40, Sayville, N.Y., vice president, Fiduciary Trust International. Confirmed dead, World Trade Center, at/in building.
Michael J. McCabe, 42, Rumson, N.J., trader, Cantor Fitzgerald. Confirmed dead, World Trade Center, at/in building.
Justin McCarthy, 30, Port Washington, N.Y., Cantor Fitzgerald. Confirmed dead, World Trade Center, at/in building.
Kevin M. McCarthy, 42, Fairfield, Conn., bond trader, Cantor Fitzgerald. Confirmed dead, World Trade Center, at/in building.
Michael Desmond McCarthy, 33, Huntington, N.Y., trader, Carr Futures. Confirmed dead, World Trade Center, at/in building.
Robert Garvin McCarthy, 33, Stony Point, N.Y., trader, Cantor Fitzgerald. Confirmed dead, World Trade Center, at/in building.
Stanley McCaskill, 47, New York, N.Y., security guard, Advantage Security. Confirmed dead, World Trade Center, at/in building.
Katie Marie McCloskey, 25, Mount Vernon, N.Y., Marsh Inc. Confirmed dead, World Trade Center, at/in building.
Tara McCloud-Gray, 30, New York, N.Y., switch operations technician, General Telecom. Confirmed dead, World Trade Center, at/in building.
Charles Austin McCrann, 55, New York, N.Y., senior vice president, Marsh & McLennan Cos. Inc. Confirmed dead, World Trade Center, at/in building.
Tonyell McDay, 25, Colonia, N.J., computer technician, Marsh Inc. Confirmed dead, World Trade Center, at/in building.
Matthew T. McDermott, 34, Basking Ridge, N.J., equity trader, Cantor Fitzgerald. Confirmed dead, World Trade Center, at/in building.
Joseph P. McDonald, 43, Livingston, N.J., broker, Cantor Fitzgerald. Confirmed dead, World Trade Center, at/in building.
Michael McDonnell, 34, Red Bank, N.J., accounting manager, Keefe, Bruyette & Woods. Confirmed dead, World Trade Center, at/in building.
John F. McDowell, 33, New York, N.Y., vice president in equities, Sandler O'Neill & Partners. Confirmed dead, World Trade Center, at/in building.
Eamon J. McEneaney, 46, New Canaan, Conn., senior vice president and limited partner, Cantor Fitzgerald. Confirmed dead, World Trade Center, at/in building.
John Thomas McErlean, 39, Larchmont, N.Y., vice president and partner, Cantor Fitzgerald. Confirmed dead, World Trade Center, at/in building.

Katherine (Katie) McGarry-Noack, 30, Hoboken, N.J., senior sales executive, Telekurs USA. Confirmed dead, World Trade Center, at/in building.
Daniel F. McGinley, 40, Ridgewood, N.J., senior vice president, Keefe, Bruyette & Woods. Confirmed dead, World Trade Center, at/in building.
Mark Ryan McGinly, 26, New York, N.Y., futures trader, Carr Futures. Reported dead, World Trade Center, at/in building.
Thomas H. McGinnis, 41, Oakland, N.J., broker, Carr Futures. Confirmed dead, World Trade Center, at/in building.
Michael Gregory McGinty, 42, Foxboro, Mass., senior vice president for power and utilities practice, Marsh Inc. Confirmed dead, World Trade Center, at/in building.
Ann McGovern, 68, East Meadow, N.Y., claims analyst, ARS Retail Group, Aon Corp. Confirmed dead, World Trade Center, at/in building.
Scott Martin McGovern, 35, Wyckoff, N.J., bond broker, Euro Brokers Inc. Confirmed dead, World Trade Center, at/in building.
Stacey S. McGowan, 38, Basking Ridge, N.J., senior trader, Sandler O'Neill & Partners. Confirmed dead, World Trade Center, at/in building.
Francis Noel McGuinn, 48, Rye, N.Y., managing director of emerging markets, Cantor Fitzgerald. Confirmed dead, World Trade Center, at/in building.
Patrick J. McGuire, 40, Madison, N.J., Euro Brokers Inc. Confirmed dead, World Trade Center, at/in building.
Thomas McHale, 33, Huntington, N.Y., broker, Cantor Fitzgerald. Confirmed dead, World Trade Center, at/in building.
Keith McHeffey, 31, Monmouth Beach, N.J., equities trader, Cantor Fitzgerald. Confirmed dead, World Trade Center, at/in building.
Ann M. McHugh, 35, New York, N.Y., Euro Brokers Inc. Confirmed dead, World Trade Center, at/in building.
Denis J. McHugh, 36, New York, N.Y., Euro Brokers Inc. Confirmed dead, World Trade Center, at/in building.
Michael Edward McHugh, 35, Tuckahoe, N.Y., director of sales at TradeSpark, Cantor Fitzgerald. Confirmed dead, World Trade Center, at/in building.
Robert G. McIlvaine, 26, New York, N.Y., assistant vice president of media relations, Merrill Lynch. Confirmed dead, World Trade Center, at/in building.
Stephanie McKenna, 45, New York, N.Y., accounting department, Reinsurance Solutions Inc. Confirmed dead, World Trade Center, at/in building.
Barry J. McKeon, 47, Yorktown Heights, N.Y., executive vice president, Fiduciary Trust International. Confirmed dead, World Trade Center, at/in building.
Evelyn C. McKinnedy, 60, New York, N.Y., Cantor Fitzgerald. Confirmed dead, World Trade Center, at/in building.
Darryl Leron McKinney, 26, New York, N.Y., Cantor Fitzgerald. Confirmed dead, World Trade Center, at/in building.
George Patrick McLaughlin, 36, Hoboken, N.J., Carr Futures. Confirmed dead, World Trade Center, at/in building.
Robert C. McLaughlin, 29, Westchester, N.Y., vice president for emerging markets, Cantor Fitzgerald. Confirmed dead, World Trade Center, at/in building.
Gavin McMahon, 35, Bayonne, N.J., Aon Corp. Confirmed dead, World Trade Center, at/in building.
Edmund M. McNally, 41, Fair Haven, N.J., senior vice president/director of technology, Fiduciary Trust International. Confirmed dead, World Trade Center, at/in building.
Daniel McNeal, 29, N.J., analyst, Sandler O'Neill & Partners. Confirmed dead, World Trade Center, at/in building.
Christine Sheila McNulty, 42, Peterborough, England. Confirmed dead, World Trade Center, at/in building. *British.*
Sean Peter McNulty, 30, New York, N.Y., trader, international desk, Cantor Fitzgerald. Confirmed dead, World Trade Center, at/in building.
Rocco A. Medaglia, 49, Melville, N.Y., construction supervisor, G.M.P. Inc. Confirmed dead, World Trade Center, at/in building.
Abigail Medina, 46, New York, N.Y. Confirmed dead, World Trade Center, at/in building.
Anna Iris Medina, 39, New York, N.Y. Confirmed dead, World Trade Center, at/in building.
Deborah Medwig, 62, Dedham, Mass., systems analyst, NStar. Confirmed dead, World Trade Center, at/in building.
Damian Meehan, 32, Glen Rock, N.J., trader, Carr Futures. Confirmed dead, World Trade Center, at/in building.
William J. Meehan, 49, Darien, Conn., chief market strategist, Cantor Fitzgerald. Confirmed dead, World Trade Center, at/in building.
Alok Mehta, 23, Cantor Fitzgerald. Reported missing, World Trade Center, at/in building.
Manuel Emilio Mejia, 54, New York, N.Y., kitchen worker, Windows on the World. Confirmed dead, World Trade Center, at/in building.
Eskedar Melaku, 31, New York, N.Y., assistant vice president, Marsh & McLennan Cos. Inc. Confirmed dead, World Trade Center, at/in building.
Antonio Melendez, 30, New York, N.Y., Windows on the World. Confirmed dead, World Trade Center, at/in building. *Mexican.*
Mary Melendez, 44, Stroudsburg, Pa., legal secretary, Fiduciary Trust International. Confirmed dead, World Trade Center, at/in building.
Yelena Melnichenko, 28, New York, N.Y., Marsh & McLennan Cos. Inc. Confirmed dead, World Trade Center, at/in building.
Stuart Todd Meltzer, 32, Syosett, N.Y., head of West Coast power management at TradeSpark, Cantor Fitzgerald. Confirmed dead, World Trade Center, at/in building.

Diarelia Jovannah Mena, 30, New York, N.Y., computer programmer, Cantor Fitzgerald. Confirmed dead, World Trade Center, at/in building.
Lizette Mendoza, 33, North Bergen, N.J., Aon Corp. Confirmed dead, World Trade Center, at/in building.
Shevonne Mentis, 25, New York, N.Y., clerk, Marsh & McLennan Cos. Inc. Confirmed dead, World Trade Center, at/in building.
Wesley Mercer, 70, New York, N.Y., vice president, corporate security, Morgan Stanley. Confirmed dead, World Trade Center, at/in building.
Ralph Joseph Mercurio, 47, Rockville Centre, N.Y., coal broker, Cantor Fitzgerald. Confirmed dead, World Trade Center, at/in building.
Alan H. Merdinger, 47, Allentown, Pa., accountant, Cantor Fitzgerald. Confirmed dead, World Trade Center, at/in building.
George C. Merino, 39, New York, N.Y., securities analyst, Fiduciary Trust International. Confirmed dead, World Trade Center, at/in building.
Yamel Merino, 24, Yonkers, N.Y., emergency medical technician, Metrocare. Confirmed dead, World Trade Center, at/in building.
George Merkouris, 35, Levittown, N.Y., Carr Futures. Confirmed dead, World Trade Center, at/in building.
Deborah Merrick, 45. Confirmed dead, World Trade Center, at/in building.
Raymond J. Metz, 37, Trumbull, Conn., currency broker, Euro Brokers Inc. Confirmed dead, World Trade Center, at/in building.
Jill A. Metzler, 32, Franklin Square, N.Y., Aon Corp. Confirmed dead, World Trade Center, at/in building.
David R. Meyer, 57, Glen Rock, N.J., bond trader, Cantor Fitzgerald. Confirmed dead, World Trade Center, at/in building.
Nurul Huq Miah, 35, New York, N.Y., audiovisual technologist, Marsh & McLennan Cos. Inc. Confirmed dead, World Trade Center, at/in building.
William Edward Micciulli, 30, Matawan, N.J., partner and senior vice president, Cantor Fitzgerald. Confirmed dead, World Trade Center, at/in building.
Martin Paul Michelstein, 57, Morristown, N.J. Confirmed dead, World Trade Center, at/in building.
Luis Clodoaldo Revilla Mier, 54, Washington Group International. Confirmed dead, World Trade Center, at/in building. *Peruvian.*
Peter T. Milano, 43, Middletown, N.J., Cantor Fitzgerald. Confirmed dead, World Trade Center, at/in building.
Gregory Milanowycz, 25, Cranford, N.J., insurance broker, Aon Corp. Confirmed dead, World Trade Center, at/in building.
Lukasz T. Milewski, 21, New York, N.Y., food service handler, Forte Food Service. Confirmed dead, World Trade Center, at/in building.
Corey Peter Miller, 34, New York, N.Y., Cantor Fitzgerald. Confirmed dead, World Trade Center, at/in building.
Craig James Miller, 29, Va. Confirmed dead, World Trade Center, at/in building.
Joel Miller, 55, Baldwin, N.Y. Confirmed dead, World Trade Center, at/in building.
Michael Matthew Miller, 39, Englewood, N.J., bond trader, Cantor Fitzgerald. Confirmed dead, World Trade Center, at/in building.
Phillip D. Miller, 53, New York, N.Y., Aon Corp. Confirmed dead, World Trade Center, at/in building.
Robert Alan Miller, 46, Matawan, N.J., New York State Department of Taxation and Finance. Confirmed dead, World Trade Center, at/in building.
Robert C. Miller, 55, Hasbrouck Heights, N.J., Aon Corp. Confirmed dead, World Trade Center, at/in building.
Benjamin Millman, 40, New York, N.Y., carpenter. Confirmed dead, World Trade Center, at/in building.
Charles M. Mills, 61, Brentwood, N.Y., director of the Petroleum, Alcohol and Tobacco Bureau, New York State Department of Taxation and Finance. Confirmed dead, World Trade Center, at/in building.
Ronald Keith Milstein, 54, New York, N.Y. Confirmed dead, World Trade Center, at/in building.
William G. Minardi, 46, Bedford, N.Y., broker, Cantor Fitzgerald. Confirmed dead, World Trade Center, at/in building.
Louis Joseph Minervino, 54, Middletown, N.J., senior vice president, Marsh USA. Confirmed dead, World Trade Center, at/in building.
Nana Akwasi Minkah, New York, N.Y., Windows on the World. Reported missing, World Trade Center, at/in building.
Wilbert Miraille, 29, New York, N.Y., computer technician, Cantor Fitzgerald. Confirmed dead, World Trade Center, at/in building.
Domenick Mircovich, 40, Closter, N.J., Euro Brokers Inc. Confirmed dead, World Trade Center, at/in building.
Rajesh A. Mirpuri, 30, Englewood Cliffs, N.J., sales vice president, Data Synapse. Confirmed dead, World Trade Center, at/in building.
Joseph Mistrulli, 31, Wantagh, N.Y., subcontractor, Bronx Builders. Confirmed dead, World Trade Center, at/in building.
Susan Miszkowicz, 37, New York, N.Y. Confirmed dead, World Trade Center, at/in building.
Richard Miuccio, 55, New York, N.Y., supervisor, New York State Department of Taxation and Finance. Confirmed dead, World Trade Center, at/in building.
Frank V. Moccia, 57, Hauppauge, N.Y., facility planner, Washington Group International. Confirmed dead, World Trade Center, at/in building.
Boyie Mohammed, 50, New York, N.Y., Carr Futures. Confirmed dead, World Trade Center, at/in building.
Manuel Dejesus Molina, 31, New York, N.Y., janitorial, cleaner, ABM Industries. Confirmed dead, World Trade Center, at/in building.
Justin J. Molisani, 42, Middletown Township, N.J., senior vice president, Euro Brokers Inc. Confirmed dead, World Trade Center, at/in building.
Brian Patrick Monaghan, 21, New York, N.Y., carpenter, Certified Installation Services. Confirmed dead, World Trade Center, at/in building.

Franklin Monahan, 45, Roxbury, N.Y., Cantor Fitzgerald. Confirmed dead, World Trade Center, at/in building.
John G. Monahan, 47, Ocean Township, N.J., operations supervisor, Cantor Fitzgerald. Reported dead, World Trade Center, at/in building.
Kristen Montanaro, 34, New York, N.Y., Marsh & McLennan Cos. Inc. Confirmed dead, World Trade Center, at/in building.
Craig D. Montano, 38, Glen Ridge, N.J., government agencies securities broker, Cantor Fitzgerald. Confirmed dead, World Trade Center, at/in building.
Cheryl A. Monyak, 43, Greenwich, Conn., executive, Marsh & McLennan Cos. Inc. Confirmed dead, World Trade Center, at/in building.
Sharon Moore, 37, New York, N.Y., vice president, Sandler O'Neill & Partners. Confirmed dead, World Trade Center, at/in building.
Krishna Moorthy, Briarcliff Manor, N.Y., programmer, Fiduciary Trust International. Confirmed dead, World Trade Center, at/in building.
Abner Morales, 37, New York, N.Y., Lotus software programmer, Fiduciary Trust International. Confirmed dead, World Trade Center, at/in building.
Carlos Morales, 29, New York, N.Y., technician, Cantor Fitzgerald. Confirmed dead, World Trade Center, at/in building.
Paula Morales, 42, New York, N.Y., financial services department, Aon Corp. Confirmed dead, World Trade Center, at/in building.
John Christopher Moran, 38, Haslemere, Surrey, England. Confirmed dead, World Trade Center, at/in building. *English.*
Kathleen Moran, 42, New York, N.Y. Confirmed dead, World Trade Center, at/in building.
Lindsay S. Morehouse, 24, New York, N.Y., research assistant, Keefe, Bruyette & Woods. Confirmed dead, World Trade Center, at/in building.
George Morell, 47, Mt. Kisco, N.Y., partner and vice president of mortgage department, Cantor Fitzgerald. Confirmed dead, World Trade Center, at/in building.
Steven P. Morello, 52, Bayonne, N.J., facilities manager, Marsh & McLennan Cos. Inc. Confirmed dead, World Trade Center, at/in building.
Arturo Alva Moreno, Mexico City, Mexico. Reported missing, World Trade Center, at/in building. *Mexican.*
Roy Wallace Moreno, 42, bank employee. Reported dead, World Trade Center, at/in building.
Yvette Nicole Moreno, 25, New York, N.Y., receptionist, Carr Futures. Confirmed dead, World Trade Center, at/in building.
Dorothy Morgan, 47, Hempstead, N.Y., Marsh & McLennan Cos. Inc. Confirmed dead, World Trade Center, at/in building.
Richard Morgan, 63, Glen Rock, N.J. Confirmed dead, World Trade Center, at/in building.
Nancy Morgenstern, 32, travel agent, Cantor Fitzgerald. Reported missing, World Trade Center, at/in building.
Sanae Mori, 27, Tokyo, Japan. Confirmed dead, World Trade Center, at/in building. *Japanese.*
Blanca Morocho, 26, New York, N.Y., Windows on the World. Confirmed dead, World Trade Center, at/in building.
Leonel Morocho, 36, New York, N.Y., chef, Windows on the World. Confirmed dead, World Trade Center, at/in building.
Dennis G. Moroney, 39, Eastchester, N.Y., senior vice president, Cantor Fitzgerald. Confirmed dead, World Trade Center, at/in building.
John Morris, 46, N.J. Reported missing, World Trade Center, at/in building.
Lynne Irene Morris, 22, Monroe, N.Y., equities p&s clerk, Cantor Fitzgerald. Confirmed dead, World Trade Center, at/in building.
Seth A. Morris, 35, Kinnelon, N.J., managing director, Cantor Fitzgerald. Confirmed dead, World Trade Center, at/in building.
Stephen Philip Morris, 31, Ormond Beach, Fla. Confirmed dead, World Trade Center, at/in building.
Christopher M. Morrison, 34, Charlestown, Mass., senior vice president, Zurich Scudder Investments. Confirmed dead, World Trade Center, at/in building.
William David Moskal, 50, Brecksville, Ohio, Marsh USA. Confirmed dead, World Trade Center, at/in building.
Marco Motroni, 57, Fort Lee, N.J., broker-trader, Carr Futures. Confirmed dead, World Trade Center, at/in building.
Chung Mou, tourist. Reported missing, World Trade Center, at/in building. *Taiwanese.*
Iouri A. Mouchinski, 55, New York, N.Y. Confirmed dead, World Trade Center, at/in building.
Jude J. Moussa, 35, New York, N.Y., bond trader, Cantor Fitzgerald. Confirmed dead, World Trade Center, at/in building.
Peter C. Moutos, 44, Chatham, N.J., Marsh USA. Confirmed dead, World Trade Center, at/in building.
Damion Mowatt, 21, New York, N.Y., food service handler, Forte Food Service. Confirmed dead, World Trade Center, at/in building. *Jamaican.*
Stephen V. Mulderry, 33, New York, N.Y., vice president, equity trading, Keefe, Bruyette & Woods. Confirmed dead, World Trade Center, at/in building.
Peter James Mulligan, 28, New York, N.Y., Cantor Fitzgerald. Confirmed dead, World Trade Center, at/in building.
Michael Joseph Mullin, 27, Hoboken, N.J., trader, Cantor Fitzgerald. Confirmed dead, World Trade Center, at/in building.
James Donald Munhall, 45, Ridgewood, N.J., managing director, Sandler O'Neill & Partners. Confirmed dead, World Trade Center, at/in building.
Nancy Muniz, 45, New York, N.Y., office worker. Confirmed dead, World Trade Center, at/in building.
Carlos Mario Munoz, 43, Windows on the World. Confirmed dead, World Trade Center, at/in building. *Colombian.*

Theresa (Terry) Munson, 54, New York, N.Y., technical assistant, Aon Corp. Confirmed dead, World Trade Center, at/in building.
Robert M. Murach, 45, Montclair, N.J., senior vice president, Cantor Fitzgerald. Confirmed dead, World Trade Center, at/in building.
Cesar Augusto Murillo, 32, New York, N.Y., international trader, Cantor Fitzgerald. Confirmed dead, World Trade Center, at/in building. *Colombian.*
Marc A. Murolo, 28, Maywood, N.J., vice president, government bonds, Cantor Fitzgerald. Confirmed dead, World Trade Center, at/in building.
Brian Joseph Murphy, 41, New York, N.Y., electronic bond trading coordinator, Cantor Fitzgerald. Confirmed dead, World Trade Center, at/in building.
Charles Murphy, 38, New York, N.Y., broker, Cantor Fitzgerald. Confirmed dead, World Trade Center, at/in building.
Christopher W. Murphy, 35, Easton, Md., senior research analyst, Keefe, Bruyette & Woods. Confirmed dead, World Trade Center, at/in building.
Edward C. Murphy, 42, Clifton, N.J., managing director, Cantor Fitzgerald. Confirmed dead, World Trade Center, at/in building.
James F. Murphy, 30, Garden City, N.Y., Thomson Financial Services. Confirmed dead, World Trade Center, at/in building.
James Thomas Murphy, 35, Middletown, N.J., Cantor Fitzgerald. Confirmed dead, World Trade Center, at/in building.
Kevin James Murphy, 40, Northport, N.Y., claims consultant, Marsh & McLennan Cos. Inc. Confirmed dead, World Trade Center, at/in building.
Patrick Sean Murphy, 36, Millburn, N.J., vice president, Marsh & McLennan Cos. Inc. Confirmed dead, World Trade Center, at/in building.
Robert Eddie Murphy, 56, New York, N.Y. Confirmed dead, World Trade Center, at/in building.
John Joseph Murray, 52, Colts Neck, N.J., Industrial Bank of Japan. Confirmed dead, World Trade Center, at/in building.
John Joseph Murray, 32, Hoboken, N.J., partner and director, Cantor Fitzgerald. Confirmed dead, World Trade Center, at/in building.
Susan D. Murray, 54, Summit, N.J., Marsh & McLennan Cos. Inc. Confirmed dead, World Trade Center, at/in building.
Valerie Victoria Murray, 65, New York, N.Y., secretary, Ohrenstein & Brown. Confirmed dead, World Trade Center, at/in building.
Yuriy Mushynskyi, 55. Reported missing, World Trade Center, at/in building. *Ukranian.*
Richard Todd Myhre, 37, New York, N.Y., operations department, Cantor Fitzgerald. Confirmed dead, World Trade Center, at/in building.

– N –

Takuya Nakamura, 30, Tuckahoe, N.Y., section chief, New York branch, Nishi-Nippon Bank. Confirmed dead, World Trade Center, at/in building.
Alexander J.R. Napier, 38, Morris Township, N.J., Aon Corp. Confirmed dead, World Trade Center, at/in building.
Frank Joseph Naples, 29, Cliffside Park, N.J., broker, Cantor Fitzgerald. Reported missing, World Trade Center, at/in building.
Catherine A. Nardella, 40, Bloomfield, N.J., insurance consultant, Aon Corp. Confirmed dead, World Trade Center, at/in building.
Mario Nardone, 32, New York, N.Y., bond broker, Euro Brokers Inc. Confirmed dead, World Trade Center, at/in building.
Manika Narula, 22, Kings Park, N.Y., Cantor Fitzgerald. Confirmed dead, World Trade Center, at/in building.
Narender Nath, 33, Colonia, N.J. Confirmed dead, World Trade Center, at/in building.
Karen S. Navarro, 30, New York, N.Y., Carr Futures. Confirmed dead, World Trade Center, at/in building.
Francis J. Nazario, 28, Jersey City, N.J., back office operations manager, Cantor Fitzgerald. Confirmed dead, World Trade Center, at/in building.
Glenroy Neblett, 42, New York, N.Y., consultant at Marsh & McLennan Cos. Inc. Confirmed dead, World Trade Center, at/in building.
Marcus R. Neblett, 31, Roslyn Heights, N.Y., Aon Corp. Confirmed dead, World Trade Center, at/in building.
Jerome O. Nedd, 39, New York, N.Y., Windows on the World. Confirmed dead, World Trade Center, at/in building.
Laurence Nedell, 51, Lindenhurst, N.Y., Aon Corp. Confirmed dead, World Trade Center, at/in building.
Luke G. Nee, 44, Stony Point, N.Y., Cantor Fitzgerald. Confirmed dead, World Trade Center, at/in building.
Ann Nicole Nelson, 30, New York, N.Y., bond broker in the agencies department, Cantor Fitzgerald. Confirmed dead, World Trade Center, at/in building.
David William Nelson, 50, New York, N.Y., senior vice president, Carr Futures. Confirmed dead, World Trade Center, at/in building.
Michelle Ann Nelson, 27, Valley Stream, N.Y., benefits specialist, Cantor Fitzgerald. Confirmed dead, World Trade Center, at/in building.
Oscar Nesbitt, 58, New York, N.Y., New York State Department of Taxation and Finance. Confirmed dead, World Trade Center, at/in building.
Nancy Yuen Ngo, 36, Harrington Park, N.J., network consultant, Marsh & McLennan Cos. Inc. Confirmed dead, World Trade Center, at/in building.
Jody Tepedino Nichilo, 39, New York, N.Y., executive assistant, Cantor Fitzgerald. Reported dead, World Trade Center, at/in building.
Martin Niederer, 23, Hoboken, N.J., securities trader, Cantor Fitzgerald. Confirmed dead, World Trade Center, at/in building.

Frank John Niestadt, 55, Ronkonkoma, N.Y., operations director, Aon Corp. Confirmed dead, World Trade Center, at/in building.
Gloria Nieves, 48, New York, N.Y., Fiduciary Trust International. Confirmed dead, World Trade Center, at/in building.
Juan Nieves, 56, New York, N.Y., salad maker, Windows on the World. Confirmed dead, World Trade Center, at/in building.
Troy Edward Nilsen, 33, New York, N.Y., network engineer for eSpeed division, Cantor Fitzgerald. Confirmed dead, World Trade Center, at/in building.
Paul R. Nimbley, 42, Middletown, N.J., vice president, Cantor Fitzgerald. Confirmed dead, World Trade Center, at/in building.
John Ballantine Niven, 44, New York, N.Y., senior vice president in mergers and acquisitions, Aon Corp. Reported dead, World Trade Center, at/in building.
Curtis Terrence Noel, 22, Poughkeepsie, N.Y., switch operations technician, General Telecom. Confirmed dead, World Trade Center, at/in building.
Daniel R. Nolan, 44, Hopatcong, N.J., assistant vice president for computer technology services, Johnson & Higgins/March McLennan. Confirmed dead, World Trade Center, at/in building.
Robert Walter Noonan, 36, Norwalk, Conn., trader, Cantor Fitzgerald. Reported dead, World Trade Center, at/in building.
Daniela R. Notaro, 25, New York, N.Y., receptionist and secretary, Carr Futures. Confirmed dead, World Trade Center, at/in building.
Brian Novotny, 33, Hoboken, N.J., Cantor Fitzgerald. Confirmed dead, World Trade Center, at/in building.
Soichi Numata, 45, Irvington, N.Y., deputy general manager, Fuji Bank. Reported missing, World Trade Center, at/in building. *Japanese.*
Brian Felix Nunez, 29, New York, N.Y., office manager for eSpeed division, Cantor Fitzgerald. Confirmed dead, World Trade Center, at/in building.
Jose R. Nunez, 42, New York, N.Y., food runner, Windows on the World. Confirmed dead, World Trade Center, at/in building.
Jeffrey Nussbaum, 37, Oceanside, N.Y., trader, Carr Futures. Confirmed dead, World Trade Center, at/in building.

– O –

James A. Oakley, 52, Cortlandt Manor, N.Y., senior vice president for information technology, Marsh & McLennan Cos. Inc. Confirmed dead, World Trade Center, at/in building.
James P. O'Brien, 33, New York, N.Y., bond trader, Cantor Fitzgerald. Confirmed dead, World Trade Center, at/in building.
Michael O'Brien, 42, Cedar Knolls, N.J., municipal bond desk senior vice president, Cantor Fitzgerald. Confirmed dead, World Trade Center, at/in building.
Scott J. O'Brien, 40, New York, N.Y., manager, Slam Dunk Networks. Confirmed dead, World Trade Center, at/in building.
Timothy Michael O'Brien, 40, Brookville, N.Y., Cantor Fitzgerald. Confirmed dead, World Trade Center, at/in building.
Jefferson Ocampo, 28. Reported dead, World Trade Center, at/in building. *Colombian.*
Dennis J. O'Connor, 34, New York, N.Y., Cantor Fitzgerald. Confirmed dead, World Trade Center, at/in building.
Diana J. O'Connor, 38, Eastchester, N.Y., Sandler O'Neill & Partners. Confirmed dead, World Trade Center, at/in building.
Keith K. O'Connor, 28, Hoboken, N.J., sales trader, Keefe, Bruyette & Woods. Confirmed dead, World Trade Center, at/in building.
Richard J. O'Connor, 49, Poughkeepsie, N.Y., senior vice president, Marsh & McLennan Cos. Inc. Confirmed dead, World Trade Center, at/in building.
Amy O'Doherty, 23, New York, N.Y., broker's assistant, Cantor Fitzgerald. Confirmed dead, World Trade Center, at/in building.
Marni Pont O'Doherty, 31, Armonk, N.Y., senior vice president, Keefe, Bruyette & Woods. Confirmed dead, World Trade Center, at/in building.
Takashi Ogawa, 37, Tokyo, Japan. Confirmed dead, World Trade Center, at/in building. *Japanese.*
Albert Ogletree, 49, New York, N.Y., food service handler, Forte Food Service. Confirmed dead, World Trade Center, at/in building.
Philip Paul Ognibene, 39, New York, N.Y., Keefe, Bruyette & Woods. Confirmed dead, World Trade Center, at/in building.
James Andrew O'Grady, 32, Harrington Park, N.J., managing director, Sandler O'Neill & Partners. Confirmed dead, World Trade Center, at/in building.
Gerald Michael Olcott, 55, New Hyde Park, N.Y., Marsh & McLennan Cos. Inc. Confirmed dead, World Trade Center, at/in building.
Gerald O'Leary, 34, Stony Point, N.Y., chef, Forte Food Service. Confirmed dead, World Trade Center, at/in building.
Christine Anne Olender, 39, New York, N.Y., Windows on the World. Confirmed dead, World Trade Center, at/in building.
Elsy Carolina Osorio Oliva, 27, New York, N.Y., junior translation engineer, General Telecom. Confirmed dead, World Trade Center, at/in building.
Linda Mary Oliva, 44, New York, N.Y., executive assistant to the president of the New York office, Carr Futures. Confirmed dead, World Trade Center, at/in building.
Edward K. Oliver, 31, Jackson, N.J., broker, Carr Futures. Confirmed dead, World Trade Center, at/in building.
Leah E. Oliver, 24, New York, N.Y., technical sales consultant, Marsh & McLennan Cos. Inc. Confirmed dead, World Trade Center, at/in building.
Maureen L. Olson, 50, Rockville Centre, N.Y., insurance broker, Marsh Inc. Confirmed dead, World Trade Center, at/in building.

Matthew Timothy O'Mahoney, 39, New York, N.Y., Cantor Fitzgerald. Confirmed dead, World Trade Center, at/in building.
Toshihiro Onda, 39, corporate banking senior manager, Fuji Bank. Reported missing, World Trade Center, at/in building. *Japanese.*
Seamus L. O'Neal, 52, New York, N.Y., Cantor Fitzgerald. Confirmed dead, World Trade Center, at/in building.
John P. O'Neill, 49, N.Y., former FBI counterterrorism expert and head of security, World Trade Center. Confirmed dead, World Trade Center, at/in building.
Peter J. O'Neill, 21, Amityville, N.Y., Sandler O'Neill & Partners. Confirmed dead, World Trade Center, at/in building.
Sean Gordon Corbett O'Neill, 34, Rye, N.Y., equities trader, Cantor Fitzgerald. Confirmed dead, World Trade Center, at/in building.
Michael C. Opperman, 45, Selden, N.Y., vice president, Aon Risk Services, Aon Corp. Confirmed dead, World Trade Center, at/in building.
Christopher Orgielewicz, 35, Larchmont, N.Y., analyst, Sandler O'Neill & Partners. Confirmed dead, World Trade Center, at/in building.
Margaret Orloske, 50, Windsor, Conn., manager, Marsh & McLennan Cos. Inc. Confirmed dead, World Trade Center, at/in building.
Virginia A. Ormiston-Kenworthy, 42, New York, N.Y., Marsh & McLennan Cos. Inc. Confirmed dead, World Trade Center, at/in building.
Juan Romero Orozco, Acatlan de Osorio, Puebla, Mexico. Reported missing, World Trade Center, at/in building. *Mexican.*
Ronald Orsini, 59, Hillsdale, N.J., bond broker, Cantor Fitzgerald. Confirmed dead, World Trade Center, at/in building.
Peter K. Ortale, 37, New York, N.Y., bond broker, Euro Brokers Inc. Reported dead, World Trade Center, at/in building.
Alexander Ortiz, 36, Ridgewood, N.Y. Confirmed dead, World Trade Center, at/in building.
Emilio (Peter) Ortiz, 38, New York, N.Y., Carr Futures. Confirmed dead, World Trade Center, at/in building.
Paul Ortiz, 21, New York, N.Y., computer technician, Bloomberg L.P. Confirmed dead, World Trade Center, at/in building.
Sonia Ortiz, 58, New York, N.Y., janitorial, elevator operator, ABM Industries. Confirmed dead, World Trade Center, at/in building.
Masaru Ose, 36, Fort Lee, N.J., manager, Mizuho Capital Markets Corp. Confirmed dead, World Trade Center, at/in building. *Japanese.*
Patrick J. O'Shea, 45, Farmingdale, N.Y., first vice president of futures, Carr Futures. Confirmed dead, World Trade Center, at/in building.
Robert W. O'Shea, 47, Wall, N.J., Carr Futures. Confirmed dead, World Trade Center, at/in building.
James Robert Ostrowski, 37, Garden City, N.Y., Cantor Fitzgerald. Confirmed dead, World Trade Center, at/in building.
Timothy O'Sullivan, 68, Albrightsville, Pa., financial consultant, Cultural Institution of Retirement Systems. Confirmed dead, World Trade Center, at/in building.
Jason Douglas Oswald, 28, New York, N.Y., bond broker, Cantor Fitzgerald. Confirmed dead, World Trade Center, at/in building.
Isidro Ottenwalder, 35, New York, N.Y., Windows on the World. Confirmed dead, World Trade Center, at/in building.
Michael Ou, 53, New York, N.Y., New York State Department of Taxation and Finance. Confirmed dead, World Trade Center, at/in building.
Todd Joseph Ouida, 25, River Edge, N.J., options broker, Cantor Fitzgerald. Confirmed dead, World Trade Center, at/in building.
Jesus Ovalles, 60, New York, N.Y., Windows on the World. Confirmed dead, World Trade Center, at/in building.
Peter J. Owens, 42, Williston Park, N.Y., government agencies, Cantor Fitzgerald. Confirmed dead, World Trade Center, at/in building.
Adianes Oyola, 23, New York, N.Y., human resources/payroll employee, Fuji Bank. Confirmed dead, World Trade Center, at/in building.

– P –

Angel M. Pabon, 54, New York, N.Y., manager of international equities, Cantor Fitzgerald. Confirmed dead, World Trade Center, at/in building.
Israel Pabon, 31, New York, N.Y., food service handler, Forte Food Service. Confirmed dead, World Trade Center, at/in building.
Roland Pacheco, 25, New York, N.Y., data administrator, Alliance Consulting. Confirmed dead, World Trade Center, at/in building.
Michael Benjamin Packer, 45, New York, N.Y., managing director of corporate & institutional client group, Merrill Lynch. Confirmed dead, World Trade Center, at/in building.
Deepa K. Pakkala, 31, Stewartsville, N.J., consultant at Marsh & McLennan Cos. Inc. Confirmed dead, World Trade Center, at/in building.
Thomas Anthony Palazzo, 44, Armonk, N.Y., bond trader, Cantor Fitzgerald. Confirmed dead, World Trade Center, at/in building.
Richard (Rico) Palazzolo, 39, New York, N.Y., mortgage security broker, Cantor Fitzgerald. Confirmed dead, World Trade Center, at/in building.
Alan N. Palumbo, 42, New York, N.Y., broker, Cantor Fitzgerald. Confirmed dead, World Trade Center, at/in building.
Christopher M. Panatier, 36, Rockville Centre, N.Y., foreign currency trader, Cantor Fitzgerald. Confirmed dead, World Trade Center, at/in building.
Dominique Pandolfo, 27, Hoboken, N.J., Marsh & McLennan Cos. Inc. Confirmed dead, World Trade Center, at/in building.

Edward J. Papa, 47, Oyster Bay, N.Y., vice president, partner, government securities, Cantor Fitzgerald. Confirmed dead, World Trade Center, at/in building.
Salvatore Papasso, 34, New York, N.Y., tax fraud investigator, New York State Department of Taxation and Finance. Confirmed dead, World Trade Center, at/in building.
Vinod K. Parakat, 34, Sayreville, N.J., programmer, central development, Cantor Fitzgerald. Confirmed dead, World Trade Center, at/in building.
Vijayashanker Paramsothy, 23, New York, N.Y., Aon Corp. Confirmed dead, World Trade Center, at/in building.
Nitin Parandkar, consultant, Marsh & McLennan Cos. Inc. Reported missing, World Trade Center, at/in building.
Hardai (Casey) Parbhu, 42, New York, N.Y., Aon Corp. Confirmed dead, World Trade Center, at/in building.
Debra (Debbie) Paris, 48, New York, N.Y., executive assistant, Sandler O'Neill & Partners. Confirmed dead, World Trade Center, at/in building.
George Paris, 33, New York, N.Y., Cantor Fitzgerald. Confirmed dead, World Trade Center, at/in building.
Gye-Hyong Park, 28, New York, N.Y., sales support associate, Metropolitan Life Insurance Co. Confirmed dead, World Trade Center, at/in building.
Philip L. Parker, 53, Skillman, N.J., senior vice president, Aon Corp. Confirmed dead, World Trade Center, at/in building.
Michael A. Parkes, 27, New York, N.Y., senior accountant, Marsh & McLennan Cos. Inc. Confirmed dead, World Trade Center, at/in building. *Jamaican.*
Robert Emmett Parks, 47, Middletown, N.J., bond broker, Cantor Fitzgerald. Confirmed dead, World Trade Center, at/in building.
Hasmukhrai Chuckulal Parmar, 48, Warren, N.J., computer systems manager, Cantor Fitzgerald. Confirmed dead, World Trade Center, at/in building.
Diane Marie Moore Parsons, 58, Malta, N.Y., New York State Department of Taxation and Finance. Reported dead, World Trade Center, at/in building.
Leobardo Lopez Pascual, 41, New York, N.Y., Windows on the World. Confirmed dead, World Trade Center, at/in building. *Mexican.*
Michael J. Pascuma, 50, Massapequa Park, N.Y., stock broker, Harvey Young Yurman Inc. Confirmed dead, World Trade Center, at/in building.
Jerrold H. Paskins, 56, Anaheim Hills, Calif., insurance executive, Devonshire Group. Confirmed dead, World Trade Center, at/in building.
Horace Robert Passananti, 55, New York, N.Y., vice president of claims, Marsh & McLennan Cos. Inc. Confirmed dead, World Trade Center, at/in building.
Suzanne H. Passaro, 38, East Brunswick, N.J., Aon Corp. Confirmed dead, World Trade Center, at/in building.
Victor Antonio Martinez Pastrana, Tlachichuca, Puebla, Mexico. Reported missing, World Trade Center, at/in building. *Mexican.*
Avnish Ramanbhai Patel, 28, New York, N.Y., research analyst, Fred Alger Management. Confirmed dead, World Trade Center, at/in building.
Dipti Patel, 38, New Hyde Park, N.Y., data systems engineer, Cantor Fitzgerald. Confirmed dead, World Trade Center, at/in building.
Manish K. Patel, 29, Edison, N.J., Euro Brokers Inc. Confirmed dead, World Trade Center, at/in building.
Steven B. Paterson, 40, Ridgewood, N.J., bond trader, Cantor Fitzgerald. Confirmed dead, World Trade Center, at/in building.
James Matthew Patrick, 30, Norwalk, Conn., bond broker, Cantor Fitzgerald. Confirmed dead, World Trade Center, at/in building.
Manuel Patrocino, 34, Windows on the World. Confirmed dead, World Trade Center, at/in building.
Bernard E. Patterson, 46, Upper Brookville, N.Y., Cantor Fitzgerald. Confirmed dead, World Trade Center, at/in building.
Cira Marie Patti, 40, New York, N.Y., trader's assistant, Keefe, Bruyette & Woods. Confirmed dead, World Trade Center, at/in building.
Robert Edward Pattison, 40, New York, N.Y. Confirmed dead, World Trade Center, at/in building.
James R. Paul, 58, New York, N.Y., executive vice president, Carr Futures. Confirmed dead, World Trade Center, at/in building.
Patrice Paz, 52, New York, N.Y., Aon Corp. Confirmed dead, World Trade Center, at/in building.
Sharon Cristina Millan Paz, 31, New York, N.Y., office services coordinator, Harris Beach LLP. Confirmed dead, World Trade Center, at/in building. *Colombian.*
Victor Paz-Gutierrez, New York, N.Y., pastry chef, Windows on the World. Confirmed dead, World Trade Center, at/in building. *Colombian.*
Stacey L. Peak, 36, New York, N.Y., energy/power stock broker, Cantor Fitzgerald. Confirmed dead, World Trade Center, at/in building.
Richard Allen Pearlman, 18, New York, N.Y., volunteer medic, Forest Hills Ambulance Corps. Confirmed dead, World Trade Center, at/in building.
Thomas E. Pedicini, 30, Hicksville, N.Y., institutional equities department, Cantor Fitzgerald. Confirmed dead, World Trade Center, at/in building.
Todd D. Pelino, 34, Fair Haven, N.J., Cantor Fitzgerald. Confirmed dead, World Trade Center, at/in building.
Michel Adrian Pelletier, 36, Greenwich, Conn., commodities broker, Cantor Fitzgerald. Confirmed dead, World Trade Center, at/in building.
Anthony Peluso, 46, New York, N.Y. Confirmed dead, World Trade Center, at/in building.
Angel Ramon Pena, 45, River Vale, N.J., Aon Corp. Confirmed dead, World Trade Center, at/in building.
Jose D. Pena, Windows on the World. Reported missing, World Trade Center, at/in building.
Richard Al Penny, 53, New York, N.Y., recycling program worker, World Trade Center Project Renewal. Confirmed dead, World Trade Center, at/in building.

Salvatore F. Pepe, 45, New York, N.Y., assistant vice president for technology, Marsh & McLennan Cos. Inc. Confirmed dead, World Trade Center, at/in building.

Carl Allen Peralta, 37, New York, N.Y., broker, Cantor Fitzgerald. Confirmed dead, World Trade Center, at/in building. *Filipino.*

Robert David Peraza, 30, New York, N.Y., bond trader, Cantor Fitzgerald. Confirmed dead, World Trade Center, at/in building.

Jon A. Perconti, 32, Brick, N.J., stock trader, Cantor Fitzgerald. Confirmed dead, World Trade Center, at/in building.

Alejo Perez, 66, Union City, N.J., Windows on the World. Confirmed dead, World Trade Center, at/in building.

Angel Perez, 43, Jersey City, N.J., Cantor Fitzgerald. Confirmed dead, World Trade Center, at/in building.

Angela Susan Perez, 35, New York, N.Y., Cantor Fitzgerald. Confirmed dead, World Trade Center, at/in building.

Anthony Perez, 33, Locust Valley, N.Y., technical specialist, eSpeed, Cantor Fitzgerald. Confirmed dead, World Trade Center, at/in building.

Ivan Perez, 37, New York, N.Y., Fiduciary Trust International. Confirmed dead, World Trade Center, at/in building.

Joseph John Perroncino, 33, Smithtown, N.Y., vice president of operations, Cantor Fitzgerald. Confirmed dead, World Trade Center, at/in building.

Edward J. Perrotta, 43, Mount Sinai, N.Y., vice president, Cantor Fitzgerald. Confirmed dead, World Trade Center, at/in building.

Emelda Perry, Washington Group International. Confirmed dead, World Trade Center, at/in building.

Franklin Allan Pershep, 59, New York, N.Y., insurance underwriter, Aon Corp. Confirmed dead, World Trade Center, at/in building.

Daniel Pesce, 34, New York, N.Y., ticket desk manager, Cantor Fitzgerald. Confirmed dead, World Trade Center, at/in building.

Michael J. Pescherine, 32, New York, N.Y., bond trader, Keefe, Bruyette & Woods. Confirmed dead, World Trade Center, at/in building.

Davin Peterson, 25, New York, N.Y., Nasdaq assistant trader, Cantor Fitzgerald. Confirmed dead, World Trade Center, at/in building.

William Russel Peterson, 46, New York, N.Y. Confirmed dead, World Trade Center, at/in building.

Mark Petrocelli, 29, New York, N.Y., commodities broker, Carr Futures. Confirmed dead, World Trade Center, at/in building.

Kaleen E. Pezzuti, 28, Fair Haven, N.J., bond broker, Cantor Fitzgerald. Confirmed dead, World Trade Center, at/in building.

Tu-Anh Pham, 42, Princeton, N.J., Fred Alger Management. Reported missing, World Trade Center, at/in building.

Eugenia Piantieri, 55, New York, N.Y., Marsh & McLennan Cos. Inc. Confirmed dead, World Trade Center, at/in building.

Ludwig John Picarro, 44, Basking Ridge, N.J., vice president, Zurich American Insurance. Confirmed dead, World Trade Center, at/in building.

Matthew Picerno, 44, Holmdel, N.J., municipal bond broker, Cantor Fitzgerald. Confirmed dead, World Trade Center, at/in building.

Joseph O. Pick, 40, Hoboken, N.J., vice president, Fiduciary Trust International. Confirmed dead, World Trade Center, at/in building.

Dennis J. Pierce, 54, New York, N.Y., New York State Department of Taxation and Finance. Confirmed dead, World Trade Center, at/in building.

Maxima J. Pierre, 40, Bellport, N.Y., food service handler, Forte Food Service. Confirmed dead, World Trade Center, at/in building.

Bernard T. Pietronico, 39, Matawan, N.J., corporate bond broker, Cantor Fitzgerald. Confirmed dead, World Trade Center, at/in building.

Nicholas P. Pietrunti, 38, Belford, N.J., data entry clerk, Cantor Fitzgerald. Confirmed dead, World Trade Center, at/in building.

Theodoros Pigis, 60, New York, N.Y., One Source (Hudson Shatz). Confirmed dead, World Trade Center, at/in building.

Susan Elizabeth Ancona Pinto, 44, New York, N.Y., vice president of systems infrastructure at eSpeed, Cantor Fitzgerald. Confirmed dead, World Trade Center, at/in building.

Joseph Piskadlo, 48, North Arlington, N.J., structural carpenter, ABM Industries. Confirmed dead, World Trade Center, at/in building.

Christopher Todd Pitman, 30, New York, N.Y., Cantor Fitzgerald. Confirmed dead, World Trade Center, at/in building.

Josh Piver, 42, Stonington, Conn., Cantor Fitzgerald. Reported dead, World Trade Center, at/in building.

Joseph Plumitallo, 45, Manalapan, N.J., bond broker, Cantor Fitzgerald. Confirmed dead, World Trade Center, at/in building.

John M. Pocher, 36, Middletown, N.J., bond broker, Cantor Fitzgerald. Confirmed dead, World Trade Center, at/in building.

William Howard Pohlmann, 56, Ardsley, N.Y., assistant deputy commissioner, New York State Department of Taxation and Finance. Confirmed dead, World Trade Center, at/in building.

Laurence M. Polatsch, 32, New York, N.Y., equities trader, Cantor Fitzgerald. Confirmed dead, World Trade Center, at/in building.

Thomas H. Polhemus, 39, Morris Plains, N.J., systems analyst, Accenture. Confirmed dead, World Trade Center, at/in building.

Steve Pollicino, 48, Plainview, N.Y., vice president, Cantor Fitzgerald. Confirmed dead, World Trade Center, at/in building.

Susan M. Pollio, 45, Long Beach Township, N.J., Euro Brokers Inc. Confirmed dead, World Trade Center, at/in building.

Joshua Poptean, 37, New York, N.Y., construction foreman, Bronx Builders. Confirmed dead, World Trade Center, at/in building.

Giovanna Porras, 24, New York, N.Y., accountant, General Telecom. Confirmed dead, World Trade Center, at/in building.
Anthony Portillo, 48, New York, N.Y., architect, Washington Group International. Confirmed dead, World Trade Center, at/in building.
James Edward Potorti, 52, Princeton, N.J., vice president, Marsh & McLennan Cos. Inc. Confirmed dead, World Trade Center, at/in building.
Daphne Pouletsos, 47, Westwood, N.J., Aon Corp. Confirmed dead, World Trade Center, at/in building.
Richard Poulos, 55, Levittown, N.Y., Cantor Fitzgerald. Reported dead, World Trade Center, at/in building.
Stephen E. Poulos, 45, Basking Ridge, N.J., information technology manager, Aon Corp. Confirmed dead, World Trade Center, at/in building.
Brandon Jerome Powell, 26, New York, N.Y., food service handler, Forte Food Service. Confirmed dead, World Trade Center, at/in building.
Tony Pratt, 43, New York, N.Y., food service handler, Forte Food Service. Reported missing, World Trade Center, at/in building.
Gregory M. Preziose, 34, Holmdel, N.J., bond trader, Cantor Fitzgerald. Confirmed dead, World Trade Center, at/in building.
Wanda Ivelisse Prince, 30, New York, N.Y., foreign trader, Fiduciary Trust International. Confirmed dead, World Trade Center, at/in building.
Everett Martin (Marty) Proctor, 44, New York, N.Y., equities controller, Cantor Fitzgerald. Confirmed dead, World Trade Center, at/in building.
Carrie B. Progen, 25, New York, N.Y., assistant office manager, Aon Corp. Confirmed dead, World Trade Center, at/in building.
David Lee Pruim, 53, Upper Montclair, N.J., senior vice president of risk services, Aon Corp. Confirmed dead, World Trade Center, at/in building.
John F. Puckett, 47, Glen Cove, N.Y., sound engineer, Windows on the World. Confirmed dead, World Trade Center, at/in building.
Robert D. Pugliese, 47, East Fishkill, N.Y., assistant vice president, Marsh & McLennan Cos. Inc. Confirmed dead, World Trade Center, at/in building.
Edward F. Pullis, 34, Hazlet, N.J., consultant, Aon Corp. Confirmed dead, World Trade Center, at/in building.
Patricia Ann Puma, 33, New York, N.Y., administrator, Julien J. Studley Inc. Confirmed dead, World Trade Center, at/in building.
Hemanth Kumar Puttur, 26, White Plains, N.Y., Marsh & McLennan Cos. Inc. Confirmed dead, World Trade Center, at/in building.
Edward R. Pykon, 33, Princeton, N.J., senior vice president, Fred Alger Management. Confirmed dead, World Trade Center, at/in building.

– Q –

Christopher Quackenbush, 44, Manhasset, N.Y., executive in charge of investment banking, Sandler O'Neill & Partners. Confirmed dead, World Trade Center, at/in building.
Lars Peter Qualben, 49, New York, N.Y., senior vice president, Marsh & McLennan Cos. Inc. Confirmed dead, World Trade Center, at/in building.
Beth Ann Quigley, 25, New York, N.Y., trader, Cantor Fitzgerald. Confirmed dead, World Trade Center, at/in building.
James Francis Quinn, 23, New York, N.Y., trade support staff, Cantor Fitzgerald. Confirmed dead, World Trade Center, at/in building.

– R –

Carol Rabalais, 38, New York, N.Y., administrative assistant, Aon Corp. Confirmed dead, World Trade Center, at/in building. *Jamaican.*
Christopher Peter A. Racaniello, 30, New York, N.Y., operations department, Cantor Fitzgerald. Confirmed dead, World Trade Center, at/in building.
Laura Marie Ragonese-Snik, 41, Bangor, Pa., special risk insurance specialist, Aon Corp. Confirmed dead, World Trade Center, at/in building.
Peter F. Raimondi, 46, New York, N.Y., vice president, Carr Futures. Confirmed dead, World Trade Center, at/in building.
Harry A. Raines, 37, New York, N.Y., vice president of global networking for eSpeed, Cantor Fitzgerald. Confirmed dead, World Trade Center, at/in building.
Ehtesham U. Raja, 28, Clifton, N.J., TCG Software. Confirmed dead, World Trade Center, at/in building.
Valsa Raju, 39, Yonkers, N.Y., Carr Futures. Confirmed dead, World Trade Center, at/in building.
Lukas (Luke) Rambousek, 27, New York, N.Y., temporary worker at Cantor Fitzgerald, United Staffing. Reported dead, World Trade Center, at/in building.
Julio Fernandez Ramirez, 47, painting company employee. Confirmed dead, World Trade Center, at/in building. *Peruvian.*
Maria Isabel Ramirez, 25, New York, N.Y., executive secretary, Lanagan Engineering and Environmental Services. Confirmed dead, World Trade Center, at/in building.
Harry Ramos, 45, Newark, N.J., head trader, May Davis Group. Confirmed dead, World Trade Center, at/in building.
Vishnoo Ramsaroop, 44, New York, N.Y., janitorial, cleaner, ABM Industries. Confirmed dead, World Trade Center, at/in building.
Lorenzo Ramzey, 48, East Northport, N.Y., casualty broker, Aon Corp. Confirmed dead, World Trade Center, at/in building.
A. Todd Rancke, 42, Summit, N.J., Sandler O'Neill & Partners. Confirmed dead, World Trade Center, at/in building.

Jonathan C. Randall, 26, New York, N.Y., Marsh & McLennan Cos. Inc. Confirmed dead, World Trade Center, at/in building.

Srinivasa Shreyas Ranganath, 26, Hackensack, N.J., consultant at Marsh & McLennan Cos. Inc. Confirmed dead, World Trade Center, at/in building.

Anne Rose T. Ransom, 45, Edgewater, N.J., travel department, American Express. Confirmed dead, World Trade Center, at/in building.

Faina Rapoport, 45, New York, N.Y., consultant at Marsh & McLennan Cos. Inc. Confirmed dead, World Trade Center, at/in building.

Robert Arthur Rasmussen, 42, Hinsdale, Ill., financial analyst, Vestek. Confirmed dead, World Trade Center, at/in building.

Amenia Rasool, 33, New York, N.Y., accountant, Marsh & McLennan Cos. Inc. Confirmed dead, World Trade Center, at/in building.

Roger Mark Rasweiler, 53, Flemington, N.J., vice president, Marsh Inc. Confirmed dead, World Trade Center, at/in building.

David Alan James Rathkey, 47, Mountain Lakes, N.J. sales executive, IQ Financial Systems. Confirmed dead, World Trade Center, at/in building.

William R. Raub, 38, Saddle River, N.J., institutional stock trader, Cantor Fitzgerald. Confirmed dead, World Trade Center, at/in building.

Gerard Rauzi, 42, New York, N.Y., New York State Department of Taxation and Finance. Confirmed dead, World Trade Center, at/in building. *Italian.*

Alexey Razuvaev, 40, New York, N.Y., Euro Brokers Inc. Confirmed dead, World Trade Center, at/in building.

Gregory Reda, 33, New Hyde Park, N.Y., e-mail coordinator, Marsh & McLennan Cos. Inc. Confirmed dead, World Trade Center, at/in building.

Sarah (Prothero) Redheffer, 35, London, England, conferences operations manager, Risk Waters Group. Reported missing, World Trade Center, at/in building. *British.*

Michele Reed, 26, Ringoes, N.J., Aon Corp. Reported missing, World Trade Center, at/in building.

Judith A. Reese, 56, Kearny, N.J. Confirmed dead, World Trade Center, at/in building.

Thomas M. Regan, 43, Cranford, N.J., Aon Corp. Confirmed dead, World Trade Center, at/in building.

Howard Reich, 59, New York, N.Y., mail clerk, Pitney Bowes. Confirmed dead, World Trade Center, at/in building.

Gregg Reidy, 26, Holmdel, N.J., trader, Cantor Fitzgerald. Confirmed dead, World Trade Center, at/in building.

James B. Reilly, 25, Huntington Station, N.Y., bond trader, Keefe, Bruyette & Woods. Reported dead, World Trade Center, at/in building.

Timothy E. Reilly, 40, New York, N.Y., vice president, Marsh USA. Confirmed dead, World Trade Center, at/in building.

Joseph Reina, 32, New York, N.Y., manager of operations, Cantor Fitzgerald. Confirmed dead, World Trade Center, at/in building.

Thomas Barnes Reinig, 48, Bernardsville, N.J., investment banker, Cantor Fitzgerald. Confirmed dead, World Trade Center, at/in building.

Frank B. Reisman, 41, Princeton, N.J., trader, Cantor Fitzgerald. Confirmed dead, World Trade Center, at/in building.

Joshua Scott Reiss, 23, New York, N.Y., bond trader, Cantor Fitzgerald. Confirmed dead, World Trade Center, at/in building.

Karen Renda, 52, New York, N.Y., travel agent, American Express. Confirmed dead, World Trade Center, at/in building.

John Armand Reo, 28, Larchmont, N.Y., bond trader, Cantor Fitzgerald. Confirmed dead, World Trade Center, at/in building.

Richard Rescorla, 62, Morristown, N.J., security chief, Morgan Stanley. Confirmed dead, World Trade Center, at/in building.

John Thomas Resta, 40, New York, N.Y., trader, Carr Futures. Confirmed dead, World Trade Center, at/in building.

Eduvigis (Eddie) Reyes, 37, New York, N.Y., Rohde & Liesenfeld. Reported missing, World Trade Center, at/in building.

John Frederick Rhodes, 57, Howell, N.J., claims consultant, Aon Corp. Confirmed dead, World Trade Center, at/in building.

Rudolph N. Riccio, 50, New York, N.Y., Cantor Fitzgerald. Confirmed dead, World Trade Center, at/in building.

AnnMarie (Davi) Riccoboni, 58, New York, N.Y., billing supervisor, Ohrenstein & Brown. Confirmed dead, World Trade Center, at/in building.

David Rice, 31, New York, N.Y., investment banker, Sandler O'Neill & Partners. Confirmed dead, World Trade Center, at/in building.

Eileen Mary Rice, 57, New York, N.Y., executive assistant, Marsh & McLennan Cos. Inc. Confirmed dead, World Trade Center, at/in building.

Kenneth F. Rice, 34, Hicksville, N.Y., vice president technology division, Marsh & McLennan Cos. Inc. Confirmed dead, World Trade Center, at/in building.

Gregory Richards, 30, New York, N.Y., eSpeed division, Cantor Fitzgerald. Confirmed dead, World Trade Center, at/in building.

Michael Richards, 38, New York, N.Y., sculptor. Confirmed dead, World Trade Center, at/in building. *Jamaican.*

Venesha O. Richards, 26, North Brunswick, N.J., secretary, Marsh & McLennan Cos. Inc. Confirmed dead, World Trade Center, at/in building. *Jamaican.*

Alan Jay Richman, 44, New York, N.Y., vice president, employee benefits, Marsh & McLennan Cos. Inc. Confirmed dead, World Trade Center, at/in building.

John M. Rigo, 48, New York, N.Y., insurance brokerage executive, Marsh & McLennan Cos. Inc. Confirmed dead, World Trade Center, at/in building.

James Riley, 25, New York, N.Y. Confirmed dead, World Trade Center, at/in building.

Theresa (Ginger) Risco, 48, New York, N.Y., senior vice president and senior analyst, Fred Alger Management. Confirmed dead, World Trade Center, at/in building.
Rose Mary Riso, 55, New York, N.Y., New York State Department of Taxation and Finance. Confirmed dead, World Trade Center, at/in building.
Moises N. Rivas, 29, New York, N.Y., staff cafeteria cook, Windows on the World. Confirmed dead, World Trade Center, at/in building.
Carmen A. Rivera, 33, Westtown, N.Y., assistant vice president, Fiduciary Trust International. Confirmed dead, World Trade Center, at/in building.
Isaias Rivera, 51, Perth Amboy, N.J., technician, CBS. Confirmed dead, World Trade Center, at/in building.
Juan William Rivera, 27, New York, N.Y., switch engineer, General Telecom. Confirmed dead, World Trade Center, at/in building.
Linda Rivera, 26, New York, N.Y., Marsh & McLennan Cos. Inc. Confirmed dead, World Trade Center, at/in building.
David E. Rivers, 40, New York, N.Y., editorial director, *Waters* magazine, Risk Waters Group. Confirmed dead, World Trade Center, at/in building.
Joseph R. Riverso, 34, White Plains, N.Y., bond trader, Cantor Fitzgerald. Confirmed dead, World Trade Center, at/in building.
Paul Rizza, 34, Park Ridge, N.J., investors services officer, Fiduciary Trust International. Confirmed dead, World Trade Center, at/in building.
John Frank Rizzo, 50, New York, N.Y., carpenter. Confirmed dead, World Trade Center, at/in building.
Stephen Louis Roach, 36, Verona, N.J., vice president, Cantor Fitzgerald. Confirmed dead, World Trade Center, at/in building.
Joseph Roberto, 37, Midland Park, N.J., bank analyst, Keefe, Bruyette & Woods. Confirmed dead, World Trade Center, at/in building.
Leo A. Roberts, 44, Wayne, N.J., municipal bond trader, Cantor Fitzgerald. Confirmed dead, World Trade Center, at/in building.
Donald Walter Robertson, 35, Rumson, N.J., bond trader, Cantor Fitzgerald. Confirmed dead, World Trade Center, at/in building.
Catherina Robinson, 45, New York, N.Y., Wachovia Corp. Confirmed dead, World Trade Center, at/in building.
Jeffrey Robinson, 38, Monmouth Junction, N.J., systems analyst, Marsh & McLennan Cos. Inc. Confirmed dead, World Trade Center, at/in building.
Michell Lee Robotham, 32, Kearny, N.J., help desk manager, Aon Corp. Confirmed dead, World Trade Center, at/in building.
Donald Robson, 52, Manhasset, N.Y., partner and bond broker, Cantor Fitzgerald. Confirmed dead, World Trade Center, at/in building.
Antonio Augusto Tome Rocha, 34, East Hanover, N.J., bond broker, Cantor Fitzgerald. Confirmed dead, World Trade Center, at/in building. *Portuguese.*
Raymond J. Rocha, 29, Malden, Mass., bond trader, Cantor Fitzgerald. Confirmed dead, World Trade Center, at/in building.
Laura Rockefeller, 41, New York, N.Y., freelance delegate coordinator, Risk Waters Group. Confirmed dead, World Trade Center, at/in building.
John M. Rodak, 39, Mantua, N.J., managing director, Sandler O'Neill & Partners. Confirmed dead, World Trade Center, at/in building.
Carlos Cortez Rodriguez. Reported missing, World Trade Center, at/in building. *Colombian.*
Carmen Milagros Rodriguez, 46, Freehold, N.J., Aon Corp. Confirmed dead, World Trade Center, at/in building.
Gregory E. Rodriguez, 31, White Plains, N.Y., assistant vice president, information security, Cantor Fitzgerald. Confirmed dead, World Trade Center, at/in building.
Marsha A. Rodriguez, 41, West Paterson, N.J. Confirmed dead, World Trade Center, at/in building.
David B. Rodriguez-Vargas, 44, New York, N.Y., Windows on the World. Confirmed dead, World Trade Center, at/in building.
Karlie Barbara Rogers, 25, London, England, divisional sponsorship manager, Risk Waters Group. Confirmed dead, World Trade Center, at/in building.
Scott Rohner, 22, Hoboken, N.J., foreign exchange trader, Cantor Fitzgerald. Confirmed dead, World Trade Center, at/in building.
Joseph M. Romagnolo, 37, Coram, N.Y., electrical worker, IPC Kleinknect Electric Co. Confirmed dead, World Trade Center, at/in building.
Efrain Franco Romero, 57, Hazleton, Pa., painter, Fine Painting and Decorating. Confirmed dead, World Trade Center, at/in building.
Elvin Santiago Romero, 34, Matawan, N.J., vice president of international equities, Cantor Fitzgerald. Confirmed dead, World Trade Center, at/in building.
Sean Rooney, 50, Stamford, Conn., risk management services, Aon Corp. Confirmed dead, World Trade Center, at/in building.
Eric Thomas Ropiteau, 24, New York, N.Y., Cantor Fitzgerald. Confirmed dead, World Trade Center, at/in building.
Aida Rosario, 42, Jersey City, N.J., assistant manager, Marsh Inc. Confirmed dead, World Trade Center, at/in building.
Angela Rosario, 27, New York, N.Y., Cantor Fitzgerald. Confirmed dead, World Trade Center, at/in building.
Mark H. Rosen, 45, West Islip, N.Y., partner, fixed income division, Sandler O'Neill & Partners. Confirmed dead, World Trade Center, at/in building.
Brooke David Rosenbaum, 31, Franklin Square, N.Y., supervisor, overseas division, Cantor Fitzgerald. Confirmed dead, World Trade Center, at/in building.
Linda Rosenbaum, 41, Little Falls, N.J. Confirmed dead, World Trade Center, at/in building.
Sheryl Lynn Rosenbaum, 33, Warren, N.J., accountant and partner, Cantor Fitzgerald. Confirmed dead, World Trade Center, at/in building.

Lloyd D. Rosenberg, 31, Morganville, N.J., junk bond dealer, Cantor Fitzgerald. Confirmed dead, World Trade Center, at/in building.

Mark Louis Rosenberg, 26, Teaneck, N.J., software developer, Cantor Fitzgerald. Confirmed dead, World Trade Center, at/in building.

Andrew I. Rosenblum, 45, Rockville Centre, N.Y., bond trader, Cantor Fitzgerald. Confirmed dead, World Trade Center, at/in building.

Joshua M. Rosenblum, 28, Hoboken, N.J., Cantor Fitzgerald. Confirmed dead, World Trade Center, at/in building.

Joshua A. Rosenthal, 44, New York, N.Y., senior vice president, Fiduciary Trust International. Confirmed dead, World Trade Center, at/in building.

Richard David Rosenthal, 50, Fair Lawn, N.J., vice president of finance, Cantor Fitzgerald. Confirmed dead, World Trade Center, at/in building.

Daniel Rossetti, 32, Bloomfield, N.J., carpenter, Certified Installation Services. Confirmed dead, World Trade Center, at/in building.

Norman Rossinow, 39, Cedar Grove, N.J., senior vice president, Aon Corp. Confirmed dead, World Trade Center, at/in building.

Michael Craig Rothberg, 39, Greenwich, Conn., bonds manager, Cantor Fitzgerald. Confirmed dead, World Trade Center, at/in building.

Donna Marie Rothenberg, 53, New York, N.Y., global affairs executive, Aon Corp. Confirmed dead, World Trade Center, at/in building.

Nick Rowe, 29, Hoboken, N.J., UME Voice. Confirmed dead, World Trade Center, at/in building.

Ronald J. Ruben, 36, Hoboken, N.J., vice president, equity trading, Keefe, Bruyette & Woods. Confirmed dead, World Trade Center, at/in building.

Joanne Rubino, 45, New York, N.Y., Marsh & McLennan Cos. Inc. Confirmed dead, World Trade Center, at/in building.

David Michael Ruddle, 31, New York, N.Y., carpenter, Reliable. Reported dead, World Trade Center, at/in building.

Bart Joseph Ruggiere, 32, New York, N.Y., broker, Cantor Fitzgerald. Confirmed dead, World Trade Center, at/in building.

Susan Ann Ruggiero, 30, Plainview, N.Y., assistant vice president, Marsh Technologies, Marsh & McLennan Cos. Inc. Confirmed dead, World Trade Center, at/in building.

Adam K. Ruhalter, 40, Plainview, N.Y., controller, Cantor Fitzgerald. Confirmed dead, World Trade Center, at/in building.

Gilbert Ruiz, 45, New York, N.Y., Windows on the World. Confirmed dead, World Trade Center, at/in building.

Steven Harris Russin, 32, Mendham, N.J., partner, Cantor Fitzgerald. Confirmed dead, World Trade Center, at/in building.

Wayne Alan Russo, 37, Union, N.J., accountant, Marsh & McLennan Cos. Inc. Confirmed dead, World Trade Center, at/in building.

Edward Ryan, 42, Scarsdale, N.Y., first vice president, Carr Futures. Confirmed dead, World Trade Center, at/in building.

John J. Ryan, 45, West Windsor, N.J., vice president, Keefe, Bruyette & Woods. Confirmed dead, World Trade Center, at/in building.

Jonathan Stephan Ryan, 32, Bayville, N.Y., Euro Brokers Inc. Confirmed dead, World Trade Center, at/in building.

Tatiana Ryjova, 36, South Salem, N.Y., Regus. Confirmed dead, World Trade Center, at/in building.

Christina Sunga Ryook, 25, New York, N.Y., human resources department, Cantor Fitzgerald. Confirmed dead, World Trade Center, at/in building.

– S –

Thierry Saada, 27, New York, N.Y., trader, Cantor Fitzgerald. Confirmed dead, World Trade Center, at/in building.

Jason E. Sabbag, 26, New York, N.Y., Fiduciary Trust International. Confirmed dead, World Trade Center, at/in building.

Scott Saber, 38, New York, N.Y., UBS Warburg. Confirmed dead, World Trade Center, at/in building.

Joseph Sacerdote, 48, Freehold, N.J., Cantor Fitzgerald. Confirmed dead, World Trade Center, at/in building.

Francis J. Sadocha, 41, Huntington, N.Y., manager, Forte Food Service. Confirmed dead, World Trade Center, at/in building.

Jude Elias Safi, 24, New York, N.Y., assistant trader, Cantor Fitzgerald. Confirmed dead, World Trade Center, at/in building. *Lebanese.*

Brock Joel Safronoff, 26, New York, N.Y., computer systems analyst, Marsh & McLennan Cos. Inc. Confirmed dead, World Trade Center, at/in building.

Edward Saiya, 49, New York, N.Y. Confirmed dead, World Trade Center, at/in building.

John Patrick Salamone, 37, North Caldwell, N.J., broker, Cantor Fitzgerald. Confirmed dead, World Trade Center, at/in building.

Hernando R. Salas, 71, New York, N.Y., clerk, Civilian Complaint Review Board. Confirmed dead, World Trade Center, at/in building. *Colombian.*

Juan Salas, 35, New York, N.Y., Windows on the World. Confirmed dead, World Trade Center, at/in building.

Esmerlin Salcedo, 36, New York, N.Y., security officer, Summit Security Services. Confirmed dead, World Trade Center, at/in building.

John Salvatore Salerno, 31, Westfield, N.J., broker, Cantor Fitzgerald. Confirmed dead, World Trade Center, at/in building.

Richard L. Salinardi, 32, Hoboken, N.J., general manager for food services, Aramark Corp. Confirmed dead, World Trade Center, at/in building.

Wayne John Saloman, 43, Seaford, N.Y., vice president, government bond broker, Cantor Fitzgerald. Confirmed dead, World Trade Center, at/in building.

Nolbert Salomon, 33, New York, N.Y., security guard, Morgan Stanley. Confirmed dead, World Trade Center, at/in building.
Catherine Patricia Salter, 37, New York, N.Y., Aon Corp. Confirmed dead, World Trade Center, at/in building.
Frank Salvaterra, 41, Manhasset, N.Y., partner, Sandler O'Neill & Partners. Confirmed dead, World Trade Center, at/in building.
Paul R. Salvio, 27, New York, N.Y., broker, Carr Futures. Confirmed dead, World Trade Center, at/in building.
Samuel R. Salvo, 59, Yonkers, N.Y., vice president, Aon Corp. Confirmed dead, World Trade Center, at/in building.
Carlos Samaniego, 29, New York, N.Y., Cantor Fitzgerald. Confirmed dead, World Trade Center, at/in building.
Rena Sam-Dinnoo, 28, New York, N.Y., accounting division, Marsh & McLennan Cos. Inc. Confirmed dead, World Trade Center, at/in building.
James Kenneth Samuel, 29, Hoboken, N.J., commodities trader, Carr Futures. Confirmed dead, World Trade Center, at/in building.
Michael V. San Phillip, 55, Ridgewood, N.J., Sandler O'Neill & Partners. Confirmed dead, World Trade Center, at/in building.
Hugo Sanay-Perafiel, 41, New York, N.Y., Euro Brokers Inc. Confirmed dead, World Trade Center, at/in building.
Alva J. Sanchez, 41, Hempstead, N.Y., Marsh & McLennan Cos. Inc. Confirmed dead, World Trade Center, at/in building.
Erick Sanchez, 41, floor covering installer and foreman, Soundtone. Reported missing, World Trade Center, at/in building.
Jacquelyn P. Sanchez, 23, New York, N.Y., compliance assistant, Cantor Fitzgerald. Confirmed dead, World Trade Center, at/in building.
Eric Sand, 36, Westchester, N.Y., stock trader, Cantor Fitzgerald. Confirmed dead, World Trade Center, at/in building.
Stacey Leigh Sanders, 25, New York, N.Y., Marsh & McLennan Cos. Inc. Confirmed dead, World Trade Center, at/in building.
Herman Sandler, 57, New York, N.Y., chief executive, Sandler O'Neill & Partners. Confirmed dead, World Trade Center, at/in building.
James Sands, 39, Bricktown, N.J., strategic development engineer, eSpeed, Cantor Fitzgerald. Confirmed dead, World Trade Center, at/in building.
Sylvia SanPio Resta, 27, New York, N.Y., trader, Carr Futures. Confirmed dead, World Trade Center, at/in building.
Ayleen J. Santiago, 40, New York, N.Y., Blue Cross Blue Shield. Confirmed dead, World Trade Center, at/in building.
Kirsten Santiago, 26, New York, N.Y., Insurance Overload Systems. Confirmed dead, World Trade Center, at/in building.
Maria Theresa Santillan, 27, Morris Plains, N.J., customer service representative for eSpeed, Cantor Fitzgerald. Confirmed dead, World Trade Center, at/in building.
Susan G. Santo, 24, New York, N.Y., Marsh & McLennan Cos. Inc. Confirmed dead, World Trade Center, at/in building.
Mario L. Santoro, 28, New York, N.Y., emergency medical technician, New York Presbyterian Hospital. Confirmed dead, World Trade Center, at/in building.
Rafael Humberto Santos, 42, New York, N.Y., Cantor Fitzgerald. Confirmed dead, World Trade Center, at/in building. *Colombian.*
Rufino Conrado F. (Roy) Santos, 37, New York, N.Y., computer consultant for Guy Carpenter, Accenture. Confirmed dead, World Trade Center, at/in building. *Filipino.*
Jorge Octavio Santos Anaya, Aguascalientes, Aguascalientes, Mexico. Reported missing, World Trade Center, at/in building. *Mexican.*
Chapelle Sarker, Marsh & McLennan Cos. Inc. Reported missing, World Trade Center, at/in building.
Paul F. Sarle, 38, Babylon, N.Y., MBS broker, mortgages, Cantor Fitzgerald. Confirmed dead, World Trade Center, at/in building.
Deepika K. Sattaluri, 33, Edison, N.J., consultant at Marsh & McLennan Cos. Inc. Confirmed dead, World Trade Center, at/in building.
Susan Sauer, 48, Chicago, Ill., managing director, Marsh Inc., Marsh & McLennan Cos. Inc. Confirmed dead, World Trade Center, at/in building.
Vladimir Savinkin, 21, New York, N.Y., Cantor Fitzgerald. Confirmed dead, World Trade Center, at/in building.
Jackie Sayegh Duggan, 34, banquet and party planner, Windows on the World. Confirmed dead, World Trade Center, at/in building.
John Sbarbaro, 45, New York, N.Y., MBS desk, Cantor Fitzgerald. Confirmed dead, World Trade Center, at/in building.
Robert L. Scandole, 36, Pelham Manor, N.Y., vice president, Cantor Fitzgerald. Confirmed dead, World Trade Center, at/in building.
Michelle Scarpitta, 26, New York, N.Y., Euro Brokers Inc. Confirmed dead, World Trade Center, at/in building.
John G. Scharf, 29, Manorville, N.Y. Confirmed dead, World Trade Center, at/in building.
Angela Susan Scheinberg, 46, New York, N.Y., manager, Blue Cross Blue Shield. Confirmed dead, World Trade Center, at/in building.
Scott M. Schertzer, 28, Edison, N.J., human resources department, Cantor Fitzgerald. Confirmed dead, World Trade Center, at/in building.
Sean Schielke, 27, New York, N.Y., trader, Cantor Fitzgerald. Confirmed dead, World Trade Center, at/in building.
Steven Francis Schlag, 41, Franklin Lakes, N.J., Cantor Fitzgerald. Confirmed dead, World Trade Center, at/in building.

Jon S. Schlissel, 51, Jersey City, N.J., mediator, New York State Department of Taxation and Finance. Reported dead, World Trade Center, at/in building.
Karen Helene Schmidt, 42, Bellmore, N.Y. Confirmed dead, World Trade Center, at/in building.
Ian Schneider, 45, Short Hills, N.J., senior managing director, Cantor Fitzgerald. Confirmed dead, World Trade Center, at/in building.
Marisa Di Nardo Schorpp, 38, White Plains, N.Y., commodities broker, Cantor Fitzgerald. Confirmed dead, World Trade Center, at/in building. *Italian*.
Frank G. Schott, 39, Massapequa, N.Y., assistant vice president for technology, Marsh & McLennan Cos. Inc. Confirmed dead, World Trade Center, at/in building.
Jeffrey Schreier, 48, New York, N.Y., mailroom clerk and messenger, Cantor Fitzgerald. Confirmed dead, World Trade Center, at/in building.
John T. Schroeder, 31, Hoboken, N.J., Fred Alger Management. Confirmed dead, World Trade Center, at/in building.
Susan Lee Kennedy Schuler, 55, Allentown, N.J., securities operations consultant, Singer Frumento LLP. Confirmed dead, World Trade Center, at/in building.
Edward W. Schunk, 54, Baldwin, N.Y., bond broker, Cantor Fitzgerald. Confirmed dead, World Trade Center, at/in building.
Mark E. Schurmeier, 44, McLean, Va., director of strategic engineering, Federal Home Loan Mortgage Corp. Confirmed dead, World Trade Center, at/in building.
Clarin Shellie Schwartz, 51, New York, N.Y., senior vice president, Aon Corp. Confirmed dead, World Trade Center, at/in building.
John Schwartz, 49, Goshen, Conn., bond broker, Cantor Fitzgerald. Reported dead, World Trade Center, at/in building.
Mark Schwartz, 50, West Hempstead, N.Y., emergency medical technician. Confirmed dead, World Trade Center, at/in building.
Adriane Victoria Scibetta, 31, New York, N.Y., accountant, Cantor Fitzgerald. Confirmed dead, World Trade Center, at/in building.
Raphael Scorca, 61, Beachwood, N.J., Marsh & McLennan Cos. Inc. Confirmed dead, World Trade Center, at/in building.
Randolph Scott, 48, Stamford, Conn., broker, Euro Brokers Inc. Confirmed dead, World Trade Center, at/in building.
Christopher J. Scudder, 34, Monsey, N.Y., computer technician, EnPointe Technologies. Confirmed dead, World Trade Center, at/in building.
Arthur Warren Scullin, 57, New York, N.Y., senior vice president and director of taxes, Marsh Inc. Confirmed dead, World Trade Center, at/in building.
Michael Seaman, 41, Manhasset, N.Y., senior vice president, Cantor Fitzgerald. Confirmed dead, World Trade Center, at/in building.
Margaret Seeliger, 34, New York, N.Y., director of underwriting, Combined Insurance, Aon Corp. Confirmed dead, World Trade Center, at/in building.
Carlos Segarra, 55, New York, N.Y., Wachovia Corp. Confirmed dead, World Trade Center, at/in building.
Jason Sekzer, 31, New York, N.Y., vice president, Cantor Fitzgerald. Confirmed dead, World Trade Center, at/in building.
Matthew Carmen Sellitto, 23, Morristown, N.J., Cantor Fitzgerald. Confirmed dead, World Trade Center, at/in building.
Howard Selwyn, 47, Hewlett, N.Y., vice president, Euro Brokers Inc. Confirmed dead, World Trade Center, at/in building. *British*.
Larry John Senko, 34, Yardley, Pa., director of recruiting, Alliance Consulting. Confirmed dead, World Trade Center, at/in building.
Arturo Angelo Sereno, 29, New York, N.Y. Confirmed dead, World Trade Center, at/in building.
Frankie Serrano, 23, Elizabeth, N.J. Confirmed dead, World Trade Center, at/in building.
Alena Sesinova, 57, New York, N.Y., information technology, Marsh Inc. Confirmed dead, World Trade Center, at/in building.
Adele Sessa, 36, New York, N.Y., sales associate, Cantor Fitzgerald. Confirmed dead, World Trade Center, at/in building.
Sita Nermalla Sewnarine, 37, New York, N.Y., disaster recovery agent, Fiduciary Trust International. Confirmed dead, World Trade Center, at/in building.
Karen Lynn Seymour-Dietrich, 40, Millington, N.J., technology specialist, Garban Intercapital. Confirmed dead, World Trade Center, at/in building.
Davis (Deeg) Sezna, 22, New York, N.Y., Sandler O'Neill & Partners. Reported dead, World Trade Center, at/in building.
Thomas Joseph Sgroi, 45, New York, N.Y., Marsh & McLennan Cos. Inc. Confirmed dead, World Trade Center, at/in building.
Jayesh Shah, 38, Edgewater, N.J., Cantor Fitzgerald. Confirmed dead, World Trade Center, at/in building.
Khalid M. Shahid, 35, Union, N.J., systems administrator, eSpeed, Cantor Fitzgerald. Confirmed dead, World Trade Center, at/in building.
Mohammed Shajahan, 41, Spring Valley, N.Y., computer administrator, Marsh & McLennan Cos. Inc. Confirmed dead, World Trade Center, at/in building.
Gary Shamay, 23, New York, N.Y., Cantor Fitzgerald. Confirmed dead, World Trade Center, at/in building.
Earl Richard Shanahan, 50, New York, N.Y. Confirmed dead, World Trade Center, at/in building.
Shiv Shankar, New York, N.Y. Reported missing, World Trade Center, at/in building.
Neil G. Shastri, 25, New York, N.Y., consultant to Cantor Fitzgerald, Scient. Confirmed dead, World Trade Center, at/in building.
Kathryn Anne Shatzoff, 37, New York, N.Y., consultant's assistant, Marsh & McLennan Cos. Inc. Confirmed dead, World Trade Center, at/in building.
Barbara A. Shaw, 57, Morris Township, N.J. Confirmed dead, World Trade Center, at/in building.
Jeffrey J. Shaw, 42, Levittown, N.Y., electrician, Forest Electric Corp. Confirmed dead, World Trade Center, at/in building.

Robert J. Shay, 27, New York, N.Y., bond broker, Cantor Fitzgerald. Confirmed dead, World Trade Center, at/in building.
Daniel James Shea, 37, Pelham Manor, N.Y., managing director and partner, Cantor Fitzgerald. Confirmed dead, World Trade Center, at/in building.
Joseph Patrick Shea, 47, Pelham, N.Y., senior executive, Cantor Fitzgerald. Confirmed dead, World Trade Center, at/in building.
Linda Sheehan, 40, New York, N.Y., vice president, Sandler O'Neill & Partners. Confirmed dead, World Trade Center, at/in building.
Hagay Shefi, 34, Tenafly, N.J., founder, GoldTier Technologies. Confirmed dead, World Trade Center, at/in building.
Terrance H. Shefield, 34, Newark, N.J. Reported missing, World Trade Center, at/in building.
John Anthony Sherry, 34, Rockville Centre, N.Y., trader, Euro Brokers Inc. Confirmed dead, World Trade Center, at/in building.
Atsushi Shiratori, 36, New York, N.Y., dollar/yen options trader, Cantor Fitzgerald. Confirmed dead, World Trade Center, at/in building.
Thomas Shubert, 43, New York, N.Y., international trader, Cantor Fitzgerald. Confirmed dead, World Trade Center, at/in building.
Mark Shulman, 44, Old Bridge, N.J., fire prevention and risk consultant, Marsh & McLennan Cos. Inc. Confirmed dead, World Trade Center, at/in building.
See-Wong Shum, 44, Westfield, N.J., New York State Department of Transportation. Confirmed dead, World Trade Center, at/in building.
Allan Shwartzstein, 37, Chappaqua, N.Y., equities trader, Cantor Fitzgerald. Reported missing, World Trade Center, at/in building.
Carmen Sierra, 46, Orange, N.J. Reported missing, World Trade Center, at/in building.
Johanna Sigmund, 25, Syndmoor, Pa., Fred Alger Management Confirmed dead, World Trade Center, at/in building.
Dianne T. Signer, 32, New York, N.Y., Fred Alger Management. Confirmed dead, World Trade Center, at/in building.
David Silver, 35, New Rochelle, N.Y., vice president for eSpeed, Cantor Fitzgerald. Confirmed dead, World Trade Center, at/in building.
Craig A. Silverstein, 41, Wyckoff, N.J., equities trader, Sandler O'Neill & Partners. Confirmed dead, World Trade Center, at/in building.
Nasima H. Simjee, 38, New York, N.Y., Fiduciary Trust International. Confirmed dead, World Trade Center, at/in building.
Bruce Edward Simmons, 41, Ridgewood, N.J., partner, Sandler O'Neill & Partners. Confirmed dead, World Trade Center, at/in building.
Arthur Simon, 57, Thiells, N.Y., equities trader, Fred Alger Management. Confirmed dead, World Trade Center, at/in building.
Kenneth Alan Simon, 34, Secaucus, N.J., equities trader, Cantor Fitzgerald. Confirmed dead, World Trade Center, at/in building.
Michael John Simon, 40, Harrington Park, N.J., energy broker, Cantor Fitzgerald. Confirmed dead, World Trade Center, at/in building.
Paul Joseph Simon, 54, New York, N.Y., computer consultant, Marsh & McLennan Cos. Inc. Confirmed dead, World Trade Center, at/in building.
Marianne Simone, 62, New York, N.Y., communications specialist, Cantor Fitzgerald. Confirmed dead, World Trade Center, at/in building.
Barry Simowitz, 64, New York, N.Y., auditor, New York State Department of Taxation and Finance. Confirmed dead, World Trade Center, at/in building.
Jeff Simpson, 38, Lake Ridge, Va., Oracle. Confirmed dead, World Trade Center, at/in building.
George V. Sims, 46, Newark, N.J. Reported missing, World Trade Center, at/in building.
Khamladai K. (Khami) Singh, 25, New York, N.Y., assistant banquet manager, Windows on the World. Confirmed dead, World Trade Center, at/in building.
Roshan R. (Sean) Singh, 21, New York, N.Y., equipment technician, Windows on the World. Confirmed dead, World Trade Center, at/in building.
Thomas Sinton, 44, Croton-on-Hudson, N.Y., senior vice president, Cantor Fitzgerald. Confirmed dead, World Trade Center, at/in building.
Peter A. Siracuse, 29, New York, N.Y., bond broker, Cantor Fitzgerald. Confirmed dead, World Trade Center, at/in building.
Muriel F. Siskopoulos, 60, New York, N.Y., secretary, Keefe, Bruyette & Woods. Confirmed dead, World Trade Center, at/in building.
Joseph M. Sisolak, 35, New York, N.Y., senior vice president, Marsh & McLennan Cos. Inc. Confirmed dead, World Trade Center, at/in building.
Francis J. Skidmore, 58, Mendham, N.J., Euro Brokers Inc. Confirmed dead, World Trade Center, at/in building.
Toyena Corliss Skinner, 27, Kingston, N.J., Wachovia Corp. Confirmed dead, World Trade Center, at/in building.
Paul A. Skrzypek, 37, New York, N.Y., broker at eSpeed division, Cantor Fitzgerald. Confirmed dead, World Trade Center, at/in building.
Christopher Paul Slattery, 31, New York, N.Y., trader, Cantor Fitzgerald. Confirmed dead, World Trade Center, at/in building.
Vincent R. Slavin, 41, Belle Harbor, N.Y., vice president, partner, equities, Cantor Fitzgerald. Confirmed dead, World Trade Center, at/in building.
Robert Sliwak, 42, Wantagh, N.Y., bond trader, Cantor Fitzgerald. Confirmed dead, World Trade Center, at/in building.
Paul K. Sloan, 26, New York, N.Y., research department, Keefe, Bruyette & Woods. Confirmed dead, World Trade Center, at/in building.
Wendy L. Small, 26, New York, N.Y., secretary, Cantor Fitzgerald. Confirmed dead, World Trade Center, at/in building.
Catherine T. Smith, 44, West Haverstraw, N.Y., division vice president, Marsh & McLennan Cos. Inc. Confirmed dead, World Trade Center, at/in building.

Daniel Laurence Smith, 47, Northport, N.Y., Euro Brokers Inc. Confirmed dead, World Trade Center, at/in building.
George Eric Smith, 38, West Chester, Pa., senior business analyst, SunGard Asset Management Systems/ Global Plus. Confirmed dead, World Trade Center, at/in building.
James G. Smith, 43, Garden City, N.Y., trader, Cantor Fitzgerald. Confirmed dead, World Trade Center, at/in building.
Jeffrey Randall Smith, 36, New York, N.Y., equity research analyst, Sandler O'Neill & Partners. Confirmed dead, World Trade Center, at/in building.
Joyce Smith, 55, New York, N.Y., food service handler, Forte Food Service. Confirmed dead, World Trade Center, at/in building. *Jamaican.*
Karl Trumbull Smith, 44, Little Silver, N.J., municipal bond broker, Cantor Fitzgerald. Confirmed dead, World Trade Center, at/in building.
Rosemary A. Smith, 61, New York, N.Y., receptionist, Sidley Austin Brown & Wood. Confirmed dead, World Trade Center, at/in building.
Sandra Fajardo Smith, 37, New York, N.Y., accountant, Marsh & McLennan Cos. Inc. Confirmed dead, World Trade Center, at/in building.
Bonnie S. Smithwick, 54, Quogue, N.Y., Fred Alger Management. Confirmed dead, World Trade Center, at/in building.
Rochelle Monique Snell, 24, Mount Vernon, N.Y., administrative assistant, Regus. Confirmed dead, World Trade Center, at/in building. *Jamaican.*
Leonard J. Snyder, 35, Cranford, N.J., vice president of special risks, Aon Corp. Confirmed dead, World Trade Center, at/in building.
Astrid Elizabeth Sohan, 32, Freehold, N.J., manager, Marsh Inc. Confirmed dead, World Trade Center, at/in building.
Sushil Solanki, 35, New York, N.Y., computer operator, Cantor Fitzgerald. Reported missing, World Trade Center, at/in building.
Ruben Solares, Cantor Fitzgerald. Reported missing, World Trade Center, at/in building.
Naomi Leah Solomon, 52, New York, N.Y., vice president of business development, Callixa. Confirmed dead, World Trade Center, at/in building.
Daniel W. Song, 34, New York, N.Y., bond broker, Cantor Fitzgerald. Confirmed dead, World Trade Center, at/in building.
Michael C. Sorresse, 34, Morris Plains, N.J., vice president, Marsh Inc. Confirmed dead, World Trade Center, at/in building.
Fabian Soto, 31, Harrison, N.J., janitorial, window cleaner, ABM Industries. Confirmed dead, World Trade Center, at/in building.
Timothy P. Soulas, 35, Basking Ridge, N.J., managing director of foreign currencies, Cantor Fitzgerald. Confirmed dead, World Trade Center, at/in building.
Gregory T. Spagnoletti, 32, New York, N.Y., bond salesman, Keefe, Bruyette & Woods. Confirmed dead, World Trade Center, at/in building.
Donald F. Spampinato, 39, Manhasset, N.Y., corporate bond trader, Cantor Fitzgerald. Confirmed dead, World Trade Center, at/in building.
Thomas Sparacio, 35, New York, N.Y., currency trader, Euro Brokers Inc. Confirmed dead, World Trade Center, at/in building.
John Anthony Spataro, 32, Mineola, N.Y., Marsh & McLennan Cos. Inc. Confirmed dead, World Trade Center, at/in building.
Maynard S. Spence, 42, Douglasville, Ga., construction safety consultant, Marsh & McLennan Cos. Inc. Confirmed dead, World Trade Center, at/in building.
George E. Spencer, 50, West Norwalk, Conn., Euro Brokers Inc. Confirmed dead, World Trade Center, at/in building.
Robert Andrew Spencer, 35, Red Bank, N.J., foreign exchange broker, Cantor Fitzgerald. Confirmed dead, World Trade Center, at/in building.
Mary Rubina Sperando, 39, New York, N.Y., director of marketing and communications, Encompys. Confirmed dead, World Trade Center, at/in building.
Frank J. Spinelli, 44, Short Hills, N.J., foreign exchange broker, Cantor Fitzgerald. Confirmed dead, World Trade Center, at/in building.
William E. Spitz, 49, Oceanside, N.Y., Cantor Fitzgerald. Confirmed dead, World Trade Center, at/in building.
Klaus Johannes Sprockamp, 42, Muhltal, Germany, chief financial officer, LION Bioscience AG. Confirmed dead, World Trade Center, at/in building. *German.*
Saranya Srinuan, 23, New York, N.Y., bond trader, Cantor Fitzgerald. Confirmed dead, World Trade Center, at/in building.
Fitzroy St. Rose, 40, New York, N.Y., computer technician, General Telecom. Confirmed dead, World Trade Center, at/in building.
Michael F. Stabile, 50, New York, N.Y., currency broker, Euro Brokers Inc. Confirmed dead, World Trade Center, at/in building.
Richard James Stadelberger, 55, Middletown, N.J., Fiduciary Trust International. Reported missing, World Trade Center, at/in building.
Eric A. Stahlman, 43, Holmdel Township, N.J., money trader, Cantor Fitzgerald. Confirmed dead, World Trade Center, at/in building.
Alexandru Liviu Stan, 34, New York, N.Y., consultant at Cantor Fitzgerald. Confirmed dead, World Trade Center, at/in building.
Corina Stan, 31, Cantor Fitzgerald. Confirmed dead, World Trade Center, at/in building.
Mary D. Stanley, 53, New York, N.Y., vice president and technical analyst, Marsh & McLennan Cos. Inc. Confirmed dead, World Trade Center, at/in building.
Joyce Stanton. Reported missing, World Trade Center, at/in building.
Patricia Stanton. Reported missing, World Trade Center, at/in building.
Anthony M. Starita, 35, Westfield, N.J., limited partner, Cantor Fitzgerald. Confirmed dead, World Trade Center, at/in building.

Derek James Statkevicus, 30, Norwalk, Conn., research department, Keefe, Bruyette & Woods. Confirmed dead, World Trade Center, at/in building.
Craig William Staub, 30, Basking Ridge, N.J., Keefe, Bruyette & Woods. Confirmed dead, World Trade Center, at/in building.
William V. Steckman, 56, West Hempstead, N.Y., engineer, WNBC-TV. Confirmed dead, World Trade Center, at/in building.
Eric T. Steen, 32, New York, N.Y., bond trader, Euro Brokers Inc. Confirmed dead, World Trade Center, at/in building.
William R. Steiner, 56, New Hope, Pa., consultant at Marsh & McLennan Cos. Inc. Confirmed dead, World Trade Center, at/in building.
Alexander Robbins Steinman, 32, Hoboken, N.J., trader, Cantor Fitzgerald. Confirmed dead, World Trade Center, at/in building.
Andrew Stergiopoulos, 23, New York, N.Y., Cantor Fitzgerald. Confirmed dead, World Trade Center, at/in building.
Andrew Stern, 45, Bellmore, N.Y., broker, Cantor Fitzgerald. Confirmed dead, World Trade Center, at/in building.
Martha Stevens, Aon Corp. Reported dead, World Trade Center, at/in building.
Michael J. Stewart, 42, New York, N.Y., Carr Futures. Confirmed dead, World Trade Center, at/in building.
Richard H. Stewart, 35, New York, N.Y., corporate bond trader, Cantor Fitzgerald. Confirmed dead, World Trade Center, at/in building.
Sanford M. Stoller, 54, New York, N.Y., Accenture. Confirmed dead, World Trade Center, at/in building.
Lonny J. Stone, 43, Bellmore, N.Y., operations manager, Carr Futures. Confirmed dead, World Trade Center, at/in building.
Jimmy Nevill Storey, 58, Katy, Texas, senior vice president in Houston office, Marsh & McLennan Cos. Inc. Confirmed dead, World Trade Center, at/in building.
Timothy Stout, 42, Dobbs Ferry, N.Y., quality assurance specialist, Cantor Fitzgerald. Confirmed dead, World Trade Center, at/in building.
Thomas S. Strada, 41, Chatham, N.J., bond broker, Cantor Fitzgerald. Confirmed dead, World Trade Center, at/in building.
James J. Straine, 36, Oceanport, N.J., fixed-income investment salesman, Cantor Fitzgerald. Confirmed dead, World Trade Center, at/in building.
Edward W. Straub, 48, Morris Township, N.J., president of compensation consulting, Aon Corp. Confirmed dead, World Trade Center, at/in building.
George Strauch, 53, Avon-by-the-Sea, N.J., Aon Corp. Confirmed dead, World Trade Center, at/in building.
Steven R. Strauss, 51, Fresh Meadows, N.Y., electrical worker, Petrocelli Electric. Confirmed dead, World Trade Center, at/in building.
Steven F. Strobert, 33, Ridgewood, N.J., trader, Cantor Fitzgerald. Confirmed dead, World Trade Center, at/in building.
David S. Suarez, 24, Princeton, N.J., systems consultant, Deloitte Consulting. Confirmed dead, World Trade Center, at/in building.
Yoichi Sugiyama, 34, Fort Lee, N.J., manager, Fuji Bank. Confirmed dead, World Trade Center, at/in building. *Japanese.*
William Christopher Sugra, 30, New York, N.Y., network administrator for eSpeed, Cantor Fitzgerald. Confirmed dead, World Trade Center, at/in building.
David Marc Sullins, 30, New York, N.Y., paramedic, Cabrini Hospital. Confirmed dead, World Trade Center, at/in building. *Filipino.*
Patrick Sullivan, 32, New York, N.Y., Cantor Fitzgerald. Confirmed dead, World Trade Center, at/in building.
Thomas Sullivan, 38, Kearney, N.J., partner, Harvey Young Yurman Inc. Reported missing, World Trade Center, at/in building.
Hilario Soriano (Larry) Sumaya, 42, New York, N.Y., technology manager, Marsh & McLennan Cos. Inc. Confirmed dead, World Trade Center, at/in building. *Filipino.*
James Joseph Suozzo, 47, Hauppauge, N.Y., Cantor Fitzgerald. Confirmed dead, World Trade Center, at/in building.
Colleen Supinski, 27, New York, N.Y., assets trader, Sandler O'Neill & Partners. Confirmed dead, World Trade Center, at/in building.
Robert Sutcliffe, 39, Huntington, N.Y., broker, Harvey Young Yurman Inc. Confirmed dead, World Trade Center, at/in building.
Selina Sutter, 58, Chatham, N.J., First Liberty Investment Group. Confirmed dead, World Trade Center, at/in building.
Claudia Suzette Sutton, 34, New York, N.Y., Cantor Fitzgerald. Confirmed dead, World Trade Center, at/in building.
John F. Swaine, 36, Larchmont, N.Y., trader, Cantor Fitzgerald. Confirmed dead, World Trade Center, at/in building.
Kristine M. Swearson, 34, New York, N.Y., web designer for eSpeed, Cantor Fitzgerald. Confirmed dead, World Trade Center, at/in building.
Kenneth J. Swensen, 40, Chatham, N.J., vice president, Cantor Fitzgerald. Confirmed dead, World Trade Center, at/in building.
Thomas F. Swift, 30, Jersey City, N.J., assistant vice president, Morgan Stanley. Confirmed dead, World Trade Center, at/in building.
Derek O. Sword, 29, New York, N.Y., equities sales analyst, Keefe, Bruyette & Woods. Confirmed dead, World Trade Center, at/in building. *British.*
Kevin T. Szocik, 27, Garden City, N.Y., equity research analyst, Keefe, Bruyette & Woods. Confirmed dead, World Trade Center, at/in building.
Gina Sztejnberg, 52, Ridgewood, N.J., database architect consultant for Marsh & McLennan Cos. Inc. Confirmed dead, World Trade Center, at/in building.
Norbert P. Szurkowski, 31, New York, N.Y., wallpaper hanger, Signature Painting and Decorating. Confirmed dead, World Trade Center, at/in building.

– T –

Harry Taback, 56, New York, N.Y., managing regional director/executive vice president in risk control strategy and consulting, Marsh & McLennan Cos. Inc. Confirmed dead, World Trade Center, at/in building.
Joann Tabeek, 41, New York, N.Y., vice president, Cantor Fitzgerald. Confirmed dead, World Trade Center, at/in building.
Norma C. Taddei, 64, New York, N.Y., Marsh & McLennan Cos. Inc. Confirmed dead, World Trade Center, at/in building.
Michael Taddonio, 39, Huntington, N.Y., bond broker, Euro Brokers Inc. Confirmed dead, World Trade Center, at/in building.
Keiichiro Takahashi, 53, Port Washington, N.Y., first vice president, Euro Brokers Inc. Reported dead, World Trade Center, at/in building. *Japanese.*
Keiji Takahashi, 42, Tenafly, N.J., manager, Mizuho Capital Markets Corp. Confirmed dead, World Trade Center, at/in building. *Japanese.*
Phyllis Gail Talbot, 53, New York, N.Y., vice president, Marsh USA. Confirmed dead, World Trade Center, at/in building.
Robert R. Talhami, 40, Shrewsbury, N.J., broker, Cantor Fitzgerald. Confirmed dead, World Trade Center, at/in building.
Maurita Tam, 22, New York, N.Y., executive assistant, Aon Corp. Confirmed dead, World Trade Center, at/in building.
Rachel Tamares, 30, New York, N.Y., Aon Corp. Confirmed dead, World Trade Center, at/in building.
Hector Tamayo, 51, New York, N.Y., project manager, Vanderbilt Group Inc. Confirmed dead, World Trade Center, at/in building. *Filipino.*
Michael Andrew Tamuccio, 37, Pelham Manor, N.Y., vice president of equity trading, Fred Alger Management. Confirmed dead, World Trade Center, at/in building.
Kenichiro Tanaka, 52, Rye Brook, N.Y., corporate banking general manager, Fuji Bank. Reported missing, World Trade Center, at/in building. *Japanese.*
Rhondelle Cherie Tankard, 31, Pembroke, Bermuda, Aon Corp. Reported missing, World Trade Center, at/in building. *Bermudan.*
Michael Anthony Tanner, 44, Secaucus, N.J., trader, Cantor Fitzgerald. Confirmed dead, World Trade Center, at/in building.
Dennis G. Taormina, 36, Montville, N.J., vice president, Marsh & McLennan Cos. Inc. Confirmed dead, World Trade Center, at/in building.
Kenneth Joseph Tarantino, 39, Bayonne, N.J., currency trader, Cantor Fitzgerald. Confirmed dead, World Trade Center, at/in building.
Ronald Tartaro, 39, Bridgewater, N.J., Fred Alger Management. Confirmed dead, World Trade Center, at/in building.
Darryl Taylor, 52, New York, N.Y., computer systems analyst, General Telecom. Confirmed dead, World Trade Center, at/in building.
Donnie Brooks Taylor, 40, New York, N.Y., office services assistant, Aon Corp. Confirmed dead, World Trade Center, at/in building.
Lorisa Ceylon Taylor, 31, New York, N.Y., insurance broker, Marsh & McLennan Cos. Inc. Confirmed dead, World Trade Center, at/in building.
Michael M. Taylor, 42, New York, N.Y., high-yield bond broker, Cantor Fitzgerald. Confirmed dead, World Trade Center, at/in building.
Yesh Tembe, 59, Piscataway, N.J., New York State Department of Taxation and Finance. Reported missing, World Trade Center, at/in building.
Anthony Tempesta, 38, Elizabeth, N.J., broker, Cantor Fitzgerald. Confirmed dead, World Trade Center, at/in building.
Dorothy Temple, 52, New York, N.Y., New York State Department of Taxation and Finance. Confirmed dead, World Trade Center, at/in building.
David Tengelin, 25, New York, N.Y., accountant, Marsh & McLennan Cos. Inc. Confirmed dead, World Trade Center, at/in building. *Swedish.*
Brian J. Terrenzi, 29, Hicksville, N.Y., global network manager, Cantor Fitzgerald. Confirmed dead, World Trade Center, at/in building.
Lisa Marie Terry, 42, Rochester, Mich., vice president, Marsh & McLennan Cos. Inc. Confirmed dead, World Trade Center, at/in building.
Goumatie Thackurdeen, 35, New York, N.Y., vice president, Fiduciary Trust International. Confirmed dead, World Trade Center, at/in building.
Harshad Sham Thatte, 30, Norcross, Ga., consultant at Marsh & McLennan Cos. Inc. Confirmed dead, World Trade Center, at/in building.
Thomas F. Theurkauf, 44, Stamford, Conn., executive vice president, Keefe, Bruyette & Woods. Confirmed dead, World Trade Center, at/in building.
Lesley Thomas-O'Keefe, 40, Hoboken, N.J., Cantor Fitzgerald. Confirmed dead, World Trade Center, at/in building.
Brian T. Thompson, 49, Dix Hills, N.Y. Confirmed dead, World Trade Center, at/in building.
Clive Thompson, 43, Summit, N.J., broker, Euro Brokers Inc. Confirmed dead, World Trade Center, at/in building.
Glenn Thompson, 44, New York, N.Y., bond trader, Cantor Fitzgerald. Confirmed dead, World Trade Center, at/in building.
Nigel Bruce Thompson, 33, New York, N.Y., senior broker, Cantor Fitzgerald. Confirmed dead, World Trade Center, at/in building.
Perry Anthony Thompson, 36, Mount Laurel, N.J., accountant, Aon Corp. Confirmed dead, World Trade Center, at/in building.
Vanavah Alexi Thompson, 26, New York, N.Y., janitorial, cleaner, ABM Industries. Confirmed dead, World Trade Center, at/in building.

Capt. William Harry Thompson, 51, New York, N.Y., associate court officer, New York state courts. Confirmed dead, World Trade Center, at/in building.
Eric Raymond Thorpe, 35, New York, N.Y., Keefe, Bruyette & Woods. Confirmed dead, World Trade Center, at/in building.
Nichola A. Thorpe, 22, New York, N.Y., accounting department, Keefe, Bruyette & Woods. Confirmed dead, World Trade Center, at/in building. *Jamaican.*
Sal Tieri, 40, Shrewsbury, N.J., managing director, Marsh & McLennan Cos. Inc. Reported dead, World Trade Center, at/in building.
William R. Tieste, 54, Basking Ridge, N.J., executive vice president of equity sales, Cantor Fitzgerald. Confirmed dead, World Trade Center, at/in building.
Stephen Edward Tighe, 41, Rockville Centre, N.Y., Cantor Fitzgerald. Confirmed dead, World Trade Center, at/in building.
Scott C. Timmes, 28, Ridgewood, N.Y., commodities customer service clerk, Carr Futures. Confirmed dead, World Trade Center, at/in building.
Michael E. Tinley, 56, Dallas, Texas, vice president, Marsh Inc. Confirmed dead, World Trade Center, at/in building.
Jennifer M. Tino, 29, Livingston, N.J., Marsh & McLennan Cos. Inc. Confirmed dead, World Trade Center, at/in building.
Robert Frank Tipaldi, 25, New York, N.Y., assistant trader, Cantor Fitzgerald. Confirmed dead, World Trade Center, at/in building.
David Tirado, 26, New York, N.Y., technical services representative, Rent-a-PC. Confirmed dead, World Trade Center, at/in building.
Michelle Titolo, 34, Copaigue, N.Y., equity controller, Cantor Fitzgerald. Confirmed dead, World Trade Center, at/in building.
John J. Tobin, 47, Kenilworth, N.J., senior vice president, Marsh & McLennan Cos. Inc. Confirmed dead, World Trade Center, at/in building.
Richard J. Todisco, 61, Wyckoff, N.J., vice president, Sandler O'Neill & Partners. Confirmed dead, World Trade Center, at/in building.
Vladimir Tomasevic, 36, Etobicoke, Ontario, Canada, vice president of software development, Optus. Confirmed dead, World Trade Center, at/in building. *Canadian.*
Stephen K. Tompsett, 39, Garden City, N.Y., computer scientist and vice president, Instinet (Reuters). Confirmed dead, World Trade Center, at/in building.
Thomas Tong, 31, New York, N.Y. Confirmed dead, World Trade Center, at/in building.
Doris Torres, 32. Confirmed dead, World Trade Center, at/in building.
Luis Eduardo Torres, 31, Cantor Fitzgerald. Confirmed dead, World Trade Center, at/in building. *Colombian.*
Amy E. Toyen, 24, Newton, Mass., marketing for sales and trading group, Thomson Financial Services. Confirmed dead, World Trade Center, at/in building.
Christopher M. Traina, 25, Bricktown, N.J., Carr Futures. Confirmed dead, World Trade Center, at/in building.
Daniel Patrick Trant, 40, Northport, N.Y., trader, Cantor Fitzgerald. Confirmed dead, World Trade Center, at/in building.
Abdoul Karim Traore, 41, New York, N.Y., Windows on the World. Confirmed dead, World Trade Center, at/in building.
Glenn J. Travers, 53, Tenafly, N.J., electrician, Forest Electric Corp. Confirmed dead, World Trade Center, at/in building.
Walter (Wally) P. Travers, 44, Upper Saddle River, N.J., bond broker, Cantor Fitzgerald. Confirmed dead, World Trade Center, at/in building.
Felicia Traylor-Bass, 38, New York, N.Y., office manager, Alliance Consulting. Confirmed dead, World Trade Center, at/in building.
Karamo Trerra, 40, New York, N.Y., computer technician, ASAP NetSource. Confirmed dead, World Trade Center, at/in building.
Michael Trinidad, 33, New York, N.Y., telecommunications accounting, Cantor Fitzgerald. Confirmed dead, World Trade Center, at/in building.
Francis Joseph Trombino, 68, Clifton, N.J., security guard, Brinks. Confirmed dead, World Trade Center, at/in building.
Gregory J. Trost, 26, New York, N.Y., research analyst, Keefe, Bruyette & Woods. Confirmed dead, World Trade Center, at/in building.
William Tselepis, 33, New Providence, N.J., broker, Cantor Fitzgerald. Reported missing, World Trade Center, at/in building.
Zhanetta Tsoy, 32, Jersey City, N.J., accountant, Marsh & McLennan Cos. Inc. Confirmed dead, World Trade Center, at/in building.
Michael Patrick Tucker, 40, Rumson, N.J., vice president, Cantor Fitzgerald. Reported dead, World Trade Center, at/in building.
Lance Richard Tumulty, 32, Bridgewater, N.J., distressed trading manager, Euro Brokers Inc. Confirmed dead, World Trade Center, at/in building.
Ching Ping Tung, 44, New York, N.Y. Confirmed dead, World Trade Center, at/in building.
Simon James Turner, 39, London, England, publishing director, Risk Waters Group. Confirmed dead, World Trade Center, at/in building. *British.*
Donald Joseph Tuzio, 51, Goshen, N.Y., former systems programmer, Bear Stearns. Confirmed dead, World Trade Center, at/in building.
Robert T. Twomey, 48, New York, N.Y., trader, Harvey Young Yurman Inc. Confirmed dead, World Trade Center, at/in building.
Jennifer Tzemis, 26, New York, N.Y., financial analyst, Fred Alger Management. Confirmed dead, World Trade Center, at/in building.

– U –

John G. Ueltzhoeffer, 36, Roselle Park, N.J., Marsh & McLennan Cos. Inc. Confirmed dead, World Trade Center, at/in building.
Tyler Ugolyn, 23, Ridgefield, Conn., Fred Alger Management. Reported dead, World Trade Center, at/in building.
Michael A. Uliano, 42, Aberdeen, N.J., options broker, Cantor Fitzgerald. Confirmed dead, World Trade Center, at/in building.
Jonathan J. Uman, 33, Westport, Conn., managing director for eSpeed, Cantor Fitzgerald. Confirmed dead, World Trade Center, at/in building.
Anil Shivhari Umarkar, 34, Hackensack, N.J., computer programmer/consultant for eSpeed, Cantor Fitzgerald. Confirmed dead, World Trade Center, at/in building.
Allen V. Upton, 44, New York, N.Y., first vice president, corporate bonds, Cantor Fitzgerald. Confirmed dead, World Trade Center, at/in building.
Diane Maria Urban, 50, Malverne, N.Y., tax auditor, New York State Department of Taxation and Finance. Confirmed dead, World Trade Center, at/in building.

– V –

John Damien Vaccacio, 30, New York, N.Y., bond broker, Cantor Fitzgerald. Confirmed dead, World Trade Center, at/in building.
Bradley H. Vadas, 37, Westport, Conn., senior vice president, Keefe, Bruyette & Woods. Confirmed dead, World Trade Center, at/in building.
William Valcarcel, 54, New York, N.Y., supervisor of tax conferences, bureau of conciliation, New York State Department of Taxation and Finance. Reported dead, World Trade Center, at/in building.
Mayra Valdes-Rodriguez, 39, New York, N.Y., Aon Corp. Confirmed dead, World Trade Center, at/in building.
Felix Antonio Vale, 29, New York, N.Y., manager, Cantor Fitzgerald. Confirmed dead, World Trade Center, at/in building.
Ivan Vale, 27, New York, N.Y., Cantor Fitzgerald. Confirmed dead, World Trade Center, at/in building.
Benito Valentin, 33, New York, N.Y., travel consultant at Marsh & McLennan Cos. Inc., American Express. Confirmed dead, World Trade Center, at/in building.
Carlton Francis Valvo, 38, New York, N.Y., vice president of interest rate swaps, Cantor Fitzgerald. Confirmed dead, World Trade Center, at/in building.
Erica Van Acker, 62, New York, N.Y., Aon Corp. Confirmed dead, World Trade Center, at/in building. *British.*
Kenneth W. Van Auken, 47, East Brunswick, N.J., bond trader, Cantor Fitzgerald. Confirmed dead, World Trade Center, at/in building.
Daniel M. Van Laere, 46, Glen Rock, N.J., risk analyst and underwriter, Aon Corp. Confirmed dead, World Trade Center, at/in building.
Edward Raymond Vanacore, 29, Jersey City, N.J., stock analyst, Fiduciary Trust International. Confirmed dead, World Trade Center, at/in building.
Jon C. Vandevander, 44, Ridgewood, N.J., vice president, Carr Futures. Confirmed dead, World Trade Center, at/in building.
Frederick T. Varacchi, 35, Greenwich, Conn., president of eSpeed, Cantor Fitzgerald. Confirmed dead, World Trade Center, at/in building.
Gopalakrishnan Varadhan, 32, New York, N.Y., Cantor Fitzgerald. Confirmed dead, World Trade Center, at/in building.
David Vargas, 46, New York, N.Y., manager, Pitney Bowes. Confirmed dead, World Trade Center, at/in building.
Scott C. Vasel, 32, Park Ridge, N.J., disaster recovery specialist, Marsh & McLennan Cos. Inc. Confirmed dead, World Trade Center, at/in building.
Azael Ismael Vasquez, 21, New York, N.Y., food service handler, Forte Food Service. Confirmed dead, World Trade Center, at/in building.
Santos Vasquez, 55, New York, N.Y., Cantor Fitzgerald. Confirmed dead, World Trade Center, at/in building.
Arcangel Vazquez, 47, New York, N.Y., maintenance. Confirmed dead, World Trade Center, at/in building.
Sankara S. Velamuri, 63, Avenel, N.J., auditor, New York State Department of Taxation and Finance. Confirmed dead, World Trade Center, at/in building.
Jorge Velazquez, 47, Passaic, N.J., security guard, Morgan Stanley. Confirmed dead, World Trade Center, at/in building.
Anthony M. Ventura, 41, Middletown, N.J., Fiduciary Trust International. Confirmed dead, World Trade Center, at/in building.
David Vera, 41, New York, N.Y., senior telecommunications technician, Euro Brokers Inc. Confirmed dead, World Trade Center, at/in building.
Loretta A, Vero, 51, Nanuet, N.Y. Confirmed dead, World Trade Center, at/in building.
Christopher Vialonga, 30, Demerest, N.J., foreign currency trader, Carr Futures. Confirmed dead, World Trade Center, at/in building.
Matthew Gilbert Vianna, 23, Manhasset, N.Y., Cantor Fitzgerald. Confirmed dead, World Trade Center, at/in building.
Robert A. Vicario, 40, Weehawken, N.J. Confirmed dead, World Trade Center, at/in building.
Celeste Torres Victoria, 41, New York, N.Y., conference telesales executive, Risk Waters Group. Confirmed dead, World Trade Center, at/in building.
Joanna Vidal, 26, Yonkers, N.Y., event coordinator, Risk Waters Group. Confirmed dead, World Trade Center, at/in building.
Frank J. Vignola, 44, Merrick, N.Y., senior vice president and partner, Cantor Fitzgerald. Confirmed dead, World Trade Center, at/in building.
Joseph B. Vilardo, 44, Stanhope, N.J., senior vice president, Cantor Fitzgerald. Confirmed dead, World Trade Center, at/in building.

Chantal Vincelli, 38, New York, N.Y., Data Synapse. Confirmed dead, World Trade Center, at/in building.
Melissa Vincent, 28, Hoboken, N.J., resource manager, Alliance Consulting. Confirmed dead, World Trade Center, at/in building
Francine A. Virgilio, 48, New York, N.Y., vice president, Aon Corp. Confirmed dead, World Trade Center, at/in building.
Joseph G. Visciano, 22, New York, N.Y., trader, Keefe, Bruyette & Woods. Confirmed dead, World Trade Center, at/in building.
Ramsaroop Vishnu, 45, New York, N.Y. Reported missing, World Trade Center, at/in building.
Joshua S. Vitale, 28, Great Neck, N.Y., trading sales clerk, Cantor Fitzgerald. Confirmed dead, World Trade Center, at/in building.
Maria Percoco Vola, 37, New York, N.Y., administrative assistant, Aon Corp. Confirmed dead, World Trade Center, at/in building.
Lynette D. Vosges, 48, New York, N.Y., senior vice president of reinsurance, Aon Corp. Confirmed dead, World Trade Center, at/in building.
Garo H. Voskerijian, 43, Valley Stream, N.Y., global technology services, Marsh & McLennan Cos. Inc. Confirmed dead, World Trade Center, at/in building.
Alfred Vukuosa, 32, New York, N.Y., information technology specialist, Cantor Fitzgerald. Confirmed dead, World Trade Center, at/in building.

– W –

Gregory Wachtler, 25, Ramsey, N.J., Fred Alger Management. Confirmed dead, World Trade Center, at/in building.
Gabriela Waisman, 33, office manager, Sybase. Confirmed dead, World Trade Center, at/in building.
Wendy Alice Rosario Wakeford, 40, Freehold, N.J., broker's assistant, Cantor Fitzgerald. Confirmed dead, World Trade Center, at/in building.
Courtney Wainsworth Walcott, 37, New York, N.Y., manager, IQ Financial Systems. Confirmed dead, World Trade Center, at/in building. *Jamaican.*
Victor Wald, 49, New York, N.Y., stock broker, Avalon Partners. Confirmed dead, World Trade Center, at/in building.
Benjamin Walker, 41, Suffern, N.Y., Marsh & McLennan Cos. Inc. Confirmed dead, World Trade Center, at/in building.
Glen J. Wall, 38, Rumson, N.J., senior vice president, Cantor Fitzgerald. Confirmed dead, World Trade Center, at/in building.
Mitchel Scott Wallace, 34, Mineola, N.Y., court officer, New York State Supreme Court. Confirmed dead, World Trade Center, at/in building.
Peter G. Wallace, 66, Lincoln Park, N.J., vice president, Marsh Inc. Confirmed dead, World Trade Center, at/in building.
Roy Wallace, 42, Wyckoff, N.J., broker, Cantor Fitzgerald. Confirmed dead, World Trade Center, at/in building.
Jean Marie Wallendorf, 23, New York, N.Y., Keefe, Bruyette & Woods. Confirmed dead, World Trade Center, at/in building.
Matthew Blake Wallens, 31, New York, N.Y., vice president, Cantor Fitzgerald. Confirmed dead, World Trade Center, at/in building.
John Wallice, 43, Huntington, N.Y., international equities trader, Cantor Fitzgerald. Confirmed dead, World Trade Center, at/in building.
Barbara P. Walsh, 59, New York, N.Y., administrative assistant, Marsh & McLennan Cos. Inc. Confirmed dead, World Trade Center, at/in building.
James Walsh, 37, Scotch Plains, N.J., computer programmer, Cantor Fitzgerald. Confirmed dead, World Trade Center, at/in building.
Ching Huei Wang, 59, First Commercial Bank. Confirmed dead, World Trade Center, at/in building. *Taiwanese.*
Weibin Wang, 41, Orangeburg, N.Y., analyst, Cantor Fitzgerald. Confirmed dead, World Trade Center, at/in building.
Stephen Gordon Ward, 33, Gorham, Maine, accountant, Cantor Fitzgerald. Confirmed dead, World Trade Center, at/in building.
James A. Waring, 49, New York, N.Y., Cantor Fitzgerald. Confirmed dead, World Trade Center, at/in building.
Brian G. Warner, 32, Morganville, N.J., senior systems engineer in eSpeed division, Cantor Fitzgerald. Confirmed dead, World Trade Center, at/in building.
Derrick Washington, 33, Calverton, N.Y., technician, Verizon. Confirmed dead, World Trade Center, at/in building.
Charles Waters, 44, New York, N.Y., vice president and partner, Cantor Fitzgerald. Confirmed dead, World Trade Center, at/in building.
James T. (Muddy) Waters, 39, New York, N.Y., senior vice president and head trader, Keefe, Bruyette & Woods. Confirmed dead, World Trade Center, at/in building.
Michael H. Waye, 38, Morganville, N.J., Marsh & McLennan Cos. Inc. Confirmed dead, World Trade Center, at/in building.
Todd C. Weaver, 30, New York, N.Y., vice president, Fiduciary Trust International. Confirmed dead, World Trade Center, at/in building.
Dinah Webster, 50, advertising manager, Risk Waters Group. Reported missing, World Trade Center, at/in building.
Joanne Flora Weil, 39, New York, N.Y., counsel, Harris Beach LLP. Confirmed dead, World Trade Center, at/in building.
Steven Weinberg, 41, New City, N.Y., accounting manager, Baseline (Thomson Financial). Confirmed dead, World Trade Center, at/in building.
Scott Jeffrey Weingard, 29, New York, N.Y., Cantor Fitzgerald. Confirmed dead, World Trade Center, at/in building.
Steven Weinstein, 50, New York, N.Y. Confirmed dead, World Trade Center, at/in building.

David T. Weiss, 50, New York, N.Y., vice president and deputy general counsel, Cantor Fitzgerald. Confirmed dead, World Trade Center, at/in building.

Vincent Michael Wells, 22, Redbridge, England, options broker, Cantor Fitzgerald. Confirmed dead, World Trade Center, at/in building. *British.*

Christian Hans Rudolf Wemmers, 43, San Francisco, Calif., Callixa. Confirmed dead, World Trade Center, at/in building.

Ssu-Hui (Vanessa) Wen, 23, New York, N.Y., programmer, Cantor Fitzgerald. Confirmed dead, World Trade Center, at/in building.

Oleh D. Wengerchuk, 56, Centerport, N.Y., Washington Group International. Confirmed dead, World Trade Center, at/in building.

Peter M. West, 54, Pottersville, N.J., bond trader, Cantor Fitzgerald. Confirmed dead, World Trade Center, at/in building.

Whitfield West, 41, New York, N.Y., Cantor Fitzgerald. Confirmed dead, World Trade Center, at/in building.

Meredith Lynn Whalen, 23, Hoboken, N.J., research analyst, Fred Alger Management. Confirmed dead, World Trade Center, at/in building.

Adam S. White, 26, New York, N.Y., broker, Cantor Fitzgerald. Confirmed dead, World Trade Center, at/in building.

James Patrick White, 34, Hoboken, N.J., Cantor Fitzgerald. Confirmed dead, World Trade Center, at/in building.

John S. White, 48, New York, N.Y., janitorial cleaner, ABM Industries. Confirmed dead, World Trade Center, at/in building.

Kenneth W. White, 50, New York, N.Y., telephone technician, IPC Kleinknect Electric Co. Confirmed dead, World Trade Center, at/in building.

Leonard Anthony White, 57, New York, N.Y., technician, global communications division, Verizon. Confirmed dead, World Trade Center, at/in building.

Malissa White, 37, New York, N.Y., human resources, Marsh & McLennan Cos. Inc. Confirmed dead, World Trade Center, at/in building.

Wayne White, 38, New York, N.Y., mailroom manager, Marsh & McLennan Cos. Inc. Confirmed dead, World Trade Center, at/in building.

Leanne Marie Whiteside, 31, New York, N.Y., Aon Corp. Confirmed dead, World Trade Center, at/in building.

Mary Lenz Wieman, 43, Rockville Centre, N.Y., marketing executive, Aon Corp. Confirmed dead, World Trade Center, at/in building.

Jeffrey David Wiener, 33, New York, N.Y., manager of risk technologies group, Marsh & McLennan Cos. Inc. Confirmed dead, World Trade Center, at/in building.

William J. Wik, 44, Crestwood, N.Y., assistant director risk management service, Aon Corp. Confirmed dead, World Trade Center, at/in building.

Allison M. Wildman, 30, New York, N.Y., broker, Carr Futures. Confirmed dead, World Trade Center, at/in building.

John C. Willett, 29, Jersey City, N.J., analyst for C02e.com, Cantor Fitzgerald. Confirmed dead, World Trade Center, at/in building.

Brian Patrick Williams, 29, New York, N.Y., broker, Cantor Fitzgerald. Confirmed dead, World Trade Center, at/in building.

Crossley Williams, 28, Uniondale, N.Y., financial analyst, Fiduciary Trust International. Confirmed dead, World Trade Center, at/in building.

David Williams, 34, New York, N.Y., engineering, tenant man, ABM Industries. Confirmed dead, World Trade Center, at/in building.

Deborah Lynn Williams, 35, Hoboken, N.J. Confirmed dead, World Trade Center, at/in building.

Kevin Michael Williams, 24, New York, N.Y., Sandler O'Neill & Partners. Confirmed dead, World Trade Center, at/in building.

Louie Anthony Williams, 44, New York, N.Y. Confirmed dead, World Trade Center, at/in building.

Louis Calvin Williams, 53, Mandeville, La., vice president and investment management consultant, Vestek. Confirmed dead, World Trade Center, at/in building.

Cynthia Wilson, 52, New York, N.Y., head receptionist, International Office Centers. Confirmed dead, World Trade Center, at/in building.

Donna Wilson, 48, Williston Park, N.Y., assistant vice president, Aon Corp. Confirmed dead, World Trade Center, at/in building.

William E. Wilson, 55, New York, N.Y., Aon Corp. Confirmed dead, World Trade Center, at/in building.

David H. Winton, 29, New York, N.Y., vice president and equity research analyst, Keefe, Bruyette & Woods. Confirmed dead, World Trade Center, at/in building.

Glenn J. Winuk, 40, New York, N.Y., partner, Holland & Knight. Confirmed dead, World Trade Center, at/in building.

Thomas Francis Wise, 43, New York, N.Y. Confirmed dead, World Trade Center, at/in building.

Alan L. Wisniewski, 47, Howell, N.J., associate director, Sandler O'Neill & Partners. Confirmed dead, World Trade Center, at/in building.

Frank T. Wisniewski, 54, Basking Ridge, N.J., vice president, Cantor Fitzgerald. Confirmed dead, World Trade Center, at/in building.

David Wiswall, 54, North Massapequa, N.Y., senior vice president, Aon Corp. Confirmed dead, World Trade Center, at/in building.

Sigrid Charlotte Wiswe, 41, New York, N.Y. Confirmed dead, World Trade Center, at/in building.

Michael R. Wittenstein, 34, Hoboken, N.J., trader, Cantor Fitzgerald. Confirmed dead, World Trade Center, at/in building.

Christopher W. Wodenshek, 35, Ridgewood, N.J., director for TradeSpark, Cantor Fitzgerald. Confirmed dead, World Trade Center, at/in building.

Martin P. Wohlforth, 47, Greenwich, Conn., managing director, Sandler O'Neill & Partners. Confirmed dead, World Trade Center, at/in building.
Katherine S. Wolf, 40, New York, N.Y., Marsh & McLennan Cos. Inc. Confirmed dead, World Trade Center, at/in building.
Jennifer Y. Wong, 26, New York, N.Y., client services in risk management division, Marsh & McLennan Cos. Inc. Confirmed dead, World Trade Center, at/in building.
Jenny Seu Kueng Low Wong, 25, New York, N.Y., assistant vice president, market information group, Marsh & McLennan Cos. Inc. Confirmed dead, World Trade Center, at/in building.
Siu Cheung Wong, 34, Jersey City, N.J., Marsh & McLennan Cos. Inc. Confirmed dead, World Trade Center, at/in building.
Yin Ping (Steven) Wong, 34, New York, N.Y., Aon Corp. Confirmed dead, World Trade Center, at/in building.
Yuk Ping Wong, 47, New York, N.Y., New York State Department of Taxation and Finance. Confirmed dead, World Trade Center, at/in building.
Brent James Woodall, 31, Oradell, N.J., Keefe, Bruyette & Woods. Confirmed dead, World Trade Center, at/in building.
James J. Woods, 26, New York, N.Y., trader's assistant, Cantor Fitzgerald. Confirmed dead, World Trade Center, at/in building.
Patrick Woods, 36, New York, N.Y., carpenter. Confirmed dead, World Trade Center, at/in building.
Richard Herron Woodwell, 44, Ho-Ho-Kus, N.J., Keefe, Bruyette & Woods. Confirmed dead, World Trade Center, at/in building.
John Bentley Works, 36, Darien, Conn., trader, Keefe, Bruyette & Woods. Confirmed dead, World Trade Center, at/in building.
Martin Michael Wortley, 29, Park Ridge, N.J., Cantor Fitzgerald. Confirmed dead, World Trade Center, at/in building.
Rodney James Wotton, 36, Middletown, N.J., senior vice president of web site design, Fiduciary Trust International. Confirmed dead, World Trade Center, at/in building.
William Wren, 61, Lynbrook, N.Y., resident manager, OCS Security. Confirmed dead, World Trade Center, at/in building.
John Wright, 33, Rockville Centre, N.Y., managing director, Sandler O'Neill & Partners. Confirmed dead, World Trade Center, at/in building.
Neil R. Wright, 30, Asbury, N.J., options broker, Cantor Fitzgerald. Confirmed dead, World Trade Center, at/in building. *British.*
Sandra Wright, 57, Langhorne, Pa., Aon Corp. Confirmed dead, World Trade Center, at/in building.

– Y –

Jupiter Yambem, 41, Beacon, N.Y., banquet manager, Windows on the World. Confirmed dead, World Trade Center, at/in building.
Suresh Yanamadala, 33, Plainsboro, N.J., consultant at Marsh & McLennan Cos. Inc. Confirmed dead, World Trade Center, at/in building.
Matthew David Yarnell, 26, Jersey City, N.J., vice president of technology, Fiduciary Trust International. Confirmed dead, World Trade Center, at/in building.
Myrna Yaskulka, 59, New York, N.Y., executive secretary, Fred Alger Management. Confirmed dead, World Trade Center, at/in building.
Shakila Yasmin, 26, New York, N.Y., computer assistant, Marsh & McLennan Cos. Inc. Confirmed dead, World Trade Center, at/in building.
Olabisi L. Yee, 38, New York, N.Y., International Office Centers. Confirmed dead, World Trade Center, at/in building.
Paul Yoon. Reported missing, World Trade Center, at/in building.
Edward P. York, 45, Wilton, Conn., vice president and director of human resources, Cantor Fitzgerald. Confirmed dead, World Trade Center, at/in building.
Kevin Patrick York, 41, Princeton, N.J., senior vice president, Euro Brokers Inc. Confirmed dead, World Trade Center, at/in building.
Suzanne Youmans, 60, New York, N.Y., Aon Corp. Confirmed dead, World Trade Center, at/in building.
Barrington L. Young, 35, New York, N.Y., manager telecommunications, Euro Brokers Inc. Reported dead, World Trade Center, at/in building.
Jacqueline (Jakki) Young, 37, New York, N.Y., Marsh & McLennan Cos. Inc. Confirmed dead, World Trade Center, at/in building.
Elkin Yuen, 32, New York, N.Y., Carr Futures. Confirmed dead, World Trade Center, at/in building.

– Z –

Joseph Zaccoli, 39, Valley Stream, N.Y., broker, Cantor Fitzgerald. Confirmed dead, World Trade Center, at/in building.
Adel Agayby Zakhary, 50, North Arlington, N.J., accountant, Carr Futures. Confirmed dead, World Trade Center, at/in building.
Arkady Zaltsman, 45, New York, N.Y., architect, Skidmore, Owings & Merrill. Confirmed dead, World Trade Center, at/in building. *Moldovan.*
Edwin J. Zambrana, 24, New York, N.Y. Confirmed dead, World Trade Center, at/in building.
Robert Alan Zampieri, 30, Saddle River, N.J., trader, Carr Futures. Confirmed dead, World Trade Center, at/in building.
Mark Zangrilli, 36, Pompton Plains, N.J., insurance underwriter, Aon Corp. Confirmed dead, World Trade Center, at/in building.

Ira Zaslow, 55, North Woodmere, N.Y., assistant vice president, Lehman Brothers. Confirmed dead, World Trade Center, at/in building.
Aurelio Zedillo, Mexico, Mexico. Reported missing, World Trade Center, at/in building. *Mexican.*
Kenneth Albert Zelman, 37, Succasunna, N.J., consultant, Oracle Corp. Confirmed dead, World Trade Center, at/in building.
Abraham J. Zelmanowitz, 55, New York, N.Y., computer programmer, Empire Blue Cross and Blue Shield. Confirmed dead, World Trade Center, at/in building.
Martin Morales Zempoaltecatl, 22, New York, N.Y., assistant chef, Windows on the World. Confirmed dead, World Trade Center, at/in building. *Mexican.*
Zhe (Zack) Zeng, 28, New York, N.Y., assistant treasurer depository receipts division, Bank of New York. Confirmed dead, World Trade Center, at/in building.
Marc Scott Zeplin, 33, Harrison, N.Y., Cantor Fitzgerald. Confirmed dead, World Trade Center, at/in building.
Jie Yao Justin Zhao, 27, New York, N.Y., computer technician, Aon Corp. Confirmed dead, World Trade Center, at/in building.
Ivelin Ziminski, 40, Tarrytown, N.Y., Marsh & McLennan Cos. Inc. Confirmed dead, World Trade Center, at/in building.
Michael Joseph Zinzi, 37, Newfoundland, N.J., vice president and CPA, Marsh & McLennan Cos. Inc. Confirmed dead, World Trade Center, at/in building.
Charles A. Zion, 54, Greenwich, Conn., senior vice president, Cantor Fitzgerald. Confirmed dead, World Trade Center, at/in building.
Julie Lynne Zipper, 44, Paramus, N.J., product manager, SunGard Trading Systems/BRASS. Confirmed dead, World Trade Center, at/in building.
Salvatore J. Zisa, 45, Hawthorne, N.J., senior vice president, Marsh USA. Confirmed dead, World Trade Center, at/in building.
Prokopios Paul Zois, 46, Lynbrook, N.Y., consultant at Marsh & McLennan Cos. Inc. Confirmed dead, World Trade Center, at/in building.
Joseph J. Zuccala, 54, Croton-on-Hudson, N.Y. Confirmed dead, World Trade Center, at/in building.
Andrew Steven Zucker, 27, New York, N.Y., associate, Harris Beach LLP. Confirmed dead, World Trade Center, at/in building.
Igor Zukelman, 29, New York, N.Y., computer science, Fiduciary Trust International. Confirmed dead, World Trade Center, at/in building.

Cleanup efforts at the site of the World Trade Center terrorist attack continue Monday, Oct. 29, 2001, in New York. (AP/WideWorld Photos)

A New York City firefighter lays flowers from family members of the victims of the World Trade Center attacks after a memorial service at the site Sunday, Oct. 28, 2001, in New York. (AP/WideWorld Photos)

National Day of Prayer and Remembrance

Friday, 14 September 2001

Twelve O'Clock Noon

National Cathedral
Washington, D.C.

NATIONAL DAY OF PRAYER AND REMEMBRANCE
Friday, 14 September 2001 Twelve o'clock noon

PRELUDE

Orchestral prelude "God of Our Fathers" *sung by United States Navy Sea Chanters* "Grace" *sung by United* States *Navy Sea Chanters* "God Bless America" *performed by United States Army Orchestra* "Father, In Thy Gracious Keeping" *sung by Cathedral Choir*

PRESENTATION OF COLOR

Joint Armed Forces Color Guard

The People stand during presentation of colors and remain standing for processional hymn.

PROCESSIONAL HYMN

"O God, Our Help in Ages Past" *sung by Congregation*

WELCOME

Said by the Right Reverend Jane Holmes Dixon, Bishop of Washington, pro tempore

INVOCATION

Led by the Very Reverend Nathan D. Baxter, Dean of Washington National Cathedral.

When ancient Israel had suffered the excruciating pain and tragedy of militant aggression and destruction, God said to them through the prophet Jeremiah:

A voice is heard in Ramah, lamenting and bitter weeping, Rachel is weeping for her children; and she refuses to be comforted, because they are no more.

Today we gather to be reassured that God hears the "lamenting and bitter weeping" of Mother America, because so many of her children are no more. Let us now seek that assurance in prayer, for the healing of our grief stricken hearts, for the souls and sacred memory of those who have died. Let us also pray for Divine wisdom as our leaders consider the necessary actions for national security, that despite our grief we may not become the evil we deplore. Let us pray,

God of Abraham and Mohammed and Father of our Lord, Jesus Christ: we are today a people of heavy and distraught hearts. The evil hand of hate and cowardly aggression, which has devastated the innocent in many other lands, has visited America this week and too many of her children are no more. But we know you are not the God of hate and cowardice, but of courage and justice. So we gather this day asking that you provide us healing as a nation. Heal our grief. Soothe our suffering hearts. Save us from blind vengeance, random prejudice and crippling fear.

Guide our leaders, especially George our President. Let the deep faith that he and they share guide them in the momentous decisions they must make for our national security.

We thank you for the courage of flight crews and passengers in the face of certain death; the brave volunteers, police and emergency workers who labor tirelessly, even as we pray. We thank you for the outpouring of generosity by businesses, unions, agencies, spiritual communities and individual citizens. Your Spirit is at work. Grant us wisdom, grant us courage, grant us peace for the facing of this hour.

Amen.

The People sit after the invocation.

SOLO

"America the Beautiful" *sung by Denyce Graves, accompanied by David Perry*

PRAYER

Led by Dr. Muzammil H. Siddiqi

Imam, Islamic Society of North America

In the Name of God, most gracious, most merciful. Lord, you said and your worlds are true: If any do seek for glory and power, to God belongs all glory and power. To Him mount up all words of purity. He exalts all righteous deeds. But those that lay the plots of evil, for them is a terrible penalty; and the plotting of such will be not abide. *(Holy Qu'ran Fatir 35:10)*

Goodness and evil are not equal. Repel the evil with the good. Then will he between whom and you was hatred become as it were your friend and intimate. But no one will be granted such goodness except those who exercise patience and restraint, none but persons of the greatest good fortune. *(Holy Qu'ran Fussilat 4 1:34-35)*

We turn to you, our Lord, at this time of pain and grief in our nation. We see the evil of destruction and the suffering of the many of our people before our eyes. With broken and humble hearts and with tears in our eyes, we turn to You, 0 Lord, to give us comfort. Help us in our distress, keep us together as people of diverse faiths, colors and races, keep our country strong for the sake of good and righteousness, protect us from all evil.

SCRIPTURE READING

Lamentations 3:22-26, 31-33 *read by Rabbi Joshua O. Haherman, Rabbi Emeritus of Washington Hebrew Congregation*

A reading from the Book of Lamentations.

The steadfast love of the LORD never ceases, his mercies never come to an end; they are new every morning; great is thy faithfulness. "The LORD is my portion," says my soul, "therefore I will hope in him." The LORD is good to those who wait for him, to the soul that seeks him. It is good that one should wait quietly for the salvation of the LORD. For the Lord will not cast off forever, but though he cause grief, he will have compassion according to the abundance of his steadfast love; for he does not willingly afflict or grieve anyone.

ANTHEM – PSALM 23

Sung by the Cathedral Boy & Girl Choristers

The Lord is my shepherd, I shall not want; he makes me lie down in green pastures. He leads me beside still waters; he restores my soul. He leads me in paths of righteousness for his name's sake. Even though I walk through the valley of the shadow of death, I fear no evil; for thou art with me; thy rod and thy staff, they comfort me. Thou preparest a table before me in the presence of my enemies; thou anointest my head with oil, my cup overflows. Surely goodness and mercy shall follow me all the days of my life; and I shall dwell in the house of the Lord for ever.

SCRIPTURE READING

2 Corinthians 4:16 – 5:9 *read by Rev. Kirbyjon Caldwell, Pastor of Windsor Village United Methodist Church, Houston*

A reading from the Second Letter of St. Paul to the Corinthians.

So we do not lose heart. Even though our outer nature is wasting away, our inner nature is being renewed day by day. For this slight momentary affliction is preparing us for an eternal weight of glory beyond all measure, because we look not at what can be seen but at what cannot be seen; for what can be seen is temporary, but what cannot be seen is eternal.

For we know that if the earthly tent we live in is destroyed, we have a building from God, a house not made with hands, eternal in the heavens. For in this tent we groan, longing to be clothed with our heavenly dwelling—if indeed, when we have taken it off we will not be found naked. For while we are still in this tent, we groan under our burden, because we wish not to be unclothed but to be further clothed, so that what is mortal may be swallowed up by life. He who has prepared us for this very thing is God, who has given us the Spirit as a guarantee.

So we are always confident; even though we know that while we are at home in the body we are away from the Lord—for we walk by faith, not by sight. Yes, we do have confidence, and we would rather be away from the body and at home with the Lord. So whether we are at home or away, we make it our aim to please him.

HYMN

"A Mighty Fortress Is Our God," ***verses 1, 3-4 sung** by **the Congregation***

GOSPEL READING

Matthew 5:2-12a *read by His Eminence Theodore Cardinal McCarrick, Archbishop of Washington*

A reading from the Gospel according to St. Matthew.

Then Jesus began to speak, and taught them, saying: "Blessed are the poor in spirit, for theirs is the kingdom of heaven. "Blessed are those who mourn, for they will be comforted. "Blessed are the meek, for they will inherit the earth. "Blessed are those who hunger and thirst for righteousness, for they will be filled. "Blessed are the merciful, for they will receive mercy. "Blessed are the pure in heart, for they will see God. "Blessed are the peacemakers, for they will be called children of God. "Blessed are those who are persecuted for righteousness' sake, for theirs is the kingdom of heaven. "Blessed are you when people revile you and persecute you and utter all kinds of evil against you falsely on my account. Rejoice and be glad, for your reward is great in heaven.

SERMON

The Rev. Dr. Billy Graham

SOLO

"The Lord's Prayer" *sung by Den yce Graves, accompanied by Dr. Douglas Major, Cathedral Organist*

PRAYER FOR LEADERSHIP

Psalm 27:1-3, 13-14 *led by Rev. Caldwell*

The Lord is my light and my salvation; whom shall I fear? The Lord is the stronghold of my life; of whom shall I be afraid? When evildoers assail me to devour my flesh — my adversaries and foes — they shall stumble and fall. Though an army encamp against me, my heart shall not fear; though war rise up against me, yet I will be confident.

I believe that I shall see the goodness of the Lord in the land of the living. Wait for the Lord; be strong, and let your heart take courage; wait for the Lord!

REMARKS BY THE PRESIDENT OF THE UNITED STATES

CLOSING HYMN

"Battle Hymn of the Republic" *sung by the Congregation* Mine eyes have seen the glory of the coming of the Lord; He is tramping out the vintage where the grapes of wrath are stored; He has loosed the fateful lightning of His terrible swift sword; His truth is marching on. *Glory! Glory! Hallelujah! Glory! Glory! Hallelujah! Glory! Glory! Hallelujah! His truth is marching on.*

I have seen Him in the watch-fires of a hundred circling camps; They have builded Him an altar in the evening dews and damps; I can read His righteous sentence by the dim and glaring lamps; His day is marching on. *Refrain* I have read a fiery gospel writ in burnish'd rows of steel; "as ye deal with My contemners, so with you My grace shall deal;" Let the Hero, born of woman, crush the serpent with His heel; Since God is marching on. *Refrain* He has sounded for the trumpet that shall never call retreat; He is sifting our the hearts of men before His judgment-seat; Oh, be swift, my soul, to answer Him! Be jubilant, my feet! Our God is marching on. *Refrain* In the beauty of the lilies Christ was born across the sea, With a glory in His bosom that transfigures you and me: As He died to make men holy, let us die to make men free, While God is marching on. *Refrain*

CLOSING PRAYER

Led by Dean Baxter

O God, whose days are without end and whose mercies cannot be numbered, grant to us and to all who are bereaved the spirit of faith and courage, that we may have strength to meet the days to come with steadfastness and patience; not sorrowing as those without hope, but in thankful remembrance of your great goodness, and in the joyful expectation of eternal life with those we love; in your most holy name we pray.

BLESSING & DISMISSAL

Led by Bishop Dixon

Go forth now, into the world in Peace; Be of good courage; Hold fast to that which is good, Render to no one evil for evil; Strengthen the fainthearted; support the weak; Help the afflicted; honor everyone; Love and serve the Lord. And the blessing of God Almighty, the God who created us, the God who liberates us, and the God who stays with us throughout eternity be with you this day and forever more. Amen.

RETIREMENT OF COLORS

SILENT RECESSION

The ministers depart in recession during the tolling of the Bourdon Bell. The people remain standing until the President has departed the Cathedral.

– Courtesy of the Washington National Cathedral

AFTERWORD

This completes the lists of those who died on that fateful day in September, 2001. Because we know that the lists may not be complete, we have provided several additional blank pages where names can be added at a later date.

PERSONAL REMEMBRANCES

As September 11, 2001 has significance for every American, you may wish to use these blank pages to record your personal thoughts about the day and the ensuing weeks and months that have transpired. Here is the perfect place to set forth your own remembrances about this tragic day in American history so that your children, grandchildren and whomever else may read this copy of the National Book of Remembrance will have a greater insight into how you may have been affected.

PERSONAL REMEMBRANCES

American flags and a sign reading "We Will Never Forget" hang from the heavily damaged American Express building on West Street across from the site of the terrorist attack on the World Trade Center in lower Manhattan Monday, Sept. 24, 2001. Part of the structure of one of the destroyed World Trade Center twin towers can be seen in the foreground. (AP/WideWorld Photos)

UPDATE REQUEST

(please copy the following information on a blank sheet of paper)

Yes, I am interested in receiving a free list of the names of September 11, 2001 victims that were either inadvertently not included or incorrectly named in this *National Book of Remembrance*.

Please forward the list to:

Name ____

Address ____

City ______________________ State ________ Zip Code __________

If you would like to have your list sent via e-mail instead of U.S. Mail, please indicate your e-mail address below:
e-mail address ____________________________________

Mail request to:

J. TUMEROLL PRESS
P.O. Box 546
Farmington, NH 03835

e-mail address: tumeroll@metrocast.net